More praise for Zipline to Success!

"*Zipline to Success* is for every business owner, manager and entrepreneur who wants to optimize and even transform how their company does its marketing. Filled with practical actionable strategies and tactics, this book shows you how to make marketing happen fast and cost-effectively, how to measure and evaluate outcomes, and how to quickly course correct to gain the competitive edge."

**—Steve Harrison, Partner & Chief Instructor,
Bradley Communications Corp.**

"Competing online can be a very technical and complicated endeavor. *Zipline to Success* is one of the few books that explains this topic in an easy-to-understand manner. I highly recommend it!"

**— Eric Spellmann, President, Spellmann &
Associates, "The Technology Evangelist"**

"Reading this book was like enjoying healthy intellectual potato chips, since I just kept reading and reading, enjoying the page turning. The voice, pacing, and delivery of information in *Zipline* is beautifully executed. It's engaging and fun, without minimizing the importance and seriousness of the content."

— Dr. MaryAnne Borrelli, Professor, Connecticut College

"Becoming widely known as having an excellent reputation for meeting people's needs is essential to the success of nonprofit organizations and companies alike. *Zipline to Success* provides an effective and entertaining roadmap for understanding and using marketing tools to demonstrate and promote your reputation. Claudia then shows how to package and sell products and services in ways that generate income to ensure sustainability in addition to furthering your mission."

**— Irene van der Zande, Executive Director and Founder,
Kidpower Teenpower Fullpower International**

Zipline to Success

Fast-Track Marketing Strategies to Accelerate Your Sales & Profits

Claudia Newcorn

Acorn Oaks Press

Printed in the United States of America
First Printing, November 2016

ISBN 978-1942936244

www.ZiplineToSuccess.com

Acknowledgments

A book like *Zipline to Success* is about more than just the author writing a lot of pages. It is also about teamwork—the support, inspiration, advice, and encouragement received from many people that at last brings it to the final published piece you hold in your hands.

Many individuals have guided me through this process, and I thank them all. I would especially like to express my appreciation to my amazing Quantum Leap writing and storytelling coaches Martha Bullen, Geoffrey Berwind, and Debby Englander, who kept prodding me along despite the demands of running a full-time business. Also to Dr. MaryAnne Borrelli, Professor, Connecticut College, for her thought-provoking comments on the manuscript and Kurt Clark, Director, SBA-Alliance Small Business Development Center, for giving me the opportunity to consult for numerous companies, be inspired by their ambition and determination to succeed, and provide them with the knowledge to do so.

Plus, a special thanks to my family for their role as cheering squad: my very patient husband Patrick Walsh, who didn't object to my writing into the wee hours (much); my sister, Jodi Newcorn, who dubbed me "the Energizer Bunny" because she says I never run out of energy; and my parents, Andrew Newcorn and Ruth Duplain, who, long before it was a common parenting practice, told us that if we had the passion to pursue a dream and the willingness to acquire the knowledge to make it happen, we would succeed.

Thank you all.

Table Of Contents

Introduction

Part 1 – Look Out! Simple Steps to Avoid Smacking into Trees

Part 2 – Get Ready to Zip: The Equipment You Need for a Smooth Ride

Part 4 – Zipping for Dollars: Budget-Friendly, Proven Traditional Marketing Strategies

Part 5 – Zipping the Digital Divide

Part 6 – Zip Wild! 7 Creative, Innovative, and Eye-Catching Marketing Ideas to Set You Apart from the Crowd

Part 7 – Keeping on Course – Maintain Your Momentum for a Smooth Landing

The 27 Zipline Essentials to Successful Marketing

About the Author

Introduction

 ➤ ***There's nothing small about running a small business!***
Does this describe you? You own or manage a small business (by the way, if you have fewer than 500 employees, that's how the Small Business Administration classifies you). You're being pulled every which way because of all of the hats you wear, while at the same time, you worry about the bottom line because sales just aren't where you want them—or where you think they should be. Some days, you feel like you're riding wild on a zipline with no idea what's waiting at the bottom—or along the way—and have that ache-in-the-gut feeling of barely being in control. Sound familiar?

Of course, you just don't hop on a zipline and let go! You're guaranteed a painful landing if you try that. You've got to plan your zipline's path and know where you're headed, then choose the right gear, and understand how to use it. Once you hook up to the zipline, you'll possibly say a few prayers when you look down that l-o-n-g sloping wire, then need to watch out for trees, maybe even a confused bird, figure out how to adjust for wind gusts to avoid spinning around, and decide how to land safely.

Whether I'm speaking at an event, conducting workshops, or consulting one-on-one with clients, all I hear about is how much "marketing" stresses them out. I hear, "Claudia, I *do* marketing. I advertise. I promote. But it seems hit or miss. And I've only got so much in my budget. How can I get marketing to make money for me?" Start-ups, entrepreneurs, established companies—all managed by people like you who are passionate about what they offer, have poured money into their company, and are working hard, determined to succeed. But they're not getting the results they want. Why?

> This book is for business owners and managers like you who believe in their company's potential and want to make more money, but don't have a big marketing budget. They're looking for practical solutions to grow their sales and boost the bottom line.

Before we continue, I think it's time to upend the "Small Business" myth that a small business is easier to manage than a large company. **I believe**

1

there's nothing small about being or running a small business. Sure, the challenges may be different, but they're just as stressful—probably often more so, because it's just you and a few others striving for success.

Here are a few facts that should make you feel good. According to the SBA, 89.8% of firms have 20 or fewer employees. It gets better! **Did you know small businesses make up an amazing 99.7% of U.S. employer firms,** 64% of net new private sector jobs, and 49.2% of private sector employment? In other words, you're part of a vital economic engine. Three cheers for you!

But there is a dark side to all this. *Forbes Magazine* states that "8 out of 10 entrepreneurs who start businesses fail within the first 18 months. A whopping 80% crash and burn." For those who survive that critical period, another 50% will fail within their first 5 years. Many others will limp along, straining for that brass ring that seems just beyond reach. And while there can be many reasons for a company's failure, *Money Magazine* flat out says that "ineffective marketing is one of the top eight reasons small businesses fail."

The operative word is *ineffective:* marketing efforts that drain money and your time, but don't deliver. Ever had that happen to you?

But it doesn't have to be that way. There are marketing secrets that produce results.

After earning my MBA, I worked as a marketing executive at big corporations for nearly 20 years, managing such brands as Bartles & Jaymes at E&J Gallo Winery, Silkience Hair Care at Gillette, and the FoodSaver vacuum packaging systems at Tilia. Along the way, I acquired smart and essential business and marketing practices that can significantly can reduce the risk of failure and increase the probabilities of success. And I realized that **smaller firms often don't know these secrets.** I have also worked in retail, food services, video gaming, and various technologies, giving me priceless exposure to a diverse array of industries and business practices. Some friends asked for help with their firms, and I taught them my hard-earned marketing secrets. Seeing them run with these concepts and achieve success was fabulous.

I had found my mission: to inspire and help business owners and managers who are wrestling with marketing, and need strategies and tactics to overcome roadblocks, avoid costly mistakes that could damage, even destroy their companies, and show them ways to accelerate their success. Knowing this, I launched my award-winning consulting firm, Acorn Enterprises.

Now, *Fortune 500* companies know how to conceive and implement effective marketing strategies and tactics. I have adapted these proven marketing concepts into practical steps designed to guide and provide you with easy-to-use resources to help achieve your business goals. I call this the *Zipline to Success*™ system, and it's worked for hundreds of so-called "small" business clients across industries ranging from automotive repair shops, gourmet olive oil manufacturers, and CPA firms to wineries, cabinet manufacturers, nonprofits, and luxury home builders.

What makes the *Zipline to Success* approach so effective? Three powerful principles: speed, practical solutions, and measurable results.

Zipline to Success is all about optimizing and even transforming how a company does its marketing, how managers can make it happen fast and cost-effectively, how to measure and evaluate outcomes, and how to quickly course correct to gain the competitive edge. We talk about today's companies needing to be nimble and agile. That's exactly what a good marketing strategy can do. Able to adapt, respond, and quickly shift gears, it empowers companies to pursue and achieve success.

You may have read some books that tell you marketing is dead. Or that you don't have to worry about marketing essentials because they're not relevant. Or it's only about digital advertising; every other form of marketing is toast. Don't you believe it! If that's the case, then why do so many companies, from micros to giants, stumble when they fail to practice smart marketing strategies?

In this book, you'll find the essential, the creative, and the just plain "crazy" things you can do to maximize your marketing efforts and boost your bottom line—without necessarily having to spend lots of money. It's not a book with complex marketing jargon and advanced techniques, there are already other texts that cover that. This book is designed to let you skip around and pick and choose what you need to know and what's right for your business. At the end of each part, there's a summary of highlights for easy reference. And to make things even more interesting and get you thinking, I've included real life business situations and challenge you to come up with fix-it solutions.

I'm not going to pretend that everything I know is in this book—you would be able to use it as a doorstop! And who has the time to read all that stuff? Instead, I've distilled it down to proven and actionable marketing strategies and tactics that you can put to work and see the results.

You'll see references to free marketing tools and templates throughout the book and you can find them at www.ZiplineToSuccess.com/Resources. Just bookmark the resources page, and download what you need.

A promise: This book is all about helping you to achieve successful outcomes. When you're done with it—even as you're reading it—you can start to apply the *Zipline to Success* marketing strategies and tactics right away. You'll know the smart way to develop promotions, be amazed at how often you may be missing low/no-cost marketing opportunities, and discover how to really connect with your buyers online and in-person. You will know how to zipline your marketing in order to improve sales and profits.

> This is your book for marketing insights, tips, tools, and creative ideas, because you're a person who recognizes the need to do things differently if you want to ride the *Zipline to Success*.

Are you ready to ride the *Zipline to Success?* Then let's start!

Part 1 – Look Out! Simple Steps to Avoid Smacking into Trees

A natural practice among business owners and managers is to be inspired by an idea or suggestion, and run with it. This passion may be why you chose to start a company or work in a smaller firm. But, too often, people hop on the zipline assuming they know how to ride it, and only discover afterward that they could have created a much more profitable and smoother ride if they had first learned how to use the equipment.

The real opportunity for success lies in combining the critical zipline marketing essentials with your enthusiasm and determination to succeed. Let's start with why you need to understand your buyers, what practical steps to take to figure out who they are, and then how you're going to provide the ideal product or service that will solve their specific issues.

Chapter 1 ~ How Leaping Before You Look Is Guaranteed to Hurt You

It's a popular misperception that marketing is the cure-all for a company's problems. However, if you don't have all your essential elements—what I like to call your zipline equipment—in order, it can become nothing more than a financial drain. It's easy to say, and I hear it all the time, "Let's do marketing." And then you spend—I say, waste—money on what you think is marketing, and when you review your sales and profits, and the results aren't what you expected, you wonder what went wrong. You can avoid this problem by following the advice that I share with you in this book.

Now, a very important point. The term *marketing* is often used when what's really meant is *marketing communications*, which are all the outreach efforts used to connect with buyers. As you're about to see, marcom, as it's called, is only part of the marketing equation. While the two terms are often used interchangeably, it's essential to know the difference.

➤ *A Gizmo's Tale – why marketing can actually hurt your business*

I was chatting with a CFO at one of my workshops. He was an admitted skeptic about marketing, seeing it as a drain on the bottom line. He offered me the following true story to illustrate his point.

So, there's this fellow who's been making gizmos that secure sliding glass windows and doors. For several years, he's been selling loads of them. They're cheap, work well, and are something people really need. The perfect recipe for a successful business, right?

Problem is, the guy can't seem to make any money. After pondering about it, he comes up with the obvious solution. He's the only one making the gizmos, and that's limiting how much he can sell. He decides to hire another person to produce more gizmos, and ramp up his marketing efforts to reach more buyers.

Over a beer, he shares his plans with a buddy, who says it's a great idea; sounds like a good business strategy. So how much does it cost to make the gizmos he sells for a buck? The gizmo maker says he thinks around 90 cents, but realizes it's been a while since he actually looked at his costs because he's always so busy—not that he's complaining.

So he phones his bookkeeper, asks for a detailed cost analysis, and is shocked to discover it now costs him $1.10 to make each gizmo! He's been so focused on gross sales that he hasn't taken time to study his financial statements in detail. He's been losing a dime per unit! Imagine if he'd gone ahead. Hiring another person and ramping up his marketing would have caused him to lose even more money!

I call this the "ready, fire, aim" approach to marketing. It's "doing marketing" without understanding what's really involved—like hopping on a zipline without knowing how to ride it. And then people are surprised when they lose control, crash into trees, or even worse, fall off.

➢ The business idea! Inspiration vs. Perspiration

Companies usually start from one of two points: "I have an idea" or "I see an opportunity." Let's look at both.

- *Inspiration: I have an idea!* This is probably the most common reason a person starts a business. Say you're an experienced plumber, programmer, accountant... and you work for somebody. You're good at what you do, customers love you, and you're inspired to go out on your own. You choose a location in the town where you live, buy what you need, hang up a sign, place an ad in the yellow pages, get a website up, and brace yourself for business.
- *Perspiration: I think I see an opportunity.* You want to work for yourself, and start looking at your market for possible opportunities that would let you do this. You might research franchises. Or you have a good skill set (copy repair, landscape, computer repair) and, upon doing some research, see there's not a lot, or any, competition, and launch your business, choose a location, and... go read the last sentence of the preceding paragraph.

Can you guess where the problem is with these approaches?

Neither business owner really *knows* whether or not what they want to sell "fits" that market and will generate revenue and profits! Please read this a second time because it's a fundamental element in the zipline approach to doing business. Know your marketplace. We're going to delve into this topic in the next chapter.

In his insightful book, *Growth Hacker Marketing,* about the shifting marketing practices in the technology sector, Ryan Holiday refers to it as Product Market Fit, and says, "You know the single worst marketing decision you can make? Starting with a product nobody wants or nobody needs." He's spot on.

I think there are very few bad ideas, as long as a person genuinely believes that their idea will benefit customers. What can make or break an idea's success is whether the target market is interested in what's going to be offered, and has enough potential buyers who will buy the product or service at a price that delivers profits. The good news? Thanks to the Internet, there's a lot you can do to figure this out *before* you spend lots of money up front (more on this in Part 2).

By the way, if you're already in business, and you jumped in with both feet without having really researched your market, that's OK. Companies can gain traction because there was a need and they did a lot of things right. But don't you want to know what will help make your marketing more effective? And what will help your company grow to the next level?

I like to say that I expect to keep learning new tools and techniques until I'm burnt or in a box. Your decision to buy this book means you want to keep learning as well. Good job!

➤ *How ignoring "Assume" warning signs can knock you off your zipline*

We all know by now what "assume" spells. It doesn't matter whether you're a start-up or an established firm. Assumptions about consumers and the marketplace can lead to costly business and marketing decisions that are outright flops—or worse.

Here are **5 common "uh-oh" assumptions** that business owners and managers make when it comes to marketing. Each one of these is like having a big tree planted right in the way of your zipline. I'll show you how to spot and navigate around them as we ride along.

1. *Everybody is my buyer.* Nope. Sorry. Not true. And if you think so, I can guarantee you're wasting a lot of your marketing dollars. (Learn more in Chapter 2.)

2. *Price is the most important decision factor for my customers.* Uh-oh. If that's really true, you have a major problem on your hands. You need to fix it. (See Chapter 7.)

3. *Buyers will choose you based on superior quality and great customer service.* Everybody says this—it's expected. Do you know anybody who says they offer crappy quality and shoddy customer service? This sets you up for comparative price wars. (See Chapter 4.)

4. *Competitors are the greatest risk to my business.* They're actually only about 20% of the problem. Want to know the other 80%? Keep reading! (See Chapter 3.)

5. *I know this is a great idea; I just have to market it to enough people to succeed.* Once in a green moon (not blue—those happen once a year; greens almost never), that is true. But not usually. What you have to do is market smart!

Fact: **The marketplace controls you, not the other way around.** As successful businessman Sam Walton, founder of Wal-Mart said, "There is only one boss. The customer. And he can fire everybody in the company from the chairman on down, simply by spending his money somewhere else."

Because the marketplace is a constantly shifting landscape of competition and consumers, and most business owners and managers are too busy with day-to-day-business issues to keep on top of those changes, they're likely to "smack into trees" on the way down the zipline, which could cost them their business. Please, don't be one of them! The good news, as you'll see, is that this book provides you with useful solutions.

Now, as promised, as the book progresses, I'm going to present real-life situations I've encountered to illustrate what we're covering. In most cases, names have been changed as a client courtesy. Challenge yourself to see if you can identify the problems or why something worked, because it's a great way to learn.

What do you think? Why Won't It Catch On?

A new client came to me with a "great idea." He had invested a lot of time and money to produce a paper medical diary so people could carry all their medical records with them—a calendar, recent appointments, medications, diagnoses, etc. Paperback book size, it was over an inch thick. He offered it at events where he could fully explain the functionality and benefits, and usually sold some. He had advertised in the right magazines, but didn't seem to be getting the sales he felt this product warranted. Why didn't people grasp how great this product was, he wondered? The year was 2009.

🖋 *Jot down your answer:* _____

_____

Answer: One word: *timing*. The product concept, while clever and having great utility, was 10 years too late. People of all ages were switching over to digital devices in droves and didn't want to carry bulky paper organizers. Plus, doctors had begun the migration to electronic medical records and were sharing information, so patients didn't need to carry all their records with them. And, finally, free downloadable apps that performed similar functions were available online. Had he done his homework, he would have saved himself a lot of frustration and money—and maybe even been first to market with an app!

People are an innovative and creative bunch. New ideas for products and services can pop up at the most unexpected times. Which is wonderful. But it's what you do next that can dictate success or failure. And what I consider a critical anchor to setting up a successful zipline marketing strategy is doing the best you can to understand who your buyer is and what makes them tick. On to the next chapter!

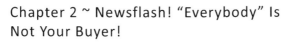

Chapter 2 ~ Newsflash! "Everybody" Is Not Your Buyer!

We're all passionate about the product or service we offer. So, why wouldn't everyone want to buy it? And the answer is... because not everyone wants or needs it. On the zipline, this is where many businesses smack into a really big tree. You've all heard, "build a better mousetrap, they'll beat a path to your door." But what if they don't want the mousetrap?

Taking the time to understand your buyer—what motivates them, what influences them, what buttons to push—is a critical anchor to a successful ride on the marketing zipline. And it's something that you can't do just one time, because consumers are always evolving. Let's look at a variety of practical approaches to getting to know your buyers.

➢ *Who the heck wants to buy what you have to offer?*

Figuring out who or even if anyone wants to buy what you plan to offer drives everything. It's the very heart of marketing, something the big companies spend tons of money on each year: researching their buyers, also known as target audience(s)—and yes, a company can have more than one audience. We're talking millions of dollars.

Imagine if Pringles potato chips had come out with yet another variety of chips in a bag. With so many other bag chips out there, another "me too" brand would have had trouble standing out in the crowd. Instead, Pringles discovered that what potato chip eaters objected to was... (wait for it)... broken chips in the bag. You know the feeling—you open the bag and it's 50% crumbs. This created an awesome marketing opportunity to be unique and different in a way that really solved a consumer issue. An innovative tubular package that popped when opened, guaranteeing freshness, and delivered uniform unbroken chips. It was a sensation!

Today, more companies are taking what I consider a proactive customer-centric approach, and trying to identify what buyers are looking for *before* they spend lots of money on product development. For all intents and purposes, the firms are looking for a way to either come up with a new idea and/or "fit" or adapt an existing product or service to satisfy an existing or even emerging buyer need.

Before the advent of the worldwide web and computers, companies did in-person surveys, mall-intercepts, focus groups, phone surveys… all of which are still in use today. Then came the Internet. It flung the door wide open on data-gathering—think cookies, Constant Contact, Survey Monkey, and other survey resources. By the way, your purchasing behavior is tracked and "known" and often sold as market research—why do you think you get all those ads popping up on Facebook or Google? Because they know what you look at as well as your demographics and try to "fit" those ads to what they think will interest you. After all, that's how they make profits; it's their business model.

What we really "need" may surprise you. Contrary to what we think, we really don't "need" much. Back in the 1943, noted psychologist Abraham Maslow came up with a theory known as the Hierarchy of Needs that continues to be used today for understanding human motivation, management training, and personal development. He determined we had a basic set of core needs upon which all our other needs are built: air, food, drink, shelter, warmth, sex, and sleep. That's pretty much it. You can't create a need because these are basic survival factors. Without most of them, we die.

This is where the **art of marketing** comes in. You *need* food, but you *want* to eat at Applebee's. You *need* to drink, but you *want* a glass of Southern Comfort. You *need* shelter, but *want* a 3,000-square-foot home at Lake Tahoe. Need vs. Want. **You can't create needs, but you sure can create wants.**

Think I'm joking? Why on earth would anybody *need* fuzzy dice to hang off their rear view mirror? A pet rock? A mood ring? Cell phone bling? Or to capture a Pokémon creature? Marketers can cleverly create a want—a desire to own or do these things. They succeed by making it a status symbol because a celebrity has it; or making it a way of being different, because we all want to stand out; or if you're not doing it, you're not "with it." You *can* create wants—that's great marketing!

I've often seen the argument put forward that people don't know what they want. I don't think that's accurate. While they may not be able to specifically articulate what they want, there are threads that tie what they wish or would like to have together, and those can be woven into a solution. Your job is to ferret out those threads and weave them into a product or service concept that people will want. It may mean you adapt or evolve an existing product or service, or develop something entirely new.

Think of smart phones. People couldn't specifically say, "I want a smart phone." But did they want something that was mobile, would give them access to email while on the go, and could conveniently consolidate phones, music, and computers in one device so they wouldn't have to lug around a pager, MP3 player, cell phone, and laptop? Of course!

Visionaries such as Steve Jobs, Mark Zuckerberg, Martha Stewart, or Oprah Winfrey can intuitively "see" these threads and successfully have woven them into things that people want. **Good marketers interpret data, spot opportunities or trends, and translate them into desirable products and services.**

Another central purpose of marketing is to *persuade* buyers that they want what a company has to offer. So, your job is to develop a marketing communications strategy that convinces people they want what you're selling. If you did your homework up front, then your product or service was "fitted" to your buyers' needs, which makes marketing so much easier. But many companies haven't done this; they already have a product or service to sell. So the only way to create want is by **figuring what motivates buyers**. I call it pushing people's buttons.

Since most of us drive cars, let's look at some examples in the auto industry. Technically, if you stop to think about it, they're all the same type of transportation—four wheels, an engine, somewhere to sit and get from point A to point B. So why are there so many different makes and models? Because different buyers *want* different things.

- **BMW**: BMWs are superbly engineered cars. Is that why most people buy them? No. The company has researched its buyers so well that it knows the vast majority buy for the status of owning a BMW. Their buyers want a luxury car that says, "Look at me. I've made it!" The firm reinforces this by positioning itself as "the ultimate driving machine," continually innovating the cars in ways that cater to its buyers' desires.

  And here's an interesting tidbit: BMW began in 1913 as a German aircraft engine manufacturer, earning a reputation for excellence. It was then forced to switch to vehicle engines after the signing of the World War I armistice. Not until the mid-1970s did it begin to focus on becoming a luxury car company, with the introduction of the 3 Series sedans.

- **Volkswagen Bugs**: This inexpensive funny-looking car was the darling of the Baby Boomer generation. Why? They wanted something that was different than what their parents drove: fun, funky, and totally acceptable with a kooky, personalized exterior paint scheme. Today's buyers have changed, as has the Bug. They are likely to be women—until recently there was a built-in dashboard flower vase!—in their 20s and 30s who want to make a statement.

- **Ram Trucks**: Built Ram tough. The ads shout, "Don't get in the way of these muscle trucks; they'll eat up anything you put in front of them." From the commanding ram's head medallion to the dominating front cab and grille, it's all about the "I'm manly" message.

Every single vehicle out there is designed to appeal to the wants of specific buyer groups, commonly known as market segments or niches. Have some fun and ask yourself: why did I buy the car I'm currently driving? Be honest. Dig deep. You'll be impressed by how much the manufacturers know about you, and how they pushed your buttons. Shouldn't you know the same about your customers?

➤ *How to find out what makes your buyer tick*

Not really knowing what makes your buyer tick is a major tree waiting to knock you off your zipline. **Defining who your buyers are is a critical anchor of any marketing effort.** The mushier the definition, the more likely you will be to spend time and money, yet achieve poor results. The more detailed the buyer profile(s), the more you will be able to push their buttons. It's as simple as that.

Everything in this book is relevant to your business, but certain concepts are zipline essentials. Whether you're a start-up or an established business, these rules apply. So, throughout the book, I'm going to flag these so you can find them for easy reference.

> *Zipline Essential #1*: You must understand your customers' "reasons why to buy."

A variety of factors, such as your industry, location, and products and services, can influence how you determine your buying audience. However, I'm going to give you practical information about what you can do to find out about them. Why?

Because doing so helps you **understand their "reasons why to buy"**— aka, what influences their buying decisions. This info will help to dramatically improve your ability to cost-effectively advertise to them. And that takes both market and consumer research.

Now, before you go screaming down the avenue at the word "research," the good news is that a lot of basic research can be done in a few hours or days, at little to no cost. The deeper you want to dig, the more time—and sometimes money—it may take. But you can assemble useful data through some straightforward techniques we cover in Chapter 3.

There are two data clusters you want to collect: Demographics and Motivators. Demographics are concrete census-type statistics about the prospects and buyers. How old are they? Did they go to college? Are they married? How much do they earn? The following are some of the things your company should be able to answer about the buyers.

1. **Age.** Yes, you may have people from ages 18 to 80 walking in the door or contacting you, but what's the sweet spot? What is the most profitable segment?

For example, Carl's Jr. fast food restaurant reinvented itself in the early 1990s by determining college-age males were its most lucrative audience. Think on it—18- to 24-year-old men who, as we all know, have bottomless appetites. The chain completely changed its advertising strategy to use messaging and visuals that young men would respond to. For example, the ads with the scantily clad girls licking their ketchup-smeared fingers suggestively? It doesn't mean older people and families don't eat there. But young men are the chain's primary target audience—the one that is the most profitable—and that's where Carl's focuses much of its marketing communication dollars.

2. **Gender.** Do your buyers skew male? Female? Is it an even split? 75%/25%? You're going to have a poor return on your advertising dollars if you're aiming at the wrong gender.

One of my clients, luxury home builder Trilogy at the Vineyards in California, knows that although couples are both involved in the home-buying process, the woman is the keystone in the decision-making process. Therefore, its model homes are designed to resonate with both genders, with a special emphasis on appliances, design elements, and floorplans that particularly appeal to age 55+ women.

3. **Income**. Income is usually defined two ways. "Per capita" refers to what an individual is earning. "Household" is what a total household earns (husband, wife, and partners living under one roof). These dollar ranges are often assigned classifications such as affluent, upper middle income, blue collar, and so on. Additionally, in society's never-ending effort to label things, researchers

often assign different income subgroups names such as DINKs (dual income, no kids) and SINKs (single income, no kids).

This data is valuable, but you should dig even deeper, because it's also about **buying power—what your audience can afford to buy,** aka "disposable" or "discretionary" income, which are often used interchangeably. To get technical for just a moment, disposable income is after tax income *before* other expenses; discretionary is disposable income less all payments necessary to meet current bills. In the purest sense, discretionary income is what buyers have left to spend on your products or services.

Another way of looking at buying power is the "cost of living" factor. Someone who lives in New York City may be making above-average income—but it also costs a lot to live there because prices are higher. Conversely, if that same person made the same amount of money, but resides in the less expensive city of Boise, Idaho, they're able to purchase a lot more.

An interesting note: some companies are now looking at starting up or relocating to the Midwest to take advantage of the lower cost of living. It gives their employees greater spending power because their dollars stretch farther. At the same time, firms are able to lower costs since they don't need to pay as large a salary as they would in an area with a higher cost of living.

4. **Education.** Did they complete high school? Some college? Earn a BA? MBA? PhD? Tech school? Education tends to correlate with income levels, outside interests, geographic location, and language sophistication.

This may come as a shocker, but the average American today reads at a sixth grade level. But that doesn't mean you write copy that way—you need to know what your buyers' reading levels are. If your audience is commercial airline pilots looking for optical wear that will protect them against idiots pointing lasers at them during flights, then you know these people are well-educated, and your marketing imagery and message need to use the proper sophistication to "connect" with them.

5. **Race.** Anglo. Latino. Afro-American. Asian. Native American. While we are all global citizens, we also come from different racial backgrounds. Some of us are "fresh off the boat," others are second or third generation, while others have been here for hundreds, even thousands, of years.

For example, in some areas in the United States, Latinos are now the predominant group. Some are third generation; some don't speak Spanish at home. For others, English is their second language. Companies targeting the

Latino buyer have to identify these nuances and adjust their communications, including using bilingual marketing tools.

Here's a really dumb marketing mistake: assuming that all Spanish is the same language. I confess I learned this the hard way in my early marketing years. I had developed a promotional piece for a wine available nationwide. We had someone in-house handle the translation. One small problem: while correct in Mexican Spanish, the translation had an obscene innuendo in Puerto Rican Spanish—and the firm got an earful of complaints.

Recognize that there are many versions of Spanish (Mexican, Californian, Cuban, Puerto Rican, etc.). While they all fall under the Spanish umbrella, some words may have different meanings among the variants—ones that only an experienced translator will know. When I have marketing materials translated, I *always* discuss who the audience is with the translator.

Consider this direct mail marketing mistake I've seen firms make when trying to reach the Latino audience: they try to get mailing lists with Spanish-sounding names. It shows a blatant lack of buyer knowledge, and an antiquated assumption that if the last name is Chavez, the person must be Hispanic.

So where you do find this demographic information? Visit ZiplinetoSuccess. com/Resources for a downloadable .pdf that lists the best free demographic resources.

Motivators are less tangible but no less important factors that influence buyer behavior patterns. They are more about consumer psychology—the things that influence the way people think, such as cultural and social factors. While there are many variables, here are some fundamental motivators to consider.

1. **Culture/Ethnic background.** While we tend to lump the terms "race" and "ethnicity" together, ethnicity is really about tradition, learned behavior, and customs. Irish. French. Indian. Japanese. East coast. West coast. Deep South. Our heritage and the environments in which we live influence how we think.

For example, in many Asian cultures, New Year's falls on a day different from the standard Roman calendar, and celebratory elements include gifting money in red envelopes and serving special foods. If you're a company that sells New Year's items, and you want to reach specific Asian groups, assuming they celebrate on December 31st and are all about funny hats and champagne would be a major gaffe.

2. **Location.** Where do people live? New England is not Mid-Atlantic is not the Pacific Northwest is not Iowa is not Alabama. And even within geographic regions, towns and communities can vary—conservative, liberal, farming, urban, or industrial.

Location can even impact the way people dress. On the East coast, business suits remain a primary form of professional attire for men; on the West coast, it's more blazers and slacks, and often it's not even that formal. As a case in point, during a recent hunt for women's business jackets at Macy's in San Francisco, I was unable to locate what I wanted. I finally asked a sales person. She directed me to a tiny area, explaining that with the technology boom, most Bay Area businesswomen dress very casually (we're talking jeans and a tank top), reflecting their companies' laid back cultures; there isn't much demand anymore for business suits. Macy's is adapting to changing local buyer needs.

3. **Social.** This is a biggie. Social influences can be within age bands—Millennials, Baby Boomers, Gen-X—as well as on more micro or macro scales. They are the ever-changing social trends that direct much of buyers' behaviors. For example, Millennials are known as "digital natives"—they don't know a world without computers, and are more likely to text than call. Baby Boomers grew up without computers until their mid-20s or later. They text, but are more likely to call. Think how many comic strips make fun of the gap in communication styles between generations!

Consider Uber or Airbnb. Both these firms rely on the digital savviness of their youthful buyers, an audience that often considers it a status symbol to say they've used those services. Other examples? Wearing a Fitbit to show you're "with it" when it comes to fitness tracking. Saying you've shopped at Forever21, Macy's, or Nordstrom's because your peer group does the same. Preordering the newest iPhone because it's a tech status symbol. Choosing your mutual fund investments based on the eco-consciousness of the companies in that fund, because you're concerned about the environment. Deciding to eat only non-GMO foods because you're worried about health and environmental issues. This is a just tiny smattering of the many social variables that influence us—and what we choose to buy. It may be a cliché, but we really are the products of our environment.

Recognize these variables can change rapidly, although some solidify and become permanent trends. Bell bottoms and smiley necklaces are a legacy of the 1960s. Ear gauges (earlobe discs) are likely to fade out and be replaced by some other ear decoration. Conversely, smart phones are not going away, but will continue to evolve.

4. **Religion.** There are an estimated 19 major world religions, subdivided into 270 large religious groups, and many smaller ones. If religion influences a buyer's purchasing process, a company needs to understand what those factors are. For example, dietary restrictions are an important issue for Hindu, Muslim, and Jewish faiths, and a food manufacturer needs to be conscious of this when developing products.

5. **Consumer expectations.** In our hyper-connected economy, most of us enter into a buying process with certain preconceived expectations. These expectations are formed from our previous experiences; word of mouth from family, friends, and colleagues; what we know about that industry, product, or service; online reviews; and research. A company needs to be aware of what their buyers' expectations are.

We've all had an experience that exceeds expectations or, conversely, is way beneath them. When our buying experience deviates from what we expect (whether good or bad), we react, usually by telling people and via online reviews and social media. For example, we expect prompt service at a retailer; that the advertised item is not out-of-stock; our dentist isn't going to hurt us; and that there won't be *E. coli* bacteria in the salad.

Note my choice of the word "expect." Very often, **companies focus their core selling points on things people *already* expect—in other words, nothing special.** We'll talk more about this in Chapter 5.

Exceeding expectations. Consider the high-end cosmetic retailer, Sephora, who is recognized for a distinctive customer service model. Positioned to appeal to women ages 20–50, products range from mid to high priced, and focus on buyers who prefer higher quality cosmetics.

I had heard about them through word of mouth as being an awesome place to buy makeup. When I visited, I was boggled at their selection; it overwhelmed me. Yet what took the experience to a whole new level was the customer transaction. No pushiness. No hard sell. No commission-motivated, aggressive sales people. Just incredibly knowledgeable, polite, skilled individuals available to listen to questions, coach on makeup application, and offer suggestions. The only thing the sales person asked me to consider was to write an online review. I left totally impressed, and I talk them up wherever I go. The experience far exceeded my expectations.

Investing the time in doing demographic and motivator research makes a world of difference. Why? Because when you're working on a new product or service concept—or starting a company—**doing this detailed analysis can save you boatloads of money** if you realize that what you thought was a market opportunity actually isn't. It applies whether you're an existing business, just starting out, or just have an idea. Consumer and market research empowers you to make smart business decisions *before* you invest lots of money and time.

A side note: Have you ever noticed that when you say you're an entrepreneur or business owner, some people wonder how you dare to take such a risk vs. being comfortably employed? Going through a buyer evaluation enables you to take *calculated risks*—in other words, you reduce risk through fact-based, well-informed decisions as much as possible.

Let's run through a quick example. Say you want to start a daycare service in your neighborhood. You've researched and defined a proposed target audience: mothers, ages 20–40, who work full- or part-time, with kids ages 5 or under. Your next step is to research the market area you want to serve. And whoa! You discover it's principally single college students under age 25. Red flag! If there are not enough potential buyers in the market—no matter how great your product or service is—you'll struggle to make a go of it. This is known as market demand: are there enough buyers who will want what you offer, and pay for it?

Got ZMOT? In 2011, Google conducted what is now known as the ZMOT study and released an excellent e-book, *The Zero Moment of Truth,* by Jim Lecinski, which illustrates how the purchasing sequence has shifted thanks to the Internet (ZeroMomentofTruth.com).

Originally, a buying decision was influenced by advertising, and then made when a buyer went to the shelf, what Lecinski refers to as the First Moment of Truth. Today, people—especially Millennials and Gen Z—rely heavily on the Internet as a key influence on their decision to buy, *before* they ever enter a store or website. The following paraphrases ZMOT as to how today's buying decision process works.

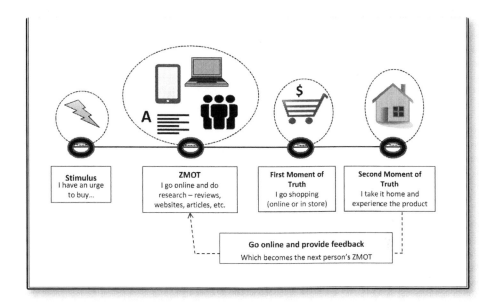

Stimulus I have an urge to buy...	ZMOT I go online and do research – reviews, websites, articles, etc.	First Moment of Truth I go shopping (online or in store)	Second Moment of Truth I take it home and experience the product

Go online and provide feedback
Which becomes the next person's ZMOT

➢ *Could your buyer be knee-high?*

Recognize that sometimes the person you think is doing the buying actually *isn't*. For example, have you ever noticed that as you mosey through the cereal aisle in grocery stores, the bright colorful kids' cereals are usually at knee or hip height? Why? That's children's eye level, and they grab the box and proceed to beg for it. The child is an *influencer*. They don't have money, but they sure have influence! Teenagers, on their limited budgets, are powerful influencers (Mom, Dad, please take notice). Often, **your marketing effort may need to be aimed most strongly at the influencers, with a different marketing approach for the actual buyer.**

A good illustration of this is LeapFrog Enterprises, a toy maker that develops interactive reading systems, educational games, books, and learning toys. Former CEO Michael Wood founded the company in 1995 because he felt the toy market offered nothing to help his three-year-old learn phonics. LeapFrog's target audience is infants and children through age nine. But since children aren't the buyers, LeapFrog actually has two primary audiences. The parents, who must be persuaded that these products—vs. a competitor's—best suit what they want for their kids. But also the children, who take on the role of influencers. How so? Because if they don't like using the products, they won't play with them and it becomes a waste of money. If they like them, they'll want more, boosting sales.

Depending on your type of business, or if you have multiple brands, products, or services, you can have more than one target audience. You need to know who the buyers are in each instance, even if there's some overlap. In the Gillette Personal Care Division, we had multiple shampoo and conditioner lines. White Rain was for the budget-conscious household. Silkience was for the woman willing to pay more for beautiful hair. Tame was for younger women trying to reduce the frizzies.

You might think the wine industry, in which I've consulted for years, has one audience: the consumer. Quite the contrary. It actually can have two or more, depending on where wines are sold. Many states require that alcohol be sold through a distributorship vs. direct to the consumer. So a winery must convince the distributorship—which carries hundreds of other products—to take on and pitch their wines to grocery or alcoholic beverage stores. In other instances, the winery must go direct to the retailer and persuade them to carry their wines. After all that, the winery has to convince the consumer to buy them.

> **"Push & Pull" marketing.** You've likely heard the terms "push" or "pull" marketing. Sounds like a monster truck rally, right? They're actually important strategic marketing tactics.
>
> "Push" refers to hard selling—taking your products or services to the buyers. A sales person makes a call. You slash prices. You put a display out on the showroom floor. You sample your product at a show or retailer. You're pushing the product or service in front of the consumer and wanting them to buy. It is usually short-term sales oriented.
>
> "Pull" is getting the customers to come to you—you're trying to pull them in, create brand loyalty, build relationships, and keep them coming back. It's a long-term sales focus. Tactics include mass media promotions, word-of-mouth referrals, and advertised sales.

If you think figuring out your buyer will take months of work and loads of money, think again. I'm able to help many of my clients go through this process within two to four weeks for a preliminary go/no go decision. Yes, one can spend a lot more time and money to really get down into more detail, but for smaller firms, that may not be an option. Now that you know what to hunt for, you can definitely get started.

Let's take a look at a simple way to visualize how different companies could define their audiences. In this case, the category is seafood restaurants. Some people will tell you the consumers are the same across the category. Not true.

This following chart is based on a visit to both local establishments, and is a sample "cheat sheet" showing how you can do "quick and dirty" research on what buyers want (more on this in Chapter 3) by eyeballing the competition. You can then do online research to round out the competitive profile.

	Red Lobster	Long John Silver's
Positioning	Fresh seafood restaurant	Fried seafood shack
Age	35+	Under 30
Location	Highway proximity	High surface traffic areas
Income	Middle–upper middle	Lower middle–middle
Gender	Male/female/family	Male/female/family
Education	High school/College	High school
Social influences	Fresh seafood is healthy	Seafood is tasty
Ethnic	Anglo	Anglo/Latino
Possible other factors		
Quality of product	Superior	Good
Price	$$	$
Setting	Sit down restaurant	Fast food
Dining experience	Pleasant, relaxing, upscale	Fun, family finger food

See how there are both similarities and differences in the diners? This is sometimes known as buyer overlap. How these companies use marketing will differ because their guests' expectations and demographics are not identical.

➢ Are there enough bodies out there?

Earlier we discussed how setting up a daycare center in a market area that's composed of mostly college-age single women won't succeed. A fundamental question you always need to ask yourself is, are there enough people who want to pay for what you have to offer in your target market area? If there's not enough sales volume because not enough people want to buy your product or service, then chances of profitability are low. Big companies call this market demand, potential demand, or "sales potential."

Once you've defined the prospective buyers, your goal is to find out where they are gathered in higher concentrations. Today, the popular term for that is **"find your tribe."** If you want to sell mountain climbing equipment in a retirement community, sales probably won't be great. Scuba gear in an area without lakes or bodies of water? A challenge. A steakhouse in a vegan neighborhood? Likely to have low traffic. So, if your product or service is location-driven—such as your town or county—then try and quantify how many possible buyers are out there. Even when you're selling over the Internet, estimating sales potential is important, because as you now know, everyone on the Internet is not your buyer.

So how do you estimate your sales potential? The demographic information you've gathered is an essential part of this process. Let's take a shot at this.

What do you think? Lock 'em Up!

You're going to sell a custom-designed security screen door for sliding glass doors. You've sold some and gotten rave reviews. You're ready to scale-up to manufacturing, subcontracting to a local facility until you see where this goes. The doors, being custom-made, are targeted at more affluent home owners, those with homes worth $400,000 or higher. The bank wants to know the potential demand before it loans you money.

Since you're the one who does the installation for the time being, you decide you're willing to drive up to 100 miles to serve customers. Now that you've defined the buyers and the parameters, what are the possible steps you could take to figure out the numbers?

🖋 *Jot down your answer:*_____

_____

_____

Answer: First, note that sometimes you have to use assumptions because the data you need just isn't readily available, or is hidden behind high price tag database options. As long as you note those assumptions, so you don't forget, that's fine. Of course, if everything is based on assumptions without any hard data for an anchor, it should raise red flags for you, and will raise red flags for the bank.

We'll use theoretical numbers to make this easy to visualize:

250,000 Number of homes in the geographic market you're going to serve

187,500 Number of homes that are owned vs. rentals (assuming home owners are more likely to spend money on home improvements): 75%

93,750 Number of owned homes with a value over $400,000: 50%

23,437 Number of these homes likely to have a sliding glass door (based on talks with area homebuilders): 25%

4,687 Number of homeowners likely to buy, based on your sales experience so far: 2 out of every 10, or 20% potential buyers.

Sure, the numbers may be more or less, but this is one approach as to how companies try to calculate how many people could be potential buyers for their products.

Note that in this case, buyers are likely to buy a door just once (vs. shampoo 6 to 12 times a year), so that means that over time, the business owner will have to look at a wider geographic area to maintain or grow sales, as he will have "saturated" his local market—meaning, most of the buyers that are going to buy already have done so.

> ### *A simple way to sabotage your sales*

Another nasty tree waiting to smack you on the zipline is complacency. You've successfully figured out who the customer is and what makes them tick, created a strong marcom campaign around those points, and enjoyed steady sales. Life is good.

If you fly, have you ever noticed the "fasten seatbelt sign" tends to come on *after* you've hit turbulence? Well, now's a good time to fasten your seatbelt.

Zipline Essential #2: Change is permanent—so enjoy the ride.

Fact: consumers are fickle and change constantly. New ideas, innovations, technologies, cultural shifts, celebrity influences… there are dozens of reasons why. But whether you like it or not, you can't count on today's customer being the same in the future.

To prove my point: as of this writing, nearly 50% of people now use *only* their cell phone—they've cut their landline's cords. Imagine being a company like AT&T or Verizon, and the billions spent on physical infrastructure to provide phone service. But their market researchers spotted this trend beginning in the 1990s, when cell phones first began to gain traction, and started to plan ahead. As the senior marketing director of a regional telephone company at the time, I experienced it first-hand.

It's hard to imagine in today's wireless society, but at the time, virtually all data transmission relied on transport over cables. Cell phones were for phone calls. The Internet was still young, and the phone companies got into data and Internet connectivity in a big way. The more capacity you wanted, the more you had to pay, choosing from basic Internet, DSL, T1 cables, and fiber optics.

Meanwhile, both AT&T and Verizon leveraged their massive infrastructure and also became involved with cell phone service. Today they are the primary carriers—other carriers are "renting" space over their existing infrastructure. Simply put, they recognized the shifting wants of buyers, and evolved their business models to adapt to them. Unlike Netscape Navigator, which didn't. Netscape who?

The business world is littered with companies that didn't spot changing consumer wants. Big and small. Remember Woolworth's, Mervyn's, and Montgomery-Ward? Major department stores. All history. Look at how Wal-Mart and Amazon are battling for "share of mind" among shoppers as online buying behavior continues to surge.

Consider the ongoing debates over Uber and Airbnb vs. traditional taxis and hotels. Millennials prefer the on-demand models, also dubbed the shared economy; Gen X and Baby Boomers less so. Think of how the automobile clobbered buggy makers, livery stables, and the demand for horse transportation. Or how trains put an end to pioneer trails, and airplanes heralded the decline of passenger trains.

Demand for products and services changes constantly for a whole slew of reasons, from outside factors over which you have no control, to inside factors which you do. Check out these examples of changing market situations that forced companies to shift gears, or fail.

• *Palm Pilot.* Introduced in 1990s, this was *the* business person's modern device for managing their schedule, keeping notes, and more—popularly known as PDAs (personal digital assistants). When did you last see one? The consolidation of computers onto mobile devices eliminated the need for a specialized product.

- *"Bag cell phones" anyone?* These early 1990s cell phones were about the size and shape of a shoe, and were transported in a bread loaf-sized carrying case. Analog-based, and much more powerful than today's phones, they had tremendous reach despite limited cell tower availability. But they were clunky. Buyers were willing to trade power and communication clarity for the smaller size and carrying convenience of digital phones. Leading to the familiar frustrations of dropped phone calls.

> **The best laid plans….** In my Gillette days, I worked on a new product called Epic Waves. In the late 1980s, perms were the hairstyle du jour. Epic Waves was the brainchild of the team's senior product manager who had overheard a stylist remarking how a perm had to be "locked in." Intrigued, she discovered that a perm could actually be locked in at different stages, resulting in looser or tighter curls.
>
> Research and focus groups indicated strong potential demand among women from mid-teens to late 40s who wanted a perm, but didn't want to spend big bucks at the salon every couple of months. Fast forward to the product launch with all sorts of marketing and wonderful fanfare. But not long after, hairstyles shifted radically to straight, and perms sagged off into history. The moral is that even when you do things correctly, external factors beyond your control can sometimes clobber a good idea.

I like to say that **change is permanent.** Put another way, change is always happening, so it's a permanent feature of the business world. If you don't recognize that the audience is evolving, then you're setting your firm up for future failure. It's vital to learn how to adapt, how to identify what's influencing buyers now, what trends are emerging that may broadside your business, and how to adjust your products and services in response. It might mean retooling a product, modifying a service, even acquiring a competitor. Are you ready?

So let's get you set up on the zipline to success with "equipment" that will enable you and your business to successfully adapt to change and have a smooth ride, such as mapping out a marketing strategy (Chapter 6), speaking from the customer's viewpoint (Chapter 8), and leveraging digital marketing (Chapter 13). Techniques that you will be able to use again and again. After all, who wants to ride only one zipline in business?

A side note: Have you ever wondered why big companies often launch multiple versions of a product (or service)? Because they prefer to cannibalize their own customers.

Huh?

Seriously, that's a genuine marketing expression. Go eyeball the toothpaste shelf. Look at most major brands and what do you see? Total Care, Sensitive Teeth, Brightening, Enamel Strengthening.... yada, yada.

Let's say the buyer currently uses Brand X Whitening, but has seen ads for a Brightening toothpaste and wants to try that. However, if Brand X doesn't carry it, the buyer will likely try a competitor's brand. And what the product manager of Brand X worries about is that the buyer may like it so much, they switch and won't return.

"Product diversification, I like that."

The product manager hopes that by introducing Brand X Brightening, it will actually steal buyers from another company who doesn't carry that type of toothpaste.

At the same time, they know it will likely cause some existing Brand X Whitening buyers to switch to Brand X Brightening. In effect, Brand X is cannibalizing its own buyers—stealing them from their own in-house products. But as long as the buyer is staying with Brand X, that's what matters, because the sales and profits stay *within* the company.

Gutenberg would be shocked…. To my mind, one thing that particularly personifies dramatic change is what has transpired in the printing industry. Local print shops were once commonplace. In the space of two decades, they have gone from the primary way of producing anything in print to battling for survival.

Computer printers, online high volume/high discount specialty providers, and rapidly evolving technologies have radically changed the industry. Paste-ups, film, and camera-ready artwork have been replaced by .pdfs and digital files. Printing press experts who used a loop to inspect color dots and plate alignment have been replaced by computerized systems. Where shops used to do everything in house, they outsource specialized work, such as foiling and embossing. To quote a colleague who has been in the printing business all his life, "Anyone looking to get into the industry, I would tell them, don't bother. It's consolidating so fast, that I don't hold out much hope for local shops in the future."

Defining your buyers, identifying their wants and needs, and evaluating the market's size and sales potential will save you a lot of money, time, and frustration. Unfortunately, many start-ups or companies launching new products or services do the exact opposite, and it's a big reason for the high failure rate. They jump on the zipline without the right equipment, and crash or fall off.

Part 1 – Zipline Highlights

✂ **Marketing can actually kill your business.** If you don't have all your zipline equipment in place and operating correctly, you're not only in for a rough ride, you may run out of money.

✂ **Do you know what "assume" spells?** Just because you want to start a business doesn't mean people want what you have to offer. Research whether or not your product or service "fits" your target buyers' wants and needs in order to generate revenue and profits.

✂ **Invest the time to understand your buyers.** Not everyone is your buyer. You need to know the details about what makes them tick so as to effectively develop and target your marketing outreach efforts to "connect" with them and persuade them to buy.

✂ **Nothing stays the same.** Change is permanent. Your market environment and buyers are constantly evolving. Are you growing and changing with them?

Part 2 – Get Ready to Zip: The Equipment You Need for a Smooth Ride

I think you'll agree that many sports need specialized equipment for optimum results. It's kind of hard to hold your breath for several hours—thank you Jacques Cousteau for the aqualung (aka scuba tank). Jumping out of a plane? I'll let you figure that one out. Even jogging is better with the proper shoes, yoga with a mat, and pole dancing with (ahem) a pole.

So what's the key equipment for ziplining? A helmet, a harness for you to ride in, a trolley to connect to the zipline, carabiners to hook you in, a zipline, and connecting points (platforms, towers, etc.) along which the zipline runs. If any of these are missing, you're going to have a very intimate relationship with the ground.

Marketing is the same. If you're missing the essential equipment, it dramatically increases your risk. The more you know how to use zipline marketing essentials, the easier it is to set your company apart, make what it offers unique and valuable, and **achieve the competitive edge that can lead to sales growth, improved profits, and loyal customers.**

Part 2 reveals to how to leverage your competitors to better position your business, be alert for situations that could put dangerous kinks in your zipline, and assemble and know how to use the five key pieces of zipline marketing equipment to optimize buyers' interest in purchasing your product or service.

Chapter 3 ~ How to Turn Your Competition into Your Best Friend

Fact: in some way, shape, or form, you face competition. Pretending you don't is almost a sure-fire guarantee for failure. Understanding your competitors' key selling points, how they try setting themselves apart from everybody else, and their pricing is a critical anchor for your marketing zipline. The more you know about your competitors, the more you can differentiate your company's products and services to boost consumer interest and sales.

➤ *Why competitors are cannibals*

The competition may be *direct*—somebody offering a service or product just like yours. Or it may be *indirect*—it's similar, or the customer can substitute something else from another company for what you offer. Let's say you're in the trucking business. Direct competition is obviously other trucking firms. But indirect competitors exist because shipping can also be done by rail, boat, and air, and probably by drone in the not-too-far-flung future. So a potential client has multiple options when it comes to shipping.

Why should you care? Ignoring competition is like ignoring branches along your zipline. Not only can they hurt, they can knock you right off. In the early 1900s, passenger train companies ignored the infant airplane and automotive industries because they felt only other railroads were competition. Instead, they should have defined themselves as being in the transportation business, and planned for emerging competitors. Today, passenger trains are often tax-payer subsidized, unable to operate profitably on their own.

By contrast, General Motors and some other big players in today's auto industry are redefining their businesses. They're evolving from being car manufacturers to makers of "personal mobility" devices, a part of the migration toward self-driving cars that are already being tested in select urban environments.

> *Zipline Essential #3:* **Knowing your competitors can give you the competitive edge.**

There's another reason you need to care: Because buyers (individuals or companies) have a finite amount of money to spend, and **you're competing for a share of their dollars**. If you're B2B (business to business), firms have specific budgets. For B2C (business to consumer), it's individuals' available discretionary income. How much money they have available is a mission critical part in evaluating who's going to buy from you (more on this in Chapter 7).

Just like you, your competitors have a primary objective—to be successful—which usually translates into capturing a big enough share of the market to meet their objectives, whether financial, market position, brand recognition, charitable, or other. Seriously, do you know any company who launches with the explicit goal to fail?

And, just like you, they're competing for a bigger share of the consumer's dollar. That means if they can be better, smarter, more appealing (and the list goes on), they'll capture more dollars than you, and eat you up. Don't think this applies to just "little companies." Haven't you read how Amazon is redefining the retail arena, forcing mega-giants such as Wal-Mart and Target to redesign their business models? Welcome to the competitive marketplace!

> ➤ *How shopping the competition can jump start your business*

You may look at competitors and only see them as "the enemy." Consider this: **your competition is actually a gold mine of information!** They can give you a leg up on starting your business, save you from having to reinvent the wheel, provide valuable buyer data and insights, and reveal marketing tools and tactics that will save you time and money. Why wouldn't you want to know more about them?

> **Super Premium Wines – Nobody's There Yet!** When I was the marketing director for Delicato Family Vineyards, the wine industry was split into three segments: jug wines, premium (under $6), and over $10. Hard to imagine today, but $7 to $10 for a 750-mL bottle was a no-man's land for wine pricing.
>
> I traveled the eastern seaboard for two weeks to evaluate competitors and to see how our wines were doing in different markets. I studied packaging, pricing, wine selection, shelf placement, and promotional materials. In the process, I noticed that Fetzer had introduced a line of varietal wines at $7 to $8 for a 750-mL bottle. I chatted up the retail managers and distributors, and they consistently reported that they were seeing buyers wanting to trade up to better quality wines, but were not willing to pay $10.

> I almost fell into the VP of Marketing's door as soon as I returned, trumpeting the void in the market. After additional research, pitching the Board of Directors on the idea, and getting everyone excited, we did the impossible. We created and released two entirely new brands within six months: Delicato Blue Label and Monterra, priced in the $7 to $9 range. This category would later be known as Super Premium—and we were among the earliest players. The rest of the story? We couldn't keep up with demand, and sold out within six months.
>
> This is just one example of how studying the competition and the market can give a company an opportunity to jump ahead of other firms, and succeed.

So, right now, let's **test how well you know your competition**, whether you're established or a start-up. Take a few minutes to write the answers to the following questions.

1. Who are the competitors in the market(s) you serve?

2. How many competitors are there—both direct and indirect?

3. Where is each one located relative to the markets your company serves (remember they may be outside your immediate market, or even on the Internet)?

4. What services or products do they offer (the same as you, more, less)?

5. Who is their target audience(s)? Who is buying from them?

6. What are they doing to set themselves apart from everybody else (also known as differentiating themselves)?

7. What are their key selling points?

8. What are they saying about themselves (because you don't want to sound just like them)?

9. What are they charging buyers; what's their pricing?

10. How do you honestly feel you stack up when compared to them? What do you feel are your strengths compared to them, and your weaknesses?

If you can answer all these questions for each competitor, you get five gold stars! If you can't, or don't (yet) see why this is important, keep reading.

➤ *7 simple ways to learn a lot about your competitors*

Thanks to the Internet, researching your competition is fairly straightforward. However, it's not the only thing you should use if you want a well-rounded picture. Follow these **seven steps to effectively shop your competitors** and gather what data you can get from each source. Task yourself with doing this not only as a business owner or manager, but as if you were the customer doing the shopping. That's what it's all about. It's a critical zipline essential.

> *Zipline Essential #4*: **Always look at things from your customer's viewpoint.**

1. Websites: An absolute data mother lode, and a great source for pricing, products, and services. You can see how up to date the firm is with today's technologies. Plus, it's where you'll find their positioning tagline or slogan, such as Red Lobster, Sea Food Differently; McDonald's, I'm Lovin' It; Visa, Everywhere you want to be; Mary Kay Cosmetics, Enriching women's lives; Subaru, Confidence in Motion; Smucker's, With a name like Smucker's it's got to be good (which has been around forever, a testament to its effectiveness).

You can also look at the type of language and "voice" used on the website—complex, simple, slang, sophisticated? Photos and graphics will reveal insights as to who the firm considers its target audience. Even their choice of logo, fonts, and colors is important to evaluate, as is the website layout, since these all may influence what you decide to do.

2. Phone book: OK, if you're under age 40, you're probably shaking your head. But seriously, this is still a very useful resource, depending on the geographic area you serve and who your customers are. First, look under the different yellow page listings for your type of business. This is a fast way to count how many potential area competitors you may have.

Next, look at the companies that have ads. From these you can often obtain website listings. But, more importantly, you can see how they position themselves, their featured selling points, and the images they use. Firms that can afford to buy yellow page ads likely are in a stronger financial position. Realize that many people actually still do start with the phone book, particularly an older audience. Should you advertise here too? We'll talk about that in Chapter 11.

3. **Online Listings:** Yelp, Yahoo, Bing, Google, among others, are all competing to provide online business listings. It's an excellent place to get an extended count of competitors, find websites, and check out key selling points, as well as any images used to showcase the company. Additional resources include industry listings and directories.

4. **Online Reviews:** Online reviews are a fabulous place to read customer comments and find out what people do and *don't* like. Let's say 12 reviewers complain that QRT Automotive Center never gets the job done on time, and they frequently have to bring back their car due to poor workmanship. If you want to open a competing shop, offering a solution to that complaint may be an opportunity to set yourself apart, and a key selling point in your messaging.

5. **Call and act like a customer:** "Shopping the competition" is a common practice. Prepare some questions so you sound like a real customer and that collect relevant information. You might ask for a quote, inquire about the firm's policies or a particular service. Is the person you speak to knowledgeable? Helpful? Do they get back to you when promised? This "transaction" is what real customers are experiencing. Are there ways you could do it better? FYI, many competitors are likely doing the same to you.

6. **Go visit:** If your competitors have a physical location, head on over. Take a look at their storefront and signage. Check out the location, foot traffic, and parking. Go in and see how it feels—welcoming, clean, cluttered, dirty? Shelves half-empty? Is there a gum-snapping cashier on a cell phone who ignores you? Do you want to stay or flee the premises? Again, you're walking in the customers' footsteps and their experience.

7. **Be a customer:** Eat a meal, have your car fixed, shop at the store, place an online order. Actually experience the process, and see what works well and what doesn't. Are you satisfied, or left wanting?

An important note: recognize that *you* may not be their target audience, and that what annoys you delights their buyers. As an example, I was shopping at a clothing boutique, and the music was rap. Looking around, it was obvious that their buyers were twenty-somethings, and they loved the music. Clearly, the retailer was tailoring the customer experience to its primary buyers.

Here's a secret on how to take advantage of the "big kids on the block." While you may not consider your company in the same league as a large competitor, still check them out thoroughly. Big companies spend hundreds of thousands, even millions of dollars on consumer and market research. You can take advantage of those results by looking at what they're doing, evaluating their best practices, and incorporating that information into how you run and market your business. You're doing that now by reading this book.

Go back to the seafood restaurant comparison chart in Chapter 2, page 23. That's an example of a competitive analysis grid—an easy way to profile your competition and compare them to each other, and to your business.

If you have a number of competitors, and would like to use our basic Zipline Competitive Analysis Grid, visit ZiplinetoSuccess.com/Resources to download it for free.

Using the competition to grow a business. Julia Rhodes is on a mission to give every student a voice. Founder and president of KleenSlate Concepts (KleenSlate.com), Julia had been a teacher for 14 years and was, in her words, "fed up with low quality dry erase products," which constantly needed to be replaced, costing teachers time and money. Determined to solve the problem, she took early retirement and invested in her dry erase idea, creating KleenSlate—customizable handheld whiteboards that enable kids to write and respond in real time while saving teachers time, energy, and resources.

Along the way, Julia discovered how challenging being a start-up can be. Big competitors copied her ideas. But contrary to what most business people would do, Julia saw it as an opportunity to allow them to spend the funds to create product awareness and interest in the market. She believed they would not be able to compete with her quality, but she didn't have the deep pockets for a major ad campaign. So while the big firms spent lots of money on ads and promotions, she concentrated on learning the ropes of running an international business, focusing on select target audiences, building a stellar reputation, and fine-tuning and expanding her products to add markers and a host of accessories.

Her unusual strategy of leveraging the competition worked. Within a couple of years, the competitors dropped out, and Julia stepped into the void with her proven products.

Today, KleenSlate products can be found around the globe. Says Julia, "Although we are first and foremost an educational company, our chief goal has always been helping people communicate. Watching our products take on a life of their own and help people in ways we never expected has inspired us to keep creating. We intend to improve education around the world, create a better future for the next generation, and help everyone find their voice."

I hope you now appreciate that far from being "the enemy," your competitors are a valuable fountain of information that can be used to your advantage, from spotting unfulfilled opportunities, to insights on how to set your firm apart in a way that connects with consumers.

A final note: smart companies monitor competitors on a regular basis, at minimum once a year. Why? Because they want to keep an eye on changes that could impact their own business. Has pricing changed? Products been introduced or discontinued? Has the website changed, or been rewritten? Do they have a new slogan? And are there any newbies who have opened? The outcome of doing a regular competitive review will influence your own business and marketing strategies to ensure you maintain a competitive edge and improve your ride on the zipline to success.

Chapter 4 ~ Setting Yourself Up for Success

Riding a zipline doesn't mean you're restricted to only one route, or that you must stick with only one way of doing things. I've seen multi-route ziplines where riders can switch off at different stages to different rides depending on their interest, skill level, or time. Running a business is the same. You plan, you prepare, you take action, yet you're flexible enough to switch ziplines as different needs arise.

Too often, though, owners and managers skip critical marketing steps that may not seem important at the time. Maybe they take a shortcut, or are too busy to notice that there are changes among their buyers, competitors, or the market that will have a direct impact on the firm's future. But the missing marketing elements gradually—or sometimes swiftly—start to set up obstructions along the zipline, roughing up the ride to the point where the rider wants to quit—or falls off.

So let's look at the steps you can take to stay ahead of the ever-changing marketplace, adapt to digital changes, ensure you offer value-added products and services, and set yourself up for success.

➤ *How shortcuts can lead to costly mistakes*

Warning! Avoid "easy" shortcuts! We're all super busy, and the temptation to cut corners or to make assumptions is natural. Maybe we skip over steps. Assume everybody is on the same page. Don't review or double check. Don't plan. Unfortunately, the outcome of doing this can be disastrous. Think about the Mars Climate Orbiter failure. NASA lost a $125 million orbiter because a Lockheed Martin engineering team used U.S. standard units of measurement while NASA's team used the more conventional SI metric system for a key spacecraft operation. People assumed things, and didn't take the time to double check. Of course the two different systems of measurements didn't dovetail. Years of work, planning, and money literally all went up in smoke.

As we know from Chapters 2 and 3, it's essential to take the steps to figure out who and where your buyers are, what makes them tick, and to understand your competitors. Failing to complete that research and have those critical anchors prepared will make it challenging to set up a successful Marketing Zipline in Part 3. If you already knew the answers, excellent. If not, invest the time to complete these action items.

By the way, if you think that a large established firm with strong brand recognition can't trip over themselves, think again. The following firms introduced products and assumed success because they were launched under recognized brand names. In hindsight, they took shortcuts by failing to probe into their buyers' interest and purchase probability, or to thoroughly assess the marketplace *before* investing millions of dollars. Here are a few legendary product mistakes. See if you can figure out what went wrong.

- *McDonald's – An Arch failure:* In 1996, McDonald's launched the Arch Deluxe, a quarter pound burger aimed at adults with more sophisticated palates. At the time, it cost around $2.29, compared with the $1.90 Big Mac. McDonald's spent $100 million advertising specifically to adults. Why do you think it flopped?
    - *Answer:* McDonald's target audience doesn't eat there for sophistication; they go for inexpensive fast food. The product didn't "fit" the buyers' wants.

- *Coca-Cola – Don't mess with success:* In the early 1980s, declining sales motivated Coca-Cola to tinker with its proprietary formula for the first time in 99 years and launch "New Coke." They also decided to discontinue the original flavor. It fizzled. Why do you think?
    - *Answer:* While not actually disliking New Coke, buyers wanted the original; they were passionate about its taste. Protest groups popped up around the country. Seventy-seven days later, the company brought back the original Coke with a new name, "Coca-Cola Classic." They lost more than $30 million.

- *Apple – Ahead of its time:* Hard to imagine Apple could stumble, but it has. In 1993, it launched the Newton MessagePad PDA. While quaint by today's standards, back then it was revolutionary—among the first devices to offer basic computing functions in a handheld unit. Handwriting recognition was the main selling point. Any idea why it bombed?
    - *Answer:* Failure to perform as promised, including the handwriting feature not working properly during the initial release. Frustrated customers complained loudly. Discontinued in 1998, it did lay the groundwork for future products such as the Palm Pilot, Blackberry, and even today's iPhone.

- *Hewlett Packard – Mine's better than yours.* In 2011, Hewlett Packard launched the TouchPad to compete with Apple's iPad. Although well-designed and promoted extensively, it failed, forcing the company to write off $885 million in assets. What happened?

    ○ *Answer:* Sometimes you can't compete head-to-head with a well-established market leader if you're offering a product or service that isn't unique enough to set it apart.

Now a word on the concept of "running it up the flagpole," which is another type of shortcut. Every so many years, this idea cycles around as a popular marketing approach touted as a fast way to get a product to market. The original mindset was actually to run *an idea* up the flagpole—meaning to test it among consumers—*prior* to investing significant amounts of time and funds into a product or service's launch.

Today, some companies will do the modern flagpole version: invest lots of dollars to get something to market as fast as possible. Frequently, it's a flop or doesn't gain the traction expected, or generate the desired revenue and profits. Why? Often it's because this flagpole method skips the research stage, which you now know is a critical zipline marketing essential. Individuals or firms with deep pockets sometimes go this route, willing to write off the loss if things don't succeed. Most companies aren't in a financial position to do this.

Now, if you can test-launch a new product or service with minimal investment, it may be worthwhile to run it up the flagpole—for example, there's no packaging, special training, or additional personnel needed, or production molds to be created, and/or it's just a logical, easy-to-implement extension of something you're already doing. Technology companies selling software, services, and apps do this all the time because of not needing to commit to tangible products and big-ticket investments—although, in reality, hundreds or thousands of people-hours still constitute an investment.

But if it's going to cost time and money to make it happen, make the effort to implement the steps in this book to increase your probabilities of success. Put it another way: if you're going to ride the zipline to success, then invest in the time and "equipment" to make it a profitable experience. Because don't you want to enjoy the ride?

No Hugs for Teddy Bear. A winery launched a new line of wines under the label Teddy Bear, building on the popularity of collecting teddy bears at that time. No market research was done; it was just "run up the flagpole" to see what would happen. Wines were created for the product line, packaging designed, and sales materials were produced.

It failed for three reasons. First, in alcoholic beverage sales, most products must pass through distributors, then through retailers—what's known as a three-tier distribution system. Both carry so many wines, liqueurs, and whatnot that it's hard for any new product to capture their attention, or for their salespeople to promote it, or for it to get a good shelf placement—without major financial incentives (aka spiffs).

Second, by the time it came out, there were so many well-established competitors in the same price segment that, without a huge investment in advertising, the products were invisible. Except for the label, it had nothing that set it apart from the hundreds of other brands. And third, people weren't keen on the idea of cute teddy bears on alcoholic beverages, and said it was inappropriate. Strike three!

➤ *Beware the "unexpected" business killers*

We all may like to think we're in control of our market environment, but the truth is we only control a fragment of our business universe. So much is going on out there that has the potential to affect sales and profits, that unless you're a mega-firm with lobbyers and people in positions of influence, you're pretty much just a leaf floating along on the current. Many of these external factors can impact a company's bottom line whether you have an idea, or are a new or established business.

Did you know that every day, thanks to the Internet, 24-hour TV, and mobile devices, we're bombarded with five times as much information as in 1986? Case in point: broadcast TV now averages 10 minutes of commercials per half hour, nearly double what it was in 1981. No wonder people record on DVRs so they can fast forward through commercials! As a result of this deluge, we shield ourselves from information overload and impose mental filters to manage our time-starved days. We're effectively tuning out what we don't think is relevant.

But here's the danger of tuning out *too* much. **Ripples occurring in one industry or market may have a domino effect on yours.** If your nose is to the grindstone managing day-to-day issues, you may not see problems coming until they smack you right in the face. I'm the first to admit you can't keep on top of every single thing, but maintaining a superficial awareness—the "topline" on what's going on in the world, and among consumers and other industries—can prove invaluable, and alert you to the winds of change.

How powerful is this domino effect? Sony, an established technology player, was at the forefront of video recording when it launched the Betamax in 1975, a technology it elected not to license to others. But a year later, another Japanese firm, JVC, released a competing technology—the Video Home System, known as VHS. Four other companies started selling VHS units by early 1977. The two formats were incompatible, forcing buyers to select between them; they went with VHS, since they had a greater selection of manufacturers. Betamax got left behind. But the story doesn't end there.

A hallmark of technology's rapid progression is that products often have very short life cycles. VHS dominated until the late 1990s, supporting such firms as Blockbuster Video. Then came DVDs, requiring new equipment, and "suddenly" VHS began to fade, forcing Blockbuster to spend millions on DVDs in attempt to straddle the shift. It finally closed its stores in 2013 as Netflix and streaming video surged in popularity. Blu-ray popped up in 2006, touted as having better visual quality, but with streaming video, it's likely to be a technology that arrived too late to market. This sequence is a strong example of an industry that is in constant flux fueling failure and success—and how companies not paying close attention get taken out.

You may be surprised by all the things shown below that can impact a business.

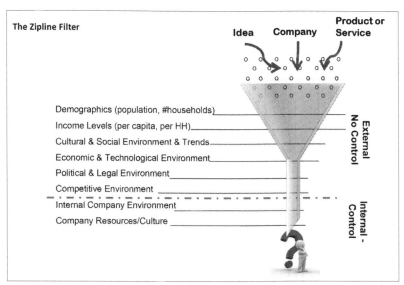

Notice how many elements are beyond your control. These external things will happen and can impact your business. A recession hammers incomes. Legislation redefines social factors. New competitors join the fray. The truth is, **you only "control" your company and how you respond to the changes and obstacles** that come at you on the zipline.

A practical way to actually gain some control over external variables is by keeping tabs on how they're shifting, in what ways those changes could affect the business—good, bad, or indifferent—and then planning how to correct your course to respond to this. Let's take a look at some of these factors, and examples of changes and their impacts.

- *Demographics* – Population shifts in towns and regions are common. Many are experiencing outmigration—people moving out in search of better paying jobs, better communities, and better schools. They leave behind older folks, usually one- or two-person households, many on fixed incomes who may not be working.
    - *Impact risks:* This can lead to a declining number of kids, schools closing and teacher layoffs, stores thinning their merchandise mix to less profitable products, and slumping real estate values due to shrinking demand for family homes.
- *Income* – You hear it all the time: roughly 70% of all U.S. economic growth is driven by consumer spending. Income expansion or shrinkage fuels economic growth or contraction, from tiny towns to giant cities.
    - *Impact risks:* Tight discretionary income leads to holding off on big ticket and even small ticket items; buying only what is needed, shopping focuses on best value. In its extreme, you have the Great Recession. Conversely, more money tends to burn holes in consumers' pockets and they spend. If you're B2B, you can get caught in a halo effect. As your clients are impacted by their customers' purchasing changes, their own buying patterns ebb and flow.
- *Cultural & Social Trends* – As seen in Chapter 2, these are constantly evolving, from fashion to media, to home styles to food choices. Look at food labeling trends—more people want to know country-of-origin, GMO, organic vs. natural vs. standard, and ingredients.

- *Impact risks:* What's hot becomes not; people shop where what they want is available; convenience is king; and social media accelerates—or short circuits—the popularity of darn near everything.

�֍ *Economic environment* – The economy is always in a state of flux; it's just a fact of business life. Dollar valuations, interest rate shifts, political changes… the list goes on. Keeping a pulse on international, national, and regional trends is essential because such variables can affect your business, shoving it up, down, or sideways.

If you're older than seven years of age, you experienced the Great Recession as an extreme economic swing. But did you know that like earthquakes, recessions of varying magnitudes hit the economy on average once every five to ten years? Take a look at the following graph of recessions of the 20th century. Study their start *and* their duration.

- *Impact risks:* Not only do recessions increase the likelihood that buyers may be more conservative in their spending, but realize there's always a laggard recovery period after a recession officially ends. Technically, the Great Recession ended in 2009. Yet in many markets, it was not until 2013 that conditions seemed to improve. If you do not plan for these inevitable contractions—in other words, have money socked away for a rainy day—you may not survive. I advise all my clients to start putting away survival capital, even if it's just $500 per month, as quickly as possible.

Recessions of the 20th Century
Dates & Months of Duration

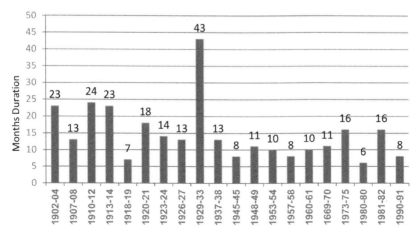

✂ *Technology* – Moore's Law states that the number of transistors on a microchip will increase exponentially, typically doubling every two years, making for the rapid progression of computer hardware—and unpredictable changes in technology that will affect our companies. In the past 30 years, technology as a variable in a firm's success or failure has exploded. Whether in the form of products, services, marketing, or operations, it impacts virtually every aspect of business.

Consider the Y2K technology crisis. Pre-existing lines of code upon which many programs were built were expected to fail at midnight at the start of the 21st century. I worked at a company specializing in business phone systems, which were considered at risk. For all of 1999, we focused on marketing new secure systems and equipment "patches" to protect companies—and had a banner sales year.

- *Impact risks:* Technology can clobber companies by making their products or services less relevant or too expensive from a buyer's viewpoint. Consider how people are migrating to online shopping. Why? It's easy, convenient, and is often perceived as cheaper than going to brick-and-mortar stores.

✂ *Political & Legal environment* – Political shifts and legal rulings can change the business climate. A more conservative or liberal body of decision makers may or may not favor company practices. Consider the issue of corporate inversions—giant firms merging with offshore corporations to reduce taxes. It's nothing new, but came under scrutiny in 2015, and new regulations may negate this practice.

- *Impact risks:* Too often companies shrug off being politically and legally aware of their industry and overall trends. New regulations and laws can severely curtail or dramatically increase costs of doing business. Being alert to emerging changes can allow a firm to respond before it's too late.

✂ *Competitive environment* – See Chapter 3! Summed up, know and keep tabs on your competitors. Watch out for new ones. And modify your course as needed to maintain a competitive edge.

➤ **The truth about the customer service digital paradigm shift**

A common objection I often hear from business owners and managers is,

"Everybody's on the Internet now, and this marketing essentials stuff can't be important anymore." Not exactly, and not true. Let's tackle both these issues.

Back in the dot.com mania of the late 1990s, everyone predicted that within just a few years, nobody would shop at stores anymore—and this was *before* smart phones! However, to adapt a famous quote from comedian Mark Twain, reports of the demise of brick-and-mortar stores have been grossly exaggerated.

Yes, the number of folks who shop on the Internet keeps growing, as evidenced during the 2015 holiday season where Black Friday online sales increased 14.3% to $2.74 billion. Look at Barnes & Noble Booksellers. Talk about a double broadside! The company's traditional sales model has been disrupted by online retail *and* they are selling books, a product also being redefined by technology. As I'm sure you'll agree, online shopping is a cultural and economic change that isn't going away.

For companies selling commodity goods (the same brands and products), it's been a nightmare slugfest. **If what you sell and how you present the business sounds the same as everybody else, then your buyers will primarily shop on price**. That's how the Internet makes it hairy for "same as everybody else" companies. Consider how during the 2000s, we had several major tech chain stores—The Good Guys, Best Buy, and Radio Shack—mostly carrying similar or the same merchandise. Today, we have Best Buy, and even it's struggling, because people go check out the products, then look online for something cheaper. Look at your own buying behavior. Can you honestly say you don't do this sometimes?

> *Zipline Essential #5:* Make buyers focus on your value, not just your price.

While consumers' shopping behavior are changing thanks to the evolving online marketplace, marketing-savvy brick-and-mortar stores are reinventing themselves to adapt to change. Those that don't are toast.

How? By seeking to make themselves stand out with special benefits, known as value-added services, which boost satisfaction and make their firm memorable to a buyer. Looked at another way, their goal is to avoid selling a commodity product or service, and to instead sell a value bundle that distinguishes what they have to offer from other competitors, and pushes the buyer's decision-making process beyond pure price comparisons.

First, they accept that people are buying online. Consequently, they have an evolving digital marketing strategy to make themselves available online, and then enhance the online shopping experience by enabling a person to either pick it up at a local store or have it delivered. Purely online retailers can't offer that, so it's one way to differentiate.

Case in point: When I bought a portable DVD player, I researched it online, read reviews, and after price-comparing, purchased online from Best Buy, even though they were $2 higher. Why? I liked the option of being able to return it to my local store, and avoiding the hassle of shipping it back if there was a problem. I was also willing to pay for the firm's reputation and proven customer service. Best Buy's ship-to-consumer with local return is a value-added service—they earned my business, even at a higher price than their competition!

Look at it this way: The Internet is no more than a much-expanded way to reach buyers. But it comes with a lot more competition. This makes zipline marketing essentials more important than ever. You have to operate with the best equipment possible to have a good ride and increase your success opportunities.

Recognize that just as they do in brick-and-mortar stores, in their "evaluation equation" buyers are still weighing your price, quality of product or service, availability, and what makes yours special. We'll get into real depth on this in Chapter 5.

Fact: The digital arena enables customers to shop beyond the limitations of their home town. **Your challenge is to give them a clear and persuasive "reason why to buy" from you—whether in person or online.** And a huge part of that is service—impeccable, customer-centric service—that sets you apart. Because *that* is what generates reviews, customer discussions, and sales, as Andy Sernovitz points out in his insightful book *Word of Mouth Marketing.*

And now I have to clamber up on my soapbox for a moment with regard to "quality customer service," "integrity/honesty," and "dependable follow up." Every single one of my clients proudly informs me they do these. Well, duh! I should hope so! I mean, seriously, do you know anybody who sells themselves saying "lousy customer service," "dishonest," and "we don't follow up"? Customers *expect* you to do this, so it's not the primary message you want to focus on as to what makes you unique. Yes, you need to mention it, depending on your products and industry, but they're not what I call Tier 1 selling points—more on this issue in Chapter 8.

If these commonplace selling points are the company's core message, you come across as sounding just like everybody else, which increases the risk of being seen as a commodity, and being compared mainly on price. The real question is, what do you do to make the customer experience exceptional? What sets it apart? *That's* what makes it memorable and unique. More on this in Chapter 5. OK, I'll hop down off my soapbox now.

The 80/20 Rule or the Golden Geese Rule. Business owners and managers often get caught up in treating all customers equally when, in fact, they're not all of equal value. Also known as Pareto's Principle, the 80/20 rule means that in any situation, a few elements (20%) are vital and many (80%) are trivial. The Pareto Principle's value for a manager is that it reminds you to focus on the 20% that's important.

From a marketing perspective, 80% of sales will come from 20% of your sales staff, or 80% of sales will come from 20% of your customers. Looked at another way, **20% of your customers are Golden Geese.** These are the ones you want to treat as VIPs, with extra bells, whistles, and benefits to secure their loyalty.

Do you know who your Golden Geese are? If the answer is no, then it's time to find out.

We humans are tactile and emotional creatures. Once we "know" the product, yes, we are more likely to buy online. However, while a piece of chocolate online can appear yummy, the pleasure of that free sample from Sees Chocolates lures me happily into the store every time. A lovely sweater that looks good in an online or print ad may be frumpy when you try it on. Brick-and-mortar stores are still going strong because we like to experience things: to interact, try, touch, and smell—not to mention, get out of the house. And knowing that about your customers is an essential part of your zipline marketing equipment.

Remember how in Chapter 2 we talked about what motivates people? **Motivations are often emotionally driven.** And those in part are fueled by tactile experiences. Consider this: Millennials are often described as a generation that seeks experiences—"experiential"—and big companies today are repackaging their products and services to showcase how they create a personalized experience that caters to the wants of this audience. The more you make your customer's experience emotional and tactile, the more likely they will be to remain loyal to you and less likely to shop around purely on price.

Now, let's start getting you equipped for the next phase of your zipline ride.

Chapter 5 ~ Five Critical Zipline Action Steps

This is it. When you assemble your zipline marketing gear, and get ready to ride the zipline. Successful zipline marketing has five critical action steps you need to determine and define if you're going to make things happen. And while I could write a book on each of these sections, this will give you a solid foundation.

We're going to cover a lot of ground, so here's a quick summary of the major essentials:

✂ Avoid believing that your product or service is a "one size fits all."

✂ Market from your customer's viewpoint to help you to stand out from the crowd.

✂ Translate what you know about your buyers into promotions and ads that will "connect."

✂ Make sure your products and services are in the right places for buyers to find.

✂ Know the key steps to creating smart pricing strategies to deliver profits.

Here's my business zipline model to help you visualize what we're tackling in this chapter. See how the zipline is anchored by the work you did in Chapters 2 and 3? Note how everything is linked. Because, **in effective marketing, all the marketing essentials are interfacing for optimum results.** And understand that this is not a "single ride" process. You are constantly riding the zipline, adjusting different essentials as new information comes in to maintain a smooth ride, and starting a new ride with each new product or service introduction.

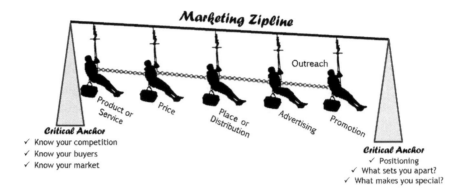

Now I'm going to respectfully disagree with some who insist that marketing essentials are dead branches in the business tree. Quite the contrary. In our fluid economy, I think they're more important than ever. Yes, implementation methods are being redefined. Communication techniques are rapidly evolving. But marketing essentials are like a skeleton—you can change flesh, skin tone, hair, eyes, and gender—but it's still a person. Take away the skeleton, and what's left? A blob with eyes.

So, let's get down to the zipline marketing essentials.

> *Zipline Essential #6*: Marketing is *not* a synonym for advertising and promotion.

Let's address one of the hurdles I have to overcome when first working with many clients: the belief that marketing is a synonym for advertising and promotion. It's not. That's like saying if you wear a helmet, you're ziplining. Both are key pieces of equipment, but are only two elements of marketing communications or what I call marketing outreach, which also includes PR, webinars, sponsorships—all the efforts to connect with customers. Marketing is so much more than ads and promos.

For a productive and enjoyable zipline ride, you have to have *all* the equipment, not just parts of it, operating correctly. Knowing this, you're now prepared for the rest of this chapter.

➢ *Why a one-size fits all approach rarely works*
  for your product or service

Many businesses make the mistake of taking a one-size-fits-all approach in the design of their product or service, instead of tailoring these to their clients' wants or needs. They assume all their customers want the same thing. Remember what assume spells? Unless you serve a very, very narrow industry segment with one specialized product, this approach usually doesn't work very well.

Often, as I work with clients, I consistently find that many are approaching marketing with this mindset, and because it fails, they complain that "marketing" is a waste of money. I've dubbed this the "chuck it at the wall and hope it sticks" method. Usually, it just slides down.

If everybody wanted the same thing, there would be only one variety of car, one perfume, one color jacket, one shoe style. There would be only one type of social media platform, one wine company, one hotel chain. Admittedly, most companies would love it if they were the only provider, and many strive to achieve that—it's called a monopoly. Which is about the time that the government evaluates the firm for anti-trust issues; think cable companies and airline mergers. While you may succeed in having a monopoly in your regional market, unless you really do make or offer something nobody else does, you know there's competition somewhere.

It's because **people *don't* want the same thing over and over again that there are opportunities for new companies, new ideas, and new ways of doing things.** As you've seen in the earlier chapters, those opportunities can be identified through researching customers, competitors, industries, and emerging socioeconomic and cultural trends—the critical anchors to the marketing zipline.

I always get a chuckle when people say, "Oooh, nobody saw the smart phone coming." Puh-lease! The fusion of phones and computers has been evolving since the early 1990s. As people have grown more mobile, they jump on new solutions to stay connected. Today's touch screen digital wristwatches—which, by the way, were "used" by Dick Tracy back in the 1930s! —are simply one more step in the merger of convenience and technology.

So what are you doing, or going to do, to avoid a one-size-fits-all mindset and make sure your products and services are tailored to the different wants and needs of your buyers?

➢ *How to talk WIFME to position yourself to stand out from the crowd*

When you're looking at your products, services, and business from a marketing perspective, you need to consider what your prospects are *really* looking for. And, if you're an established business, *why* people are buying from you. Put another way, what are their **reasons why to buy**? If you can't provide a top of mind answer, then you don't know (yet). This is a key part of how you position the business. Understanding what sets your company, product, or service apart and makes it special in the buyers' minds. As business expert and author Seth Godin says, "Marketing is a contest for people's attention."

Can you answer, **how do you solve the buyer's WIFME: "what's in it for me"?** WIFME is all about what end-benefits they get out of purchasing from you. In marketing, this is often referred to as a Problem–Solution strategy.

Is it your location? Price? Uniqueness? Exclusivity? Your reason for being in business? Does it make them look/feel/smell good? Does it make them stand out? Does it impress their friends? Does it make them feel safe/healthy/respected? Do you inspire trust/excitement/innovation/dependability? Do you bring added-value through warranties, follow up, customer service, loyalty programs, or other things that distinguish you from competitors? Is there anything you do that nobody else does, or you do better than anybody else? The answer should be a resounding "yes!" Let's take a look at a mini case history to get you thinking.

What would you do? **Creating cachet for heating and air conditioning systems**

Arthur's Heating & Air Conditioning was a 30-year-old business. His primary marketing message had been about factory-certified technicians, high-end brand name equipment, and company longevity. Business had been great due to the home-building boom when demand outstripped supply. But once the Great Recession hit, he kept losing bids to lower-priced competitors. However, he had well-established vendor relationships that he didn't want to lose. He didn't have money to spend on lots of market research or advertising. But he had to turn his business around or go under. What would you recommend he do?

*Jot down your answer:*_____

_____

_____

Answer: Leverage the existing available data. Arthur and I tackled the problem using two tools: survey data and the phone book. Yes, the "obsolete" phone book—remember how useful it is with competitive research?

Arthur regularly conducts customer surveys to measure client satisfaction, and always invites people to provide a written comment. We data-mined these for common themes, and two things that jumped out were that clients skewed female, and how much they trusted and depended upon him. Remember we're talking about equipment that can run into thousands of dollars, and letting some strange guy in your house to do repairs. It's frequently the woman who's at home to await the repair guy, so trust really *is* a key motivational factor.

Next, we looked at each competitor's ad copy in the phone book, and guess what? Everybody was mostly repeating the same selling points. After crossing out duplicated phrases, we isolated unique claims some firms were making to set themselves apart, such as: serving veterans; speaking Spanish; 24/7 emergency on-call. But nobody was "selling" trust. How could Arthur create a "trust" message that would really connect with prospects?

> We crafted a unique and innovative message: free second opinion. It implied Arthur was so confident in the quality of his technicians, service, and products, he would come in and review a competitor's bid and give an honest written opinion of what the buyer should question, or advise if it looked OK. No gimmicks. No selling. Nada.
>
> People loved it. It instilled trust and confidence. Even if a buyer went with a competitor, they often would call Arthur for repairs and advice, and subsequently even buy a system from him. He's still using the message; it's become his signature, and nobody in his market can copy the phrase because it's associated with his firm.

Another way of looking at what your product or service does for people is by identifying what problem(s) it solves, or is going to solve, for them. **People usually buy because they have a problem, need, or want that they hope to resolve.** Please re-read that last line. The washing machine broke = need a new one. There's nothing in the fridge = go to a restaurant or the grocery store. The jeans don't fit anymore = time for a new pair, or a diet. We're bored = let's go to a movie. I just got a bonus = it's time for a new car. My business isn't performing the way I want = time to consider outside expert help.

Take a look at your own purchase behaviors. Something occurs that motivates you to take action. It may be tangible, such as the jeans, or it may be emotional, a bonus, a wedding. You, for example, are seeking ways to improve your marketing—you are reading this book.

Zipline Essential #7: Clearly define how your product or service uniquely solves a customer's problem.

What are the problems that your buyers want or need solved? Take a few minutes to write them down. Note that sometimes what you think is the primary problem, isn't—there may be other underlying issues that really influence the decision-making process.

Consider Rolex watches. These fine timepieces tell the time. But is telling time the customer's real problem? Heck, they can look at their smart phone for that! Their problem is that they want to show the world—stylishly—that they've "made it" and can afford an expensive watch. Rolex caters to that. Creative marketing looks beyond the obvious.

What would you do? **Here come the Brides**

A company opened in the Sierra mountain region offering tours to popular destinations. Inspired by a European trip, the owner wanted to re-create the same enjoyable experience for tourists. Despite advertising efforts and an informative website, there was little response. Meanwhile, that first season, the firm received some calls from brides planning weddings in the area who hoped the company could provide shuttle service. Of course they accepted the jobs.

What do you think may have misfired in the original business idea?

*Jot down your answer:*_____

_____

_____

Answer: The owner had not assessed whether there was sufficient demand to base a tour company in that market. Through quick Internet research, we determined there were plenty of tour companies based in San Francisco, where most out-of-state tourists arrive. If somebody were to rent a car, they wouldn't need a tour company. Or they would go with one that could pick them up right at the airport and deliver them to their destination. So the problem that the owner thought the business was solving didn't "fit" the buyer's actual needs.

All was not lost. I had her interview the brides, and she discovered the region is popular for weddings, receptions, events, and concerts, as well as being a destination wine region. And what the customers really wanted was convenient, safe, and dependable transportation. They didn't want to worry about getting lost on the twisting roads, or drinking and driving. The firm repositioned itself as a safe and convenient concierge-style transportation service, and business took off.

We know that figuring out who your buyers are and what motivates them is essential to successful marketing. But it doesn't stop there. As you saw with these examples, identifying your prospect's problems and coming up with a desirable solution is not only what drives product development, but serves as the rootstock for what's referred to as a Positioning statement or a USP (Unique Selling Proposition), the other critical anchor for the marketing zipline. These terms are marketing lingo for what makes you special, different.... Let me ask you: in one or two lines, how do you sum up what sets you apart and makes what you do stand out from all the other companies providing the same or similar products or services?

Why is this important? Because, as you now know, **the more similar you are to competitors, the more likely a buyer is going to compare you on price.** If everybody is selling vanilla ice cream, and they don't say what makes their vanilla more special, more delicious, then it all boils down to who has the cheapest product.

Fact: Price wars are hard to win, require deep pockets, and tend to devour profits. Avoid them as much as possible. Why do you think ice cream makers tout such terms as "organic," "premium," "sustainably farmed," "hand-harvested," and "natural"? Because they're telling buyers it's *not* just about price—it's about quality, taste, how it's harvested, etc. And the WIFME from the buyer's viewpoint varies depending on what they feel is important. If I'm health conscious, then my WIFME is to buy organic. If I fancy gourmet, I want a luxury brand—hand-harvested at a higher price. Haagen-Dazs and Magnum cater to these kinds of buyers.

Let's face it—there's not much new under the sun. And we know that people have ever-shortening attention spans, which means you have to immediately seize their interest. How short? Back in the 1970s, when an ad agency designed a print ad, they knew they had about 30 seconds to get the reader's attention. By the early 2000s, that was about 10 seconds. Today, you have between 3 and 5 seconds, and fwoosh! They're moving on. So if you can't quickly establish "why you," you've lost them. How do you do that? By knowing your buyers and prospects well enough that you can choose which buttons to press, speak in WIFME, and position your product or service as the desirable solution.

A different way of telling your story to buyers: What is your Why? I'm a trend watcher—I'm constantly studying advertising (my family jokes that I'm more interested in the TV ads than the shows), and reading articles to see what's going on in marketing. And not just within my industry, because I know that stuff going on outside my field can influence what's going on within it. I've developed a distinctive ability to spot "patterns" as I digest all this information, and it contributes to my ability to help clients succeed.

One marketing concept that I find intriguing is how **some companies start their business by focusing on the "why" of getting into business vs. the product or service's functionality.** Particularly among Millennials, a company's "why" is often a critical influence in their "reason why to buy" decision-making process.

In his excellent YouTube TED talk, "Start With Your Why," author Simon Sinek talks about a different way of looking at your business—not from the viewpoint of *what* you do, but *why* you do it. Sinek says that having loyal customers is all about attracting the people who share your fundamental beliefs. People don't buy *what* you do. They buy *why* you do it.

It might be because they want to support a local business. Or your socially conscious service connects with their values, such as selling only sustainably farmed products. Understanding *why* is essential to effectively communicating *how* and *what* you do.

To illustrate this concept, he developed the Golden Circle, which has three rings:

1. *Why* – your firm's core belief, why it exists. Not about making money, but its purpose.
2. *How* – how the business fulfills that core belief.
3. *What* – what the company does to fulfill that core belief—the product or service.

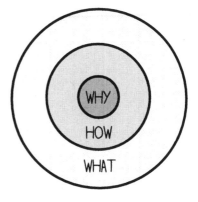

Businesses usually start from the outside and work their way in. This is what we make, this is how we make it, and this is why. Sinek challenges us to reverse this approach, and build a story around our why for being in business. In doing so, we connect emotionally with what motivates people to purchase.

> An excellent example of this is the extremely successful online business, The Grommet (TheGrommet.com), which is known for discovering and launching new products. At a Small Business Administration conference I attended, CEO Jules Pieri spoke about what drives her buyers: it's the story behind the products—the why factor. "Grommets are products with a purpose invented by people with stories."
>
> Knowing your "why" can help you build a story that will better connect with your target buyers—as long as you know what inspires them, and leverage it to motivate purchases.

Remember the competitive research you did in Chapter 3? Now you're going to see why that data is extra valuable, and how to use it make your business stand out.

First, let's define everything you feel makes your product or service special. Pull out a sheet of paper and divide it into three columns, labeled "Special," "WIFME," and "Competition." Write down all the things you can think of that you might say to a prospect as to what makes your business special, even unique, in the Special column (see the following example).

Next, in the middle column, write down what that special means from your customer's viewpoint. I often see companies failing to close the loop by not translating what they offer into an end-benefit, or the **WIFME point of view—what problem, want, or need they solve.** For example, if you're a dentist using new equipment that eliminates discomfort, your list could look like: Special = State of the art equipment. WIFME = Pain free dentistry.

In the third column, note how many competitors are saying the same "Special" or WIFME. The more that do, the less unique that factor becomes in differentiating your business.

Here's an example that a solar company did for this exercise. They have 10 competitors in their regional market that they identified by searching online and in the phone book.

Special	WIFME (Customer's viewpoint)	Competition
Customized packages to fit your budget	There's a chance I can afford to do this	3
Professional installation	They know what they're doing	8
Financing available	A convenient one-stop shop	5
Rebate program assistance	They're making it easy and turnkey	2
Specializing in solar for over 35 years	Experienced, here for the long haul	1

Do you notice how only the first one of the Specials actually is written from a true customer's viewpoint (which is the right way to do it)? The rest are just a laundry list of what the company offers or how old it is. That raises the question, **are you showcasing the product and service the right way or the weak way?**

Think like a solar buyer. What if we changed Professional Installation to read, "Certified Technicians guarantee quality installation"? Now the company has added reassurance plus touted the fact it has highly trained techs. Let's combine points 3 and 4 to read, "Convenient financing and rebate programs make us your one-stop-shop." See how by adjusting the words to solve the *problems* a prospect faces, you can connect with them on a deeper level?

Now, going back to the chart, you might think that since only one other company cited their years in business, that's the best point to highlight since it's fairly unique. But first ask yourself, is it the most important issue for the buyer?

Having been a solar panel shopper myself, I know that a top concern is cost. I had sticker shock when we looked at them for our home. From a prioritization standpoint, that means that the most important concerns pertain to cost. Which says that the most important marketing solution points that need to be communicated are cost-related—items 1, 3, and 4 in the chart. Length of time in business is important, and does need to be mentioned, but from a customer's point of view, it's not the most burning issue.

Imagine how focusing on this important solution (solar system cost) is going to affect all the marketing outreach efforts—website, ads, brochures, even the installation truck's exterior paint jobs. Voilà! Understanding your customers and knowing your competition enables you to figure out how to set yourself apart in your marketing, and reduce competing on price.

Ideally, there will be a lot more "special" things that help differentiate you. Is it guaranteed returns? One-on-one service? A live person answering the phone? 24-hour response to an email query? Is it the quality of ingredients or materials used? Where the product is manufactured? The expertise of the provider? For example, I've been doing consulting and coaching for 30 years—people hire me, listen to me speak, or attend my workshops because they want to take advantage of my in-depth expertise.

One of the most powerful sources of information for determining why people buy from you? Your customers! If you're an existing business, you have an amazing built-in database to leverage through customer surveys. More about this in Chapter 13.

Now, here's another positioning pointer. A very useful resource when it comes to developing a tagline or USP is to check out how some of the big companies summarize themselves. It should be short and clearly communicate what makes you special, written from your buyer's perspective. Here are some good examples to get you thinking:

- Nike – Just do it. (Inspirational and motivational.)

- Pizza Factory – We toss 'em. They're awesome. (Great visual, using language that appeals to a younger audience.)

- La-Z-Boy – Live Life Comfortably. (Can you see it?)

- Denny's – Welcome to America's Diner. (Great tie back to tradition and comfort food.)

- Allstate – You're in good hands with Allstate. (Awesome, and one of the more enduring positioning statements; it's been around for decades, and translates into a great visual.)

By the way, it's normal that developing a USP starts with one or more rambling sentences, and then through polishing and prioritizing, it's culled down into a one-liner. FYI, these are periodically updated as a company or their client base evolves.

> ### *Make them crave what you have to offer with targeted promotions and advertising*

You watch (or drool) as the rich dark chocolate dribbles over the moist shredded coconut on the screen. While smell-a-vision hasn't yet been invented, if you're hungry or like chocolate, it may make you think, "mmm, I'd like a Mounds or Almond Joy." Can't you almost taste it? That's what advertising's job is. To establish an image in your mind, and hopefully trigger a desire to purchase or at least learn more. We're really going to drill down into marketing outreach tactics in Part 4, but this chapter provides the summary version.

Now, advertising is not the same as promotion. Say you receive an offer in one of the ubiquitous online ads for an Almond Joy bar, "Buy 2, get a third one free!" That's a promotion: a specific offer designed to get you to take action. Advertising and promotions don't have to be mutually exclusive and often work in tandem, in the sense that an ad may feature a promotion or a promotion may be designed to do double duty as an ad.

In both advertising and promotion, as with all marketing outreach efforts, the "trick" used by successful marketers is knowing which buttons to push—through language, imagery, and pricing—to make you want to buy that product. Now or in the future.

As you know from Chapter 2, not all your buyers want the same things, and different components of your marketing message are going to push different buttons. You persuade people to want, desire, or crave your product or service not only through advertising and promotions, but at every point of consumer contact: packaging design, websites, product copy, pricing, and more. *That's* marketing.

> **Zipline Essential #8: Advertising and promotion are not the only ways to connect with customers.**

For example, if you go to Payless Shoe Stores, key buyer motivators are price, selection, styles, and availability—and the company makes sure you are aware about them all, because they know that different buyers assign different levels of importance. A 20-something may want to look on top of fashion trends to impress the guys without breaking her budget; Mom wants sturdy but affordable shoes for her toddler since he'll grow out of them in a few months.

A good example of how products are developed around the buyer's wants and needs is shampoo. Go to a store, and you'll see shelves upon shelves of brands from which to choose. Ever wonder why? Because although most people want clean, nice-looking hair, there are many other decision-making variables—other buyer WIFMEs. The big companies' marketing teams know this, and design packaging and copy specifically to connect with the target audience.

- If you're a buyer on a budget – price is a key factor. Think VO5.

- If you're status conscious – brand name, and you'll likely buy it at a salon. Think Aveda.

- If you have hard-to-style hair – a product that promises a solution drives your choice. Think Garnier.

- If you don't want your baby to cry – you select a "no more tears" type of shampoo. That's Johnson & Johnson since forever.

When I worked at Gillette on Silkience Hair Care, we decided to restage the brand to make it look more contemporary and appeal to a younger female audience, especially the yuppies (young urban professionals). We spent months developing a new sleek pearlized bottle to position the brand as edgy and "worth" a higher price. We reformulated the products with new popular scents in addition to the original "chloe" fragrance. Back panel copy described how the luxurious shampoo and conditioner would create beautiful hair. Every aspect of the marketing mix—price, product, positioning, advertising, promotion, and distribution—was thoroughly planned out, resulting in a successful restage and renewed sales growth. Proof that with planning and tying together all the marketing essentials, it can pay off.

Here's a great exercise I recommend in my workshops to help you get a better perspective on how connecting with a consumer occurs at multiple levels. Pick up products you would never buy and look at the package design and descriptive language being used. Try to determine who it's aimed at, what problem is being solved and what the WIFME is, and how the buyer's buttons are being pushed. It will help you to understand how the packaging's language and imagery are tailored to make a particular prospect want to try the product.

A common mistake many companies make is writing copy that lists features and does not include benefits. Now I'm the first to agree that writing copy is not something any smart marketer just tosses off in hopes hopes it will work, although I do see a lot of that. Really powerful copy is problem-solution driven, structured around the well-defined wants and needs of the buyer. Effective ads and promotions don't just talk about features, they talk about _____ (you should be able to fill in the blank by now).

Did you say *end benefits*? Three gold stars! What the buyer will experience and gain by making the purchase. Here are some real life WIFME examples:

- Our shampoo will make your hair look fabulous and get you noticed.
- Our dry-cleaning process does not use chemicals to protect those with sensitive skin.
- Our fish is wild-caught, to ensure the finest flavor while supporting sustainable fishing practices.
- Trust our certified CPAs to guide you through tax season.
- Our expert mechanics guarantee a safe ride because we know your family depends on us.

See how these statements connect, in part, at the emotional level? Heads up: if you're just trotting out what I call a 3B ad or promotion—Basic, Boring, Been done too much already—you're likely to get weak results. More on this in Chapter 10.

Here are **3 smart ways to find creative ideas:** some helpful tips on how to find inspiration that I share in my workshops, along with some big company secrets.

- *Be a hoarder.* Anytime you see a creative or clever ad or promotion, save it and put it in a concept file. It doesn't have to be from within your industry. When you're running around looking for inspiration, that file will be priceless.
- *Monitor your industry's big players.* Keep an eye on the visuals, images, fonts, graphics, and language they're using, in print, online, TV, and social media. These folks spend a lot of money on consumer research, and you can learn and adapt your messaging and emulate what they're doing. But please, do not plagiarize or violate copyrights.
- *Test your ideas with customers.* Big companies do focus groups, online research, etc. to evaluate ideas, concepts, or ad campaigns. While you may not have a budget for that, you do have customers from whom you can invite comments, or even offer an incentive to provide feedback. People love to share their opinions; why do you think social media is such a hit? You can do surveys in-store or online, via your website, social media, or survey programs like Constant Contact (we'll cover more on surveys in Chapter 9).

➢ *Can they find you where they need to?*

The term "global economy" gets tossed around a lot. Some firms do have international sales, and with the power of online buying escalating steadily, many smaller firms are able to take advantage of this. Whatever it is you're selling, the fundamental question is, can your buyers find you with minimum hassle? Is what you offer readily available? The harder it is to find you, the more roadblocks you're putting up, and the more likely it is they'll shop elsewhere. This is what's often referred to as Place and Distribution in marketing.

You've heard the expression, "location, location, location." It may sound humorous, but it's absolutely spot on. If you serve only a certain town, county, or geographic region, can your buyers find you in the phone book? On Yelp, Bing, and Google, or through online searches? If you have a retail establishment, is it in a convenient location with good foot traffic? Is parking available? For example, if you're a retailer and your sales depend on steady foot traffic, why would you choose a location that's only drive-by? Why do you think so many smaller stores locate in malls anchored by big name retailers? They're relying on those stores' advertising and brand recognition to draw in shoppers who will then discover all the smaller shops.

Case in point: A shoe store had found "a great low rent deal" in a downtown location. At first glance, it looked like it would have good foot traffic resulting in steady sales. But the owner soon discovered that people didn't walk much in that area, and cars passed by too quickly to see the shop. Had she first done a location analysis to assess these issues, she would have realized why the store was vacant, and looked for another place. She did ultimately relocate to a strip mall anchored by a major grocery store, and business turned around.

If you don't have geographic boundaries, can you be "found" through online directories, industry websites, trade publications, trade shows and expos, and web searches? Are your products and services available online, in-person, over the phone, or via chat on a website?

Don't forget that an underlying part of what you sell is convenience! What does everybody complain about these days? Not having enough time. So what are you doing to help them solve that? Can you work this into your message? Adapt it as a way to bring added-value to your product or service?

Think about bottled water. You're willing to pay for the convenience of not having to refill and tote around your own water bottle. But crunch the numbers. If you pay $2 for a 16.9-ounce bottle, doesn't seem like much, right? But that's 12 cents/oz. There are 128 ounces per gallon, so you're paying $15.15 per gallon! Compare that to what you pay per gallon of gas.

Consider Amazon. Part of its powerful implied advantage over other competitors is absolute convenience—all your shopping can be done from the comfort of your chair in a robe and fuzzy slippers. Point, click, pay. Amazon makes it easy, and has optimized the experience for people willing to pay for its Prime service.

In fact, it's the online shipping model that has successfully fractured the time-honored Black Friday sales pattern, where shoppers mob stores in search of great deals on one day. Now, they can find those same deals online often spread out over several days or even weeks, as Black Friday ebbs back to Halloween with early announcements and teaser sales. So, unless you're into the crush and holiday frenzy, why bother? It's a perfect example of a shift in buyer behavior patterns. And how is your business responding to all this?

Cycling back to the "frustration in finding" issue, have you ever gone to a website, found something you like, and then become so frustrated with the ordering process you "x" out? Or gone to a store and encountered empty shelf space? What's your reaction? Unless you want it really badly, you resent wasting the time, and probably do a quick Google search to find who else carries it and head out to buy it there. Today's retailers, whether online or brick-and-mortar, can't forget that availability is an essential part of effective marketing.

Choosing your location and where you're available can make or break you, no matter how good your product or service. If people can't find you, they can't buy you. And remember it's no longer just about having a website. With literally millions of websites out there, you have to have a presence at other online locations as well, and be able to provide online merchant services that today's buyers are coming to expect. More on this in Part 5.

> ### *Financial smarts – make sure sales really equal profits*

OK, for all you number haters out there, I have one thing to say: you can choose to run from numbers, or you can run them. If you're in business, you *have* to run them, or make sure you have trusted members on your team who know how. **Numbers = sales = profits.** That's the simple equation. You ignore numbers at an extreme risk.

Numbers also equal pricing. Many businesses hear the word Pricing and their eyes glaze over. Yet setting your price is an essential part of your zipline marketing strategy (more insights on this in Chapter 7). Without well-planned pricing, how are you going to achieve your profit goals?

Zipline Essential #9: Smart pricing is essential to delivering decent profits.

Fact: Smart companies should never, ever just "set a price." Several vital steps need to be taken for your price to generate both sales and profits. Let's take a closer look.

Pricing is pressured by three core factors: buyers, competition, and costs. Too high, and your buyers may not be able to afford what you have to offer or, even worse, may not think the product or service is worth it, and won't buy. If it's too far out of line with competitors, you better have a strong "reason why" to justify it, or buyers will go elsewhere. If it's not covering all your expenses, you're losing money. And presumably, you're not in business to lose money.

Too often, companies set their price on only one or, at best, two of these three variables. If they're lucky, it flies, for a while. But then things like new competitors or economic downturns hit, and suddenly the bottom line starts to bleed red ink. Or they never achieve the profitability they believe they should, but don't really know why.

Let's assume you've done your competitive market research, and have a pretty good handle on what others are charging, and what buyers are willing to pay for the same or similar services or products. Now you need to decide the initial price point. We'll run through a simplified example with an ice cream shop.

You're planning to open a gourmet ice cream shop in town. Your up-front market and buyer research indicates the town is big enough to potentially generate a lot of sales, and people are earning enough to have discretionary income to buy ice cream. Good.

Your competitive market research shows that there are only three other shops in a 30-minute drive radius, which is how far you figure people will drive to get ice cream. Going prices for a single scoop cone range between $2.99 and $3.49. But unlike everybody else, your ice cream is hand-churned and made the old fashioned way, with locally-sourced ingredients. So you're going to charge a premium price of $4 because you know it's a better product, and it's worth a higher price, right?

This is where many companies halt the pricing process and unintentionally sabotage themselves. FYI, if you're applying for a loan, the banks will make you do this next step, because they know it is absolutely essential.

You must figure out *how much it costs you* to make the ice cream cones. Here are the basics. Costs are broken into two categories: Cost of goods (COGs) and Fixed costs. **You must know both in order to figure out if you're going to make a profit.**

COGs, also known as variable costs, happen only when you *actually make or produce* a product. In this case, it's the cream, flavorings, ice, and all the ingredients that go into making ice cream. If the ice cream isn't made, no costs are incurred. For this example, let's decide that it costs $3 to make each cone.

Fixed costs are stuff like rent, utilities, janitorial services, employee costs… costs that you *have* to pay (landlords tend to get cranky when you don't) whether or not you sell a single ice cream cone. So, let's say you spend $2,000 per month on fixed costs.

Now let's quickly pencil it out. Let's assume you sell 1000 cones in one month.

Gross sales:	1000 cones × $4 = $4,000
COGs:	1000 cones × $3 = $3,000
<u>Gross profit</u>	$4,000 − $3000 = $1,000
Fixed costs	$2,000
Net profit	$1,000 − $2,000 = −$1,000 (a loss)

Uh-oh. You're actually losing money at $4 per cone! Notice how I underlined gross profit. Again, in my experience with many clients, there's a tendency to look at gross profit, but ignore fixed costs and net profit. You can see why the proposed $4 pricing is a bad idea. And realize this loss is *before* having to pay taxes!

Theoretically, the only way you can break even if you sell only 1000 cones per month is if you charge $5 per single scoop. But you know your area's buyers probably won't pay that; it's too expensive. So, you're faced with a dilemma. You can't charge more. What can you do?

The good news is that there are actually several possible solutions to explore.

1. Lower your COGs. Maybe you can source your ingredients from cheaper local vendors, or get volume discounts. You don't have to sacrifice quality.

2. Shrink the portion size. Can you scoop smaller amounts, or use smaller cones and cups? During the Great Recession, in an effort to cut costs, many manufacturers reduced portion sizes: 20-pound bags of cat food shrank to 16 pounds, 240-count tissues dropped to 184, 100-count paper plates became 64. Restaurants even started using smaller plates to give the illusion of larger portion sizes!

3. Look for ways to lower utility costs and other fixed costs. Lots of lights, running the air conditioning constantly, and using excess water can results in unnecessary expenses. Employees often don't think about these things, but as the business owner or manager, you need to change that mindset pronto.

   Here's an excellent example of firms taking action in a changing market: when electricity costs spiked in California, smart light bulb vendors promoted low wattage lights and recommended turning off 25% to 50% of a facility's lights to conserve power. It saved their customers money, and created supplier loyalty.

4. Sell more. If you can't raise prices, or lower costs, how many cones a month would you need to sell to break even? When you pencil it out, you would have to double sales.

Gross sales:	2000 cones × $4 = $8,000
COGs:	2000 cones × $3 = $6,000
Gross profit	$8,000 – $6,000 = $2,000
Fixed costs	$2,000
Net profit	$2,000 – $2,000 = $0

Can you double sales? Are there enough potential buyers in the area? And how are you going to reach them and get them to try out the ice cream? Maybe you can get them to eat ice cream more often? What types advertising and promotion can you do? Think back to the Gizmo story in Chapter 1—by not having run the numbers up front, you would be selling lots of ice cream cones, and losing money!

Of course, financial matters are usually more complex, but **doing a preliminary cost analysis is a valuable reality check when evaluating proposed pricing.**

Now, it may seem more challenging to set pricing when you're a service-based company. Not really. Labor can be considered COGs—how many hours it takes to do a project. Think about lawyers, consultants, advertising agencies, and psychologists. Basing your pricing on competitive market research and your experienced-based caliber of service is also fairly standard. Never discount the value of your experience, because that is an important part of what differentiates you from the competition.

Case in point: When I first graduated, I worked at Harvard Business School. One day, one of my friends, a secretary to a very senior professor with a pedigree a mile long, called and insisted I had to hurry down to her office immediately. There, she showed me a check her boss had just received for a week's consulting. We both stared at it, amazed. It was the first million dollar check we had ever seen that didn't have "void" written through it! This professor's experience is what earned him that million dollars; it's what set him apart. Your experience is a quantifiable asset.

Recognize that if you can create a compelling story as to why your product or service warrants a higher price, people will pay it, resulting in more profits. Hermes scarves, Rolls Royce, Apple iPhones, Godiva chocolates, NARS cosmetics... all of these luxury-priced items don't cost tons to make. But these brands have created a cachet, a perception of such added value that it makes people willing to pay premium prices to say they own and/or use them.

That's where positioning, and your entire marketing story or message, becomes so essential: it's all about knowing the buyer and persuading them that these products are designed to "fit" their wants, and are worth it—the essence of the WIFME concept. Think of L'Oréal's fabulous hair coloring campaign; the product is more expensive, but their pitch? "Because I'm worth it." Does that appeal to a person's vanity, or what?

When setting price points, remember you're in business to achieve a profit. Whether you're a for-profit business or a not-for-profit organization, this mindset is essential because profits fund salaries and bonuses, future investment in the company's growth, and, of course, marketing outreach efforts. And not just gross profit. You need to know your net (after fixed expenses), net net (after taxes), and net net net (after depreciation and amortization). You can see how easily a company that doesn't know its numbers can shoot itself in the foot... or worse.

Two final notes on pricing. Unless you're very good with numbers, I recommend you find a trustworthy CPA to keep your books current and balanced, so you know exactly how the business is performing financially. You can subcontract this to outside providers; they don't have to be on staff in the firm's early days. Plus, they can make sure you're doing the right things when it comes to federal, state, and local taxes. You don't want to mess up in those areas—it's not worth the penalties and hassles you'll incur. Note that even if you subcontract, you still need to understand how the numbers work, to ensure that the books are being kept properly and accurately, and there are no future "unpleasant" surprises.

Second, I've said this before, but as soon as you can, start socking some profit away in a special account for future economic downturns. It may make all the difference in your company's survival. As you saw in Chapter 4, recessions are an economic fact of life.

To reinforce this point, one of my clients, a construction firm, had enjoyed California's boom times of heavy commercial and residential building. When the Great Recession hit, everybody stopped building. And I mean *everybody*—individuals, private corporations, and governments. The company barely made it through, surviving through employee attrition and by cutting costs to the marrow. After the recession eased, at my advice, as soon as the firm could, it set up an independent account and now regularly makes deposits. The managers know there will be another downturn, and this time, they'll be financially prepared.

Many firms fail in recessions not because they had a bad product or service, but because they did not have the necessary financial cushion to survive the shrinking of buyers' wallets. Smart companies who put aside money actually often were able to develop and implement a business and marketing strategy to capture their failed competitors' clients—and emerge stronger than before. Make sure you're one of the survivors!

Successfully creating a smoother ride on the marketing zipline is about knowing your competitors; strategically developing positioning, product or service, pricing, and advertising and promotions in context of your buyers' wants and needs; and making sure that you are available where the can find you.

Finally, **remember: your marketplace is constantly shifting.** If you do the same thing year after year without monitoring your market, buyers, and competitors, and adjusting your course as needed to maintain a competitive edge, you will smack into branches and trees, and risk tumbling off the zipline.

Part 2 – Zipline Highlights

✵ **Know your competition.** They are your best resource for determining how to make your products and services unique.

✵ **Avoid shortcuts.** Before cutting corners, make sure they're safe to cut. Too often, companies skip steps or avoid marketing essentials in a rush to get to market. A first impression is a lasting impression with customers—especially in today's arena of online reviews.

✵ **One size rarely fits all.** If your product or service is not designed to satisfy a well-defined want or need, or solve a real or imagined problem, why should anyone buy it? This puts you in the difficult spot of battling to convince people it's worth buying, which makes for challenging marketing communication efforts.

✵ **Tell your story in their language.** Always speak in WIFME when positioning products or services. Talk end-benefits, sell solutions, satisfy their desires, wants, and needs. It's not about how you think it should be said; it's about what you know they want and expect to hear.

✵ **Make it available.** No matter how wonderful your product, if buyers can't find it, who cares? Be in the places they can and expect to find you.

✵ **Price it smart.** If your price point is not what buyers expect, what they know others are charging, or what they perceive the product or service is worth, you're setting up tree blocks on your zipline when it comes to attracting their interest. Plus, if you don't know all your costs, you may actually be setting your price too low and selling at a loss, leaving no money to invest back into the business or marketing.

Part 3 – Zip Smart – Setting Up Your Marketing Zipline

Have you been guilty of thinking of marketing and advertising as synonyms? As you now know from Part 2, they're not. I can't tell you how often I hear people insist that they're "doing marketing," but after a short review, it becomes clear that what they're really doing are ads and promos—and these are frequently implemented using an unplanned, shotgun approach. *Effective* advertising and promotion are the outcome of a well thought out marketing outreach strategy and plan, which in turn flows from a comprehensive overall marketing strategy.

Say you have a website, brochure, coupons, and a billboard; you have print ads, digital ads, and search engine optimization (SEO); and you have fancy graphics and nice copy. But if you don't have an overall marketing strategy, how can you possibly know if all of these efforts are aimed correctly, working cohesively, and helping to optimize sales and profits? Sure, you may be getting results, but are you really doing as well as you could be or achieving the return on investment you expected in the form of customers and sales?

Part 3 reveals how to map out your marketing Zipline to Success. We'll define how to create a marketing strategy and plan to use as a roadmap to guide and measure the outcomes of your marketing efforts. We'll review smart pricing strategies, look at selecting the right language to connect with customers, find out how create customer surveys that actually collect useful information, and how to avoid setting up tree blocks on your zipline.

Chapter 6 ~ So, Where Do You Want to Go?

Too often, people "do marketing" as if it was some Harry Potter-type spell that will magically produce results. Kind of like hopping on a zipline with no idea where it's going—or worse, no idea about how to use the equipment or whether there's danger up ahead.

First, let's establish the concept that **a strategy and a plan are not the same**. Big companies know this; smaller firms often lump them together. Strategy establishes the overall objectives about what you want to accomplish—The Big Picture, the main route on which you want to set up your zipline. The Plan is what detailed steps need to be taken and when—immediate, actionable steps on how to set up your zipline.

For example, you decide to visit Yosemite National Park. Your strategic objectives could be to travel by plane in the summer of next year at off peak hours to take advantage of the lowest fares. Your plan would be to research hotel availability at Yosemite within the next two weeks and book your rooms, then research fares four months ahead of your planned travel dates, book within two weeks after, etc. The plan is the nitty gritty details of making it happen.

➢ What's your Zipline marketing strategy and plan?

Marketing's fundamental job should be to support your company's overall business goals, whether you're a giant like Google or Joe's Dry Cleaning on the corner. A smart company sets an overall *business* strategy which includes the revenue and profit objectives for the next three to five years. From a zipline marketing perspective, this defines the starting point and the desired destination.

> **Zipline Essential #10: "Doing" marketing without a strategy or plan = poor results.**

The purpose of a marketing strategy and plan is to help deliver on those objectives. If I, as your marketing director, don't know how much revenue and profit needs to be made this year, how on earth can I figure out the steps I need to take to deliver those results?

Long detailed business plans are out of vogue these days given the speed at which the marketplace can change, but we have created a short form version that can serve very effectively in today's rapidly changing time-starved work environments. Visit ZiplinetoSuccess.com/Resources to download our free sample Zipline Business Plan.

At the very least, your business strategy should state sales and profit objectives for the next three years. If you're making $100,000 in sales now, and want to double revenue in two years' time, it's not going to happen by magic, or just by hoping it will occur organically and more people will call or walk in the door. Yes, your strategic business objectives may evolve in response to changing customer and market factors, but you have to pick a direction.

Big firms' senior marketing executives are tasked with determining how products and services are going to be sold to achieve specific revenue and profit objectives. In my days as a Gillette product manager, the Personal Care

Division would be given divisional sales and profit targets for the next year. In turn, each brand was assigned a portion of these. Each product manager would spend three months plotting marketing strategies and plans, and would be subsequently measured on brand performance vs. those objectives during the year. If your brand was "off-strategy," you had better be able to account for the reasons why. Now I'm not saying you need to spend months on this process, but you absolutely need to take time to set up your marketing zipline.

Important: We're focusing on marketing in this book, but I don't want you to forget that operations, human resources, and finance are three other mission-critical parts of your company's organization, and also have to support your overall business goals and objectives. In larger companies, these are departments. In mid-sized firms, they may be handled by several people. In small companies and start-ups, the business owner is typically juggling all these pieces. If you have a great marketing plan, but you don't have the operations and production capacity to make enough products to support the business goals… so much for the marketing plan. Remember the Gizmo story in Chapter 1? "More marketing" can actually do harm if a firm doesn't have the other essentials in place—you can't scale-up your company without proper internal support structures in place.

So what are the strategic factors that a company can use to set up its marketing zipline?

- *Financial goals:* how much revenue and profit do you want to make each year over the next three to five years?

- *Brands:* if you have multiple brands or service types, how much does each one need to contribute to the company's overall financial and other strategic objectives?

- *Volume:* what quantity of products or services need to be sold to support the strategic business goals?

- *Budget:* how much money do you have available to spend for marketing activities?

- *Measuring:* how are you going to measure results and course correct as needed?

Let's work through an example of how I help companies follow this marketing zipline process. Feel free to plug in your own business variables instead.

Keeping the future sweet. Carlotta's Cupcakes & Confections has been in business for five years. It's grown from a two-person food truck to a mid-sized bakery employing 30 people. The company also supplies high-end grocery stores within a two-hour driving radius. Current revenue is $2 million, with net profits of $500,000. The company would like to double its revenues to $4 million within three years. Note how specific their objectives are.

Part of a zipline marketing strategy involves breaking it down into measurable pieces. Very often, clients tell me what their sales revenue and profit objectives are. But that's where they stop. This means they have set only two performance measurements, and not broken it down into other numbers that can be used to develop a much more powerful marketing strategy and plan. Dollars should be converted into sales units—it might be number of units sold, number of transactions, number of hours by project or client, etc. But, without those numbers, marketing efforts can't be as effectively measured.

So, Carlotta's has to translate the financial goals into sales and number of customers and see what happens when they spread them across the next three years, a process we'll work our way through. This is where I like to simplify things to quickly visualize what's going on. Here's we can summarize Carlotta's proposed strategic objectives.

- Minimum revenue goal: $4,000,000 by Year 4

- Minimum net profit goal: 25% of gross revenue
  (25% × $4 million = $1 million)

- Products offered: artisan cakes, cookies, and confections

- Distribution: Bakery and high-end retailers

- Service area(s): two-hour driving radius from bakery

- Employees: 30 people through 2016; 2–5 additional
  hires in Year 2 to support growth

Here's how their initial numbers pencil out. Depending on whether you're a new or established business, the percentages of gross and net profits may be based on historic sales or on assumptions drawn from research or industry information.

	Current year	1 year	2 years	3 years
Gross Revenues	$2,000,000	$2,500,000	$3,250,000	$4,000,000
Gross Profit (50%)	$1,000,000	$1,250,000	$1,625,000	$2,000,000
Net Profit (25%)	$500,000	$625,000	$812,500	$1,000,000
Growth vs. previous year - Revenues (%)	--	25%	30%	23%
Growth vs. previous year - Gross Profits (%)	--	25%	30%	23%
Growth - Net Profits (%	--	25%	30%	23%

Next, management has to decide, are these numbers doable or is it too aggressive a growth strategy? Note how in Year 2, Carlotta's recognizes it will need to hire more staff, which would impact the bottom line. But it may also need more equipment because it only has so much production capacity. Both these issues would have to be captured in their numbers, something they haven't done yet.

This summary serves as a reality check before investing more time in planning. Of course, a more complex spreadsheet with expanded details would ultimately be developed. But it's a good "quick and dirty." Viewed from the Zipline to Success perspective, it's determined the starting and ending points for marketing. Next comes setting up the zipline.

➤ **How to map your route**

When you set up a smooth-riding zipline, you select a route that gets you from point A to B with a decent slope for speed, minimal risk of colliding with objects, and possibly even a great view. Marketing operates the same way. You're setting up a strategy and plan that enables you to deliver the revenue and profit goals.

If you're a start-up, you have to estimate these numbers, using what I call SWAG: scientific wild-ass guessing. The "scientific" part comes from having done the market and competitive research in Part 2 to collect the statistics on which to base your assumptions. If you're an existing business, there should be historical data to reference.

As the marketing director of Carlotta's Cupcakes, you know your marketing strategy has to support delivering $2.5 million in gross revenue for the upcoming year; that's your starting point. The end point is successfully achieving that. Your marketing plan is the zipline itself: the actions you're going to take to achieve your strategy.

This is where all the zipline marketing essentials you put into place in Part 2 come into play. You've set up your critical anchors on which to build your marketing strategy and plan: you know who your buyers are, and what motivates them to buy. You've shopped the competitors and know what sets your company apart. You've defined the price, product or service, and distribution.

Now come the next key pieces that set the zipline points for your marketing plan.

1. What is your average revenue per customer transaction? This is also sometimes referred to as average revenue per ticket (e.g., a register receipt or order form). In other words, how much does your customer spend each time they make a purchase?

Let's say Carlotta's had 175,000 customer transactions in the current year. That means customers on average spent $11.43 ($2 million divided by 175,000).

If you want to take this even further, which can be a good thing depending on your company's products or service segments, you may choose to break this down by average revenue per client per segment. So Carlotta's could break sales down into breads, pastries, and wedding cakes, and track the revenue and number of transactions for each segment, because the register keys have been coded to do that.

Why is this important? We know the goal is $2.5 million in sales for the upcoming year, right? So, if we divide $2.5 million by $11.43 per customer, that means we need 218,750 customer transactions to hit that objective. Put another way, in the past year we had 175,000 transactions. So that means that our marketing efforts need to generate an additional 43,750 sales transactions.

Before you fall off your feet at the sheer size of that number, let's put it into perspective. If we divide that by 12 months, it translates to an additional 3,645 transactions per month, or 841 per week. Does that help make it a little more digestible? (Sorry, I couldn't resist the pun.)

At this point, your experience in the business may say it's too big a stretch, that attracting that many more customers each week is highly unlikely. So then marketing and management sit down, discuss the situation, and determine whether the $2.5 million target revenue should be revisited. Or should marketing come up with a plan on how this could be achieved, and how much it will cost? These back and forth dialogues happen all the time at big companies.

One solution to this situation is to not only look for ways to increase number of customers, but to *increase how much they spend per transaction.* The more one customer spends each time they visit, the fewer additional customers are needed.

Even if you have a service-based business, such as a lawyer or consultant, you know your hourly or project rate, and can calculate how many more hours, clients, or projects are needed to achieve your revenue goals.

Put in terms of dollars, let's say we can get people to spend $12.43 instead of $11.43 per visit (an extra $1). Sales history shows we have had 175,000 ticket sales and we decide it's reasonable to assume the same sales quantity will occur in the upcoming year. So if all of those folks spent the extra $1, that's $175,000 toward the revenue goal.

Another approach is to raise pricing to generate that extra $1 per customer. That's why you so often see companies raising prices on a periodic, sometimes regular, basis. We'll talk further about pricing as a marketing tool in the next chapter.

2. What is your average gross profit per customer transaction? Go through the same above steps, but plug in gross profit numbers instead. After all, you're in business to make a profit.

3. What is your "customer conversion" rate? This is a fancy way of saying how many prospects do you need to connect with before (or if) they turn into a customer. This connection is made via marketing outreach efforts and/or through direct sales. It can be looked at from different angles.

Say your company sells farm equipment. For every 10 prospects contacted, how many convert to becoming a customer? If it's one, then you have a 10% conversion rate (1 divided by 10). If you're a bakery, how many people do you have to reach via marketing outreach channels to persuade some to come into your shop? If the newspaper reaches 80,000 households, you run a coupon promotion, and you get 100 people, that's a 0.1% conversion rate (100 divided by 80,000).

Another approach is converting first-timers to repeat customers, the most valuable of all. How many new customers does it take to create one regular customer in your business? If 10 people try your product or service, but only one returns, that means you need 5,000 prospects to come in the door if you're going to have a chance of hitting a goal of getting 500 new customers (1 divided by 10 = 10% conversion rate; 10% of 5,000 = 500).

You'll often hear firms talking about "keeping the sales pipeline full." This refers to marketing efforts that constantly keep a flow of new prospects coming in, because only so many will convert to actual customers. Plus, because of "churn" or customer attrition, a portion of lost customers have to be replaced with new ones; nobody stays around forever!

Why does all this matter? **Knowing your conversion rate can refocus your marketing strategy.** If you set a goal to grow your company by 100 new customers, and you get one customer per every 10, that means you have to connect with 1,000 new prospects, or figure out a way to improve the conversion rate.

I'm going to step away from Carlotta's for a moment and share with you a more complex client situation that will help illustrate this process. I was working with a communications equipment firm, and they historically had determined their sales objectives purely on total revenue. I've provided a chart to show how we worked through the numbers below.

Business Segment	Year 1 Total # of Clients	Year 1 Average Revenue/Client	Percent of Year 1 Revenue	Year 2 Target Revenues	Year 2 # of Clients Needed	Client increase vs. Year 1	# Cold Calls @ 10% conversion
	A	B	C	D	E=D/B	F=E-A	G=F/.10
Education	20	$68,000	67%	$2,000,000	29	9	90
Agriculture	8	$37,000	14%	$350,000	9	1	10
Construction	19	$8,000	7%	$200,000	25	6	60
Real Estate	14	$9,000	6%	$150,000	17	3	30
Manufacturing	12	$5,000	3%	$100,000	20	8	80
Medical	11	$2,000	1%	$25,000	13	2	20
Misc.	26	$1,000	1%	$30,000	30	4	40
Total	110	$130,000	100%	$2,855,000	143	33	330

Step 1: We broke down their revenue objective into existing business segments, such as education, manufacturing, etc. To do that, they looked at the previous year's historic sales (Year 1) by percentage for each segment, and then used that percentage to estimate the current year's revenue (Year 2). For example, the educational segment's historic sales were 67% of total revenue, so we took 67% multiplied by Year 2's total target revenue of $2,855,000, which showed education would be responsible for $2 million in sales. We also did the same thing separately for profits.

It was a shocker for my client to see how much or little revenue and profit each segment actually delivered. It raised all sorts of questions as to where to focus the sales people's efforts vs. what had originally been planned when they only looked at their business from a total revenue standpoint, and viewed all customers as being of equal value.

Step 2: Next we translated that data into a sales plan as to how many new customers were needed by segment to achieve those target revenues. By analyzing past sales calls and how many firms became regular customers, we determined my client had a 10% conversion rate. You can guess where Sales planned to focus the first phase of their efforts.

The marketing analysis helped them decide to concentrate sales efforts on education and agriculture as having the fastest return on time investment. They chose both segments because there are a finite number of educational institutions in the region. As part of the process, they also began to reevaluate all the other client segments and determine which ones they wanted to either focus on or eliminate in the future.

4. Where are the bottlenecks to growth? I mentioned earlier that marketing is just one part of the business matrix. It's great to have growth objectives, but all companies hit bottlenecks that prevent further growth without necessary and (preferably) planned changes.

If your company is producing widgets, at what point are the machines or people maxed out, requiring another investment in equipment or human capital? If you're a lawyer, what's your client capacity? If you're a dentist, what's the maximum number of patients you can see in a day? How many phone lines do you need? When does the wait time for your customer service department exceed acceptable levels?

It's a nightmare when the marketing plan successfully ramps up your business, only to then discover you can't handle all the demand! It may sound like a good problem, but it can quickly translate to upset customers who may leave, look elsewhere, and complain to others. Part of planning is anticipating when this may happen, and being prepared to act when it occurs.

> **Zipline Essential #11**: Be proactive, not reactive, when it comes to business growth.

Let's wrap up Carlotta's marketing strategy. As marketing director, you now have concrete strategic marketing objectives: $2.5 MM in gross revenue, which equates to 841 additional customers a week paying an average of $11.43 per transaction. Because you feel that's a stretch—but management has said you still have to hit that number—you now have to develop your marketing *plan* to make it happen. Here are some of the things I would evaluate:

- A price increase on high volume and/or high profit items so less customers are needed.

- Incentives to get customers to buy more frequently: loyalty programs, bundled buys such as buy one/get one.

- Referral rewards program to get existing customers to bring in new customers.

- Special events to attract attention of prospects and area publications.

- Fun recipe contests, with the winner's recipe being added to Carlotta's menu, and showcased via traditional and digital media channels.

Notice how advertising as the "instant solution" has not yet been mentioned. While yes, as I subsequently developed the marketing *plan*, advertising could be a factor, it would be more to support some of these options. As part of the plan, I would prepare a cost–benefit analysis to determine if the cost of doing these is worth the outcomes (more on this in Chapter 12).

➤ *Getting ready to zipline*

Another common cause of companies getting whacked as they ride the zipline? When they don't solidify their plan with timelines, deadlines, or details. It's like not worrying about "minor" details such as the helmet, harness, and carabiners that connect and protect you on the zipline. **When you're tangled up in day-to-day-business, it's easy to let things slip if you don't have a timeline-based marketing plan.** Consider New Year's resolutions. If they're too general or dates and deadlines haven't been attached, the chances of them happening can plummet. In his excellent book, *The Success Principles*, Jack Canfield talks in-depth about making goals detailed and concrete. The same goes for marketing plans.

He finally had time to develop a marketing plan.

According to *Forbes Magazine*, "Those who wrote down their goals accomplished significantly more than those who did not write down their goals." Imagine if you set a strategic marketing objective to add 500 new regular customers during the year. That's a good concrete objective. But don't stop there! Let's make it much more tangible: 500 new customers means you need nearly 42 customers a month. How are you going to achieve that? What steps are you going to take? When are you going to implement those steps?

This is where the marketing *plan* comes in. It's the **detailed schedule of activities that you are going to develop and implement across a certain period of time, with specific timelines and outcomes.** Think of it as a detailed trip itinerary: what you need to do, where you need to be, what you need to prepare.

> **The Whip Crack Lesson.** A freshly minted MBA, I joined Gillette as an assistant product manager. I was given a special task to resolve an ongoing problem with how to develop safety seals for shampoo bottles. Of course I was full of creative ideas. But it took a frustrated director of manufacturing to smack some sense into my head, and I've never forgotten it.
>
> "You marketing types," he growled at me. "You're always coming up with things for us to do on the production line. But you never stop to realize that it's like cracking a whip. You see only the twitch of the handle, and forget that the end of the whip snaps all over the place— and we're at the end of that whip!" He woke me up to the fact that marketing never operates in a void, and a responsible marketer takes all the other departments into consideration during the planning process.

Lewis Carroll, author of *Alice in Wonderland*, said, "Any road will get you there, if you don't know where you are going." Big companies know that when you don't organize your plan of attack, you are guaranteed to waste time and effort—and most business owners and managers don't have a lot of that to spare. And, by the way, crafting a detailed marketing plan makes it easier for you to delegate because you're handing someone a roadmap they can follow.

While some companies do a basic marketing plan, the most common missing checkpoints are projecting outcomes and costs, and then measuring results. The result is they do some form of advertising or promotion and hope for the best. Here's a sample of how failing to put into place these checkpoints can hurt your business.

What would you do? Hey, let's run a promotion!

- *Products:* Kitchen gadgets, small appliances, and supplies (1,500 square feet store; 10 employees)

- *Plan:* "25% off coupon on everything in store this weekend" in newspaper with 100,000 subscribers. (Note: This is usually where firms stop planning.)

What do you think may happen that the company hasn't considered?

🖊 *Jot down your answer.* _____

_____

_____

Answer:

- Has it planned for lots of people? If we estimate coupon redemptions at 10% of subscribers, that equals 10,000 people who will pour into the store across a two-day period.

- Has it planned for out of stocks? Does it have sufficient inventory in house? If not, will it provide rainchecks? How is it going to handle unhappy customers without rainchecks?

- Has it calculated the cost at 25% off everything? Assume an average purchase of $50, less 25%. Cost per purchase to company = $12.50. What does this do to profits? Second, since the offer is off everything, what if people are using it to buy very expensive items, or items with slim margins? This is why you see restrictions placed on offers—because companies have done the cost–benefit analysis (see Chapter 12).

- Finally, at the end of the event, how do the results compare to what was projected? What were actual sales? What items sold? How many people made purchases? What were the gross and net profits? What feedback did customers give?

Your initial marketing plan may start with a general outline, to which you will later attach specific deadlines. Organize it in a way that makes sense to you and other members of your team, but also so that it serves as an easy reference document.

Here's an example of a portion of a marketing plan for a website design company. Its strategic business goal is to grow revenues by 50% over the next 12 months. Marketing's strategic goals are to achieve that revenue target, as well as to create stronger brand awareness in the regional market, and develop more repeat business within the existing customer base.

Sample Partial Marketing Plan

1. Refresh and contemporize brand identity to better connect with business target audiences.
    a. Finalize new logo by June 1.
        i. Get three proposals and select new designer by February 1.
        ii. Review rough concepts by March 1.
        iii. Finalize top three by March 27.
            (1) Make sure all three look good in black/white, grayscale, and color at a 1-inch size before advancing.
        iv. Test top three via online and in-shop customer surveys March 27–April 15. If none achieve a 3.5 or higher score on a 1–5 scale, develop new set.
        v. Announce new logo to existing clients/customers via email blast June 5.
            (1) Explore possible promotional tie-in to increase awareness and generate "buzz" and business.
    b. Phase overall marketing materials and communications to new logo beginning early June to ensure consistent look and message to synchronize with brand identity.
        i. Digital – upon logo approval.
        ii. Print – as supplies deplete.
        iii. Letterhead/envelopes – as supplies deplete.
2. Conduct ongoing customer surveys to secure performance feedback, and potential testimonials and "stories" for use in marketing efforts.
    a. Develop in-house customer survey to be administered upon job completion.

          i. End of January.

   b. Review and act upon any problematic issues within two business days.

   c. Assemble testimonials and add to marketing materials (ongoing).

   d. Request reviews on Google+ page.

          i. Revise all digital marketing materials to request reviews by end of January.

          ii. Update print materials as in-house stocks deplete.

          iii. Add request to all customer surveys by beginning of February.

          iv. Develop outreach effort to existing customers to request feedback by March.

3. Identify new target audience segments with highest revenue and profit potential for greatest return on initial sales efforts by April 1.

   a. Proposed

          i. Professionals who market themselves as speakers, teachers, or coaches

          ii. Higher end restaurants with significant tourist trade

          iii. Businesses likely to benefit from content marketing

          iv. Graphic designers or agencies needing a subcontractor for WordPress development

          v. Organizations covered by the Brown Act, which requires that public bodies must be "open and public."

             (1) Local agencies, including counties, cities, school, and special districts.

             (2) Boards, commissions, committees, task forces, or other advisory bodies created by covered agencies.

             (3) Governing bodies of nonprofits formed by a public agency.

See how this helps to outline and determine where and how the company will be focusing their marketing efforts? Next, specific deliverables can be added to each of these. For example, let's say the decision is made, based on research, that restaurants are a key audience. So now, another objective could be to add that 10 restaurants a month will be contacted. Another deliverable could be all organizations subject to the Brown Act in a 100-mile radius will be identified and contacted within the first six months of the year.

We'll be discussing media planning in greater depth in Chapter 11, but below are two examples of how you start detailing out components of the advertising and promotion section of your marketing plan. The more detailed you are, with concrete objectives, the more likely you will be to implement the actions and to generate measurable results.

Promotion #1: Retailer

Title: "Winter Special" 25% Off Special

1. *Promotion goals:* $10,000 in sales in a month

2. *Offer period:* February 1 – March 1, 20XX

3. *Offer:* 25% off coupon on select merchandise

    a. Offer limited to one-time use; only original coupon accepted

2. *Program components:*

    a. Newspaper ad: Ad and coupon insert 1 week before offer starts

        i. Full page ad

        ii. Frequency: 4 times (same ad will run)

            (1) Ad cost: $1000

        iii. Artwork due: 5 days before run date

            (1) Copy due to ad designer by: ABC date

            (2) Photographs due to ad designer by: EFG date

            (3) Ad layout version one for review by: HIJ date

            (4) Final ad approved by: KLM date

            (5) High resolution print-optimized artwork sent by: NOP date

        iv. Review newspaper proof by: QRS date

5. *Other*

    a. Notify all service clerks; advise that only original coupons will be accepted.

b. Program registers to expedite processing and ensure accurate deductions.

c. All coupons to be turned in daily with register drawers.

Promotion #2: Restaurant
(Note: in this example, I've put actual dates so you have a concrete sense of turnaround times)
Title: "Three for the price of 2"
1. *Promotion goals:*

    a. 100 new customers

    b. $2000 revenue

3. *Offer period:* September 1 – September 15, 20XX

4. *Offer:* Buy two entrées and beverages, get the third entrée free

5. *Program components:*

    a. Digital: Facebook and website announcement and coupon: announce one week prior; link to website coupon

        i. Design online coupon with specific code by August 15

        ii. Test download on multiple browsers by August 22

    b. Print: Ad and coupon insert 1 week before offer starts

        i. Weekly magazine – due August 24

        ii. Half-page ad

        iii. Frequency: 1 time

            (1) Ad cost: $250

        iv. Artwork: due August 24

            (1) Copy due to ad designer by: August 1

            (2) Photographs due to ad designer by: August 1

            (3) Ad layout version one for review by: August 5

            (4) Final ad approved by: August 15

            (5) High resolution print-optimized artwork sent by: August 22

v. Review proof by: August 27

c. Radio: Announce offer 2 weeks before offer starts

   i. KWT5 Country

   ii. 15-second radio spot

   iii. Frequency: 5 times during peak morning commute hours

      (1) Radio spot development cost: $250

      (2) 35 spots: $1000

   iv. Radio spot: Will be done by radio station with in-house talent

      (1) Copy due to station by: August 5

      (2) Station to send draft spot back for review by: August 12

      (3) Final approval by: August 17

      (4) Final ad approved by: August 24

Now, we all have our own workstyles. I'm not saying you have to stick with the above examples' formats. You may prefer to use an Excel spreadsheet or another planning program. My goal is to get you thinking like a true zipline marketer, assembling all your equipment, and determining your direction in detail so that you have a smooth and enjoyable ride on the zipline to success. By setting your business strategic objectives, you define the starting and ending points for your zipline marketing. With that information, you can then develop your marketing strategy and your detailed marketing plan, the essential roadmap that keeps you focused, able to budget, and, as you'll learn in Chapter 14, able to measure results and adjust your course as needed. Why put kinks in the zipline that are easy to avoid?

Chapter 7 ~ Pricing Is One of Your Most Powerful Marketing Tools

Toss out the idea that pricing is a fixed factor in your business mix. It's not something you set once and wander away from. It's one of the most powerful tools you have in your zipline marketing equipment kit. Big companies spend a lot of time and effort on smart pricing strategies because they know these can make or break them.

Pricing influences everything. Sales, profits, a company's very future. When used in a smart way, it can optimize your bottom line. We're going to look at tactics to use pricing in promotions in Chapter 12, but you should know right up front that a price tells prospects a lot about your company, product or service, and there are pricing techniques that can influence buyer behavior. Add to this the pitfalls of wholesale pricing, mark-ups, and margins, and you see why pricing is so much more than "just a number."

Join me as we review the zipline marketing essentials you need to know when it comes to this (ahem) priceless piece of equipment.

➢ *Don't let your price damage your business*

So what does pricing have to do with marketing? You know from Chapter 5 that price drives the bottom line. What smart firms do is combine "cost plus" pricing with competitive analysis to identify the potential price range that their buyers will likely accept.

> ***Zipline Essential #12:*** **Choosing the wrong pricing strategy can be a costly mistake.**

Pricing is psychological as well as tactical. On the marketing zipline, pricing can help differentiate a product or service from those of the competition, since price emits signals about quality and exclusivity. If pricing is wrong, it can damage a company, hamstring growth, clobber sales, and even throttle the business.

From the marketing perspective, pricing's responsibilities are to:

- Be something your buyer is willing to pay because they think the product or service is worth it.

❊ Be competitive with other providers of the same or similar product or service.

❊ Reinforce the brand/product/company's image.

❊ Deliver a specified amount of profit.

Let's dig in a bit more and take a look at each of these to see how pricing can be leveraged as part of your zipline marketing equipment.

1. **Be something your buyer is willing to pay because they think it's worth it.** The right price can create value in a buyer's mind. It's often referred to as **"perceived value"**: what they perceive it as being worth. Perceived value tends to fall into one of three categories.

- The worth or value of the product or service is perceived as greater than its price. Luxury brands are built on this concept. The gap between the cost of making the goods or providing a service and the price can be huge.

  Think of such top-of-the-line brands as Coach, Tiffany, and Ferrari. They've created a perception of value so high that the price is irrelevant, and actually contributes to being seen a status symbol.

  "Sales" pricing also can create a similar consumer mindset when dealing with high ticket items. A buyer knows the regular retail price is $200, but it's on sale for $75. In their mind, it's a great value for the price.

- Everything that's included makes the product or service seem worth more than its actual price. By bundling multiple elements under a single price point, depending on the perceived value of those elements, buyers feel they're getting a great deal for their money. This is often known as "bundled" pricing.

  For instance, think of infomercials that offer not one but two items plus such and such—"all this and more!" Or a 20-point inspection as part of an auto repair shop's winter special. Or "bundled discounts" of services—three yoga classes, five manicures—where the discount off of multiple visits creates a sense of value, while giving the company a repeat customer.

- The promotional offers make the product or service worth more than the advertised price. In this situation, a buyer has a sense of the regular price (or it's communicated in the promotion) and the incentive being offered, aka savings, makes them feel that they're getting a great value for what they will spend.

Examples include "specials" such as BOGOs (buy one get one free), or buy one entrée and two drinks, get the second entrée free, or $10 cash back on every $50 spent.

2. **Be competitive with other providers of your product or service.** In your competitive research (see Chapter 2), you've identified the going price range for your product or service. You now know that when a prospect is ready to buy, they often already have a sense of what they will be spending, particularly these days with the ease of doing Internet research. So when they shop from you, they come with an expectation with regard to price.

If your pricing is out of line with expectations, then you better have a good marketing story to justify it, especially if it's higher. This is where companies have to define a clear reason why (aka, positioning) as to why their products or services are unique and special in order to better support their price point (see Chapter 5).

Now, logic says you should always shop for the cheapest option in tires. You use them and throw them away when worn out. But you don't. Why? Because you may feel there's more to tires than just the price. And the tire manufacturers know this. Check out how three of them go beyond price to create implied high value through positioning.

- *Michelin.* A better way forward. Because you get everything you need, in every tire. [Aimed at buyers who look for the better choice, a well-engineered tire, and consistent quality.]

- *Goodyear.* More driven. Whether it's on the road or in the air, experts choose Goodyear Tires. You should too. [Implies that savvy buyers know this is the tire to choose, and if you want to be part of that group, you will buy these.]

- *Bridgestone.* It's Your Road. Your journey to the top is full of twists and turns. That's why our tires are rigorously engineered to perform their best when you need them most. [Targeted at drivers who are more adventuresome and may use their vehicles in more challenging situations, and want superior, reliable technology.]

3. **Reinforce the brand/product/company's image.** You're walking along the streets of New York City and one of the many sidewalk vendors hawks their Ray-Ban sunglasses or Louis Vuitton handbags at incredible prices. Maybe you stop to look. And of course the prices are ridiculously low. What's your

probable reaction? Too cheap to be the real thing. There's a fine line between "a great deal" and "cheap rip off."

Big companies use pricing to support and reinforce carefully cultivated brand images. Their underlying message is often, "Sure, you can find a cheaper [fill in the blank], but it's not as good as what we offer, which delivers so much more value." Within every product or service category, there are market segments or niches that cater to different target buyers, and for which those buyers have a price expectation.

For instance, consider shaving creams. Looking for an inexpensive shaving cream that does the job? Barbasol fits that niche perfectly at around $1. At $4 to $6, Edge guarantees a closer shave and extra protection. Contrast that to Acqua de Parma Collezione de Barbiere "with a luxurious Italian heritage" at nearly 50 times Barbasol's price. They're all shaving creams, but their pricing is designed to resonate with different buyer segments.

4. **Deliver a specified amount of profit.** No profit = short company shelf life, unless you have a venture capitalist willing to bankroll you indefinitely as a tax write off. (See Chapter 5 where we discuss the importance of knowing your product costs.)

➤ *Are you thinking with your customers' wallets?*

Pricing really is so much more than a number. It's really about understanding how people think with their wallets. Done correctly, it has the power to actually direct buyer behavior. And a fascinating example of that is the "Power of 9s."

Have you ever wondered why most prices end at .99 or .49? Think about gas prices—they yo-yo, but they always end in 9. Cereals, almond milk, meat… the list is endless. Look at the success of the 99 Cents Only stores, which sold for $1.6 billion. It's a clever mind-game that should influence your price setting, and it's all about the power of suggestion.

Number 9 is a pricing sweet spot. Research has shown that buyers usually round *down* prices ending in 9 to the nearest whole number. So an $8.99 blouse is seen as $8 instead of $9. I often refer to it as **the penny that costs a dollar.** You might say, oh, let's just set the price at $9 instead of $8.99 because it's easier on the register. Or you might argue that you don't want to give up a penny per sale because it adds up. But your buyer sees it not as just a penny higher but a dollar higher. That can cause problems if they're comparison shopping and your competitor offers the same thing at $8.99.

Another problem is if you round up your pricing, and it tips the price point into the next $10 level—for example, from $9.99 to $10 or $19.99 to $20—people perceive it as a lot more expensive because "it's over $10," or "it's over $20," even though it's just a penny more.

There is also a **pricing "no man's land"** that can actually discourage a buyer from making a purchase. Notice you usually don't see everyday pricing that ends in 1 to 8, as in $31 or $38. That's because research has shown that prices ending in the number nine—as in $39—were actually *able to outsell* even lower prices for the same product! The exception occurred with sale prices—"Was $70, now just $45!" Then the sale price did beat out the number nine. Yet when the $45 sale price was adjusted up to $49, it again outperformed even the lower price point. Are we pushbutton or what?

Here's another interesting character twist to the pricing plot. Recent research shows that **the currency symbol itself can impact buyer behavior**. Have you noticed how some stores use the $ symbol on their pricing labels and some don't? For example, $9.99 vs. 9.99. Turns out that the decision as to whether or not to include the symbol does make a big difference. Pricing research has determined that it's far more effective to price goods *without* the dollar symbol. When we see a currency sign as part of the price, it triggers a psychological connection to our wallets, and we perceive the price as being higher than it really is.

Can the comma in a price cause a problem? Apparently so. Take a look at the following prices: $1,299.00, $1,299, and $1299. Can you guess what research showed? If you guessed that the first two numbers were seen as much higher than the third price, you're correct. This is caused by the way we say or think numbers to ourselves when we see commas. "One thousand two hundred and ninety-nine," vs. "twelve ninety-nine." In other words, keep the style in which you present prices as simple as possible!

Can you surge prices? Ever wondered why hotels and airlines, Uber and Lyft, movie theaters, and others charge different rates at different times or days? Why roses on Valentine's Day hit stratospheric prices? Even Universal Studios and Disney have decided to implement it at their theme parks. **It's called demand, surge, or variable pricing.**

When it's busy—weekends, rush hour—and demand is high, they know they can charge a higher price because they have a captive audience who may not be able to come at another time. When it's slow, the price is dropped. So from a revenue and profit standpoint, demand pricing delivers more to the bottom line.

However, it's also a marketing tool. Demand pricing is used to try and "push" people to use a service or go places during slow periods, therefore spreading the load more evenly across business days or hours of operation. The benefit is a company does not have to absorb the costs of more workers or overtime.

Smart firms often "package" the lower prices with additional tangible incentives and/or create added value by "selling" the advantages of coming during off peak times, such as being quieter, shorter lines, etc. Nevada casinos routinely offer free rooms Sunday through Thursday, plus gaming incentives and meal discounts to attract guests during off peak days.

➤ *Whoops... what about wholesale?*

Pricing is usually divided into retail (the price to the end-user) and wholesale—the price to a middleman who resells the product or service to the end-user. In either instance, everybody's "favorite" topic of markups and margins pop up—and we'll cover those in the next chapter.

Most of us naturally tend to shop at "aggregators"—stores with which we have established a trusting relationship and where we can conveniently find everything we want. Think Amazon, Target, Wal-Mart. These stores usually make their money on the difference between what they pay the wholesaler for a product and what they sell it for. While direct-from-manufacturer buying has skyrocketed among consumers thanks to the Internet, the aggregator model is still at the heart of retail sales.

Even service providers can resell others' services. For example, an ad or design agency may subcontract website design to an outside specialist. A law firm may subcontract work to clerk recorders. In both instances, they usually markup those services.

> **Zipline Essential #13:** Your wholesale pricing strategy is all about how much money the retailer or reseller is going to make.

While it can be a great opportunity to be able to sell your products at wholesale, strategic pricing plays a huge part in the game. Successful players have to know *all* their costs—both fixed and variable—to make a profit. Otherwise, no matter how much you sell, you risk making very little or even losing money. **Sales volume is not a substitute for profit.**

Different industries have different formulas they use to set retail pricing. They know what their buyers are willing to pay, and you have to be ready to play in their sandbox. So your wholesale pricing strategy needs to translate correctly into their retail or client pricing strategy.

That fancy blender you bought at a department store for $59.99 may be wholesale priced to the retailer from the manufacturer at $25 to $30. So in order to make a profit, the manufacturer's total product costs might be $15. That doesn't include promotional discounts, payments for prime shelf placement, etc.

And that's through just one tier of distribution: manufacturer → retailer → consumer. It gets really exciting when you have multiple distribution tiers, where products first have to go through a middleman distributor. In that case, you have manufacturer → distributor → retailer → consumer. With each successive tier, another layer of profit is added.

If you want to play in the wholesale arena, you especially need to understand…

➤ *Margins and markups, oh my!*

I think margins and markups were designed to confuse people and someday we're going to streamline the concept to have a one-size-fits-all terminology. However, until then, you have to know the difference. Markup is easier, but margin dominates in the business arena and is used for financial projections and reports. A good way of thinking about it is that markup begins with cost, margin begins with retail price.

✂ **Markup:** is a fancy way of saying "adding a percent to the cost." If your product costs $1 and you want a 50% markup, the retail price is $1.50. It's calculated by adding a percentage of the cost to the base cost in order to reach a desired price. [*Formula*: $1 × 150% =$1.50. [cost × (100% + 50% desired markup) = price].

✂ **Margin:** is the amount of profit expressed as a percentage of the price. If your price is $1.50 and your cost is $1, then your profit is 50 cents, or a 33% margin. [*Formula:* $.50 profit/ $1.50 price = .33 (33%). (profit / retail price = margin)]. You may hear the terms gross margin or net margin tossed around. Gross is based on gross profit; net on net profit.

By understanding how these two pricing tools work, you're now in a position to use them in your own pricing strategies. Will you sell your products at a 33% margin or a 50% markup? Whatever strategy you use, be consistent.

What would you do? To sell or not to sell…

Sybil's Smart Cleaner is a proprietary formula that cleans off thick, built up gook. Sybil has been selling the product via infomercials for several years at two for $24.99 plus shipping and handling, and is making a very nice profit. With all fixed and variable costs included (except for shipping), the cleaner costs her $6.77 per bottle to produce.

A major retailer has approached Sybil about carrying her cleaner at their home improvement store. They want to sell it for $19.95 for two bottles, and want a 30% markup. Should Sybil do it?

✎ *Jot down your answer:* _____

_____

_____

Answer: Do the math *and* do the projections.

At a desired retail price of $19.95, a 30% markup means the retailer needs a wholesale price of $15.35 for two bottles. In this case the "cost" for the retailer is the wholesale price. Using the markup formula, cost × (100% + 30% desired markup) = price, $15.35 × 130% = $19.95.

Right now, Sybil is making $11.45 in profit per two bottles [her retail price: $24.99 – her cost: $13.54 = $11.45]. If she sells wholesale, she will only be making $1.81 [wholesale price: $15.35 – cost: $13.54 = $1.81]. That's an 84% drop in profits. Ouch!

Knowing this, Sybil should ask for sales projections from the retailer. How many stores, what is the projected unit sales volume, etc. This serves two critical purposes. First, Sybil can contrast the projected volume vs. historic sales and crunch the numbers to compare profit potential. Since the retailer may ask her not to sell via infomercials anymore because of competing pricing, Sybil must determine if she will make more or less going with the retailer.

Let's say she has historically sold 5,000 two-bottle packs a year. So her profits are 5,000 × $11.45 = $57,250. If the retailer projects it will sell the same volume, Sybil is going to lose a lot of profit: 5,000 × $1.81 = $9,050. That's a loss of $48,200. Ouch again! But if the retailer says they could sell 50,000 two-bottle packs, now she makes $90,500 (50,000 × $1.81). See how crunching the numbers is essential? But that's only the first hurdle.

Second, Sybil has to look at production capacity issues. At 30,000 two-bottle packs, she needs to sextuple her volume to meet projections. Does she have the ability to do that without significant capital investment? If not, does she have access to capital or a loan to fund buying the equipment? And if she spends that money, what is her risk if sales don't materialize?

Other issues can include being able to handle increased customer contact volume, via phone or Internet, possible need to increase staff—and any associated costs, etc.

I've had many clients who are thrilled to be approached by retailers to carry their products. Sales increases have a domino effect throughout a company. *Always* evaluate all aspects during the decision-making process. Sometimes such a relationship is an amazing opportunity, and sometimes it can cause a company to crash and burn.

One more word on pricing: Sometimes we get hung up on cost as the only deciding factor for price planning. Technically, your cost is nobody else's business. It might cost you $1 to make, but if the buyer is willing to pay $600 because that's what they feel the product or service is worth, then you will make a lot of profit. That's why companies manufacture overseas: they're cutting their costs to maximize profits.

You can now see why strategic pricing is a zipline marketing essential, and so much more than "just a number." Pricing is not only about profits; it's about how buyers perceive and value your product or service, and reinforces the overall brand's image and positioning. And it will be a critical part of your promotional strategy, as you'll discover in Chapter 12.

Chapter 8 ~ Are You Speaking Your Customers' Language?

Companies have a tendency to get wrapped up in their products and services because they live and breathe them every day. Very often owners and managers, because they are so fluent in the business, get hung up on selling only the features of what they offer, and forget to get inside the customer's head. I call doing this **"inside out" marketing**.

➢ *Buyers' rule – it's all about them*

The real way you should be looking at marketing is "outside in"—from your customer's viewpoint. This is where the WIFME (what's in it for me) we discussed in Chapter 5 comes into play. You have to speak their language, and what they want to know is **how does your product or service benefit them and resolve their problems**?

The fundamental truth about marketing is it's all about the customer. How you communicate with them builds up **the customer life cycle of Know, Like, Trust, Try, Buy, Repeat, and Refer**. First they hear about you, next they research and learn to like and trust what your company and your products or services are about, ideally they make the decision to try, and buy. If they're satisfied, they become repeat purchasers, and tell others. This is even more true when it comes to digital marketing, which is largely relationship based.

Beware of flabby content! As I noted in Chapter 4, a common error I see companies committing is focusing on Tier 2 instead of Tier 1 selling points. Which means what?

Tier 2s are the things that people *expect* to a company to say and do. They're not special, not something that sets a business apart, that distinguishes them from the crowd. Examples of Tier 2 are "friendly customer service," "extended hours of operation," "we pride ourselves in honesty and integrity," or "workmanship you can trust." It's exactly what author Seth Godin is referring to when he says, "In a crowded marketplace, fitting in is a failure. In a busy marketplace, not standing out is the same as being invisible." It's not that you don't use Tier 2 selling points in your marketing message, but they are secondary, and not what you want to focus on for your website, ads, and promotions.

Tier 1 is all about what makes your product, service, or company *unique* and stand out from the competition. Call them your vital statistics—they are the key selling points that should be at the heart of your marketing story, and are distilled down from the WIFME factors we discussed in Chapter 5. And it's not about a list of features.

When you speak just about features, you're relying on the buyer to connect the dots and figure out the WIFME, the "Why should I care?" By tying it back to how it benefits them, you're closing the loop; showing them you understand their problems, challenges, and needs; and presenting them with a desirable solution that is better than what others have to offer. You're a problem solver!

Part of your solution is the **"intrinsic value factor"**: how your product or service makes a customer *feel*. Emotions do play a significant role in the decision-making process. So much so that they are a powerful factor in ad campaigns and positioning. Your marketing messages have to overtly or covertly address this through language and visuals. Here are just a few examples over time; see how you respond as you read them.

- *Beautiful women of the world wear Revlon.* Revlon showcased famous beautiful women of all ages, convincing women they could look that way too.

- *A Diamond is Forever.* DeBeers coined this phrase, associating its gems with eternal romance. Prior to that, the diamond solitaire as the token of engagement didn't exist.

- *Absolutely, Positively Overnight.* FedEx preyed on an employee's fear that if a critical package didn't arrive the next day, their job was history. They used superb visual imagery of a sweat-soaked office manager worrying if the package had arrived.

- *Plop plop fizz fizz, oh what a relief it is.* If you don't know Alka-Seltzer's famous line about relief from gastrointestinal discomfort, you're probably from the 21st century. In fact, I've seen the campaign reappearing, which is a testament to how memorable it is.

- *Mmm, Mmm Good.* Campbell's created a great feeling among children and moms about how wonderful its soups taste, especially on a frosty winter's day after playing in the snow.

- *Tastes great, less filling.* Miller Lite's campaign addressed the less-than-desirable outcome of drinking beer (beer guts) directly with this product's introduction.

- *Snap! Crackle! Pop!* Kellogg's Rice Crispies tackled soggy cereal head on using sound effects, and reinforced it with on-the-box characters which had the same names.

- *Let your fingers do the walking.* The Yellow Pages campaign cleverly addressed time-management issues by inviting people to use the phone book instead.

➤ *Talking in tongues – connecting with the right words*

Most target audiences have certain expressions and phrases they use that distinguish them, and these change steadily over time. You've heard of the Generation Gap? That includes not only experiences and reference points, but also the language. Cool! Gnarly! YOLO! And there you have Baby Boomers, Gen X, and Millennials. Younger groups have the trendiest language, and their expressions trickle up and out to the preceding generations as a result of child-parent-grandparent and other social interactions.

Companies also have their own lingo, with such terms as metrics, shared economy, monetize, and collaborative work environment, as well as industry-specific jargon. The cartoon strip Dilbert has been mocking this for decades. Nurses have nurse-speak. And the list goes on.

> **Zipline Essential #14: Understand how your buyer speaks to write more effective marketing messages.**

The more you know about your buyers, the better you will be at communicating with them. But it can get a bit challenging if you're a Boomer targeting a Millennial, because there may be some trouble "translating" your message into their language. So, how can you find the right words to connect with your buyers? Once again, your customers and competitors are actually among the best resources, as are publications aimed at your buyers. Even your employees can be a resource. How so? It's all about *listening*.

✂ **Customers.** They know the words they want to hear. You can interview them, using one-on-ones, online surveys or meetings, even focus groups.

Record the conversation, with their permission of course, and listen to their words as they talk about your product or service.

Sell skis or snowboards? Go to the slopes to talk with buyers. Car seats? Talk to moms. A bankruptcy lawyer? Talk to people who have suffered foreclosures, or are facing one.

- **Competitors.** Listen and check out what competitors are saying, especially the successful ones. How are they communicating with their buyers? From Chapter 2, you know how to "shop the competition" by checking out their website, visiting their location, calling, even making a purchase. Look, listen, and learn.
- **Publications.** When you study a magazine rack, what do you see? Loads of specialty publications. Each is aimed at a specific readership. And there are likely multiple print and online magazines, newspapers, trade rags, or association newsletters reaching out to your target buyers. Review them. The writers will use language and imagery proven to connect with the audience. More inspiration and translation techniques for you!
- **Employees.** Many companies have a mix of staff that cuts across age, race, and ethnic groups. They can be an excellent resource to help you frame up the right language.

  What I'm saying is don't labor to reinvent the wheel when it comes to identifying the most effective language to use in your marketing messages. You don't have the time, and it's not necessary. Leverage the free resources available. You may choose to hire an outside copywriter who has samples of having written for your target audience, but if you want to do the work in-house, this type of research is a proven technique.

➢ *Punch it up – why less really is more*

Remember how back in high school and college, we were usually instructed to write a five- or ten-page essay on a topic? We would labor to write using long sentences and big words to impress the teacher and earn a good grade.

When it comes to marketing messages, heave that approach out the window, effective immediately. Because it's all about being short and to the point. The KIS (keep it simple) principle is alive and well, especially with today's micro attention spans.

Think about it. What do we not have enough of? Time! **Lack of time makes for harried and hurried customers who tend to scan information**

quickly. If they don't find what they want to know, they move on. How hurried?

Back in the 1960s, according to some advertising executives I know, an ad was designed with the expectation that a person would read the headline in 10 seconds; if interested, they would then read the subhead and body copy in 30 seconds to a minute. Now, you're lucky to get three to five seconds of a reader's attention. Today, it's all about shrinkage. We speak in the length of email subject headers, tweets, and acronyms. So do you really think your buyer is interested in long detailed content?

Yes, as with all marketing essentials, there are exceptions. Highly technical or legal materials may have to be wordy. A particular target audience might want lots of information. Or the media channel where the ad or promotional piece is placed may warrant more content. For example, with a Canon camera or a luxury car ad in *National Geographic* magazine, there tends to be more copy. Why? Because their readers are highly educated, and seek details. But even those ads have become noticeably less wordy over time in response to people's inattention.

Consider what you see on today's websites. The well-honed home page tends to be short and to the point, with key information right up front and easy to find. If you're interested in knowing more, you click through or scroll down; the second level has more information, and so on. Remember how just a few years ago, websites contained long paragraphs of content and animated eye-candy?

The battle for mindshare has ballooned to new proportions with the Internet. Everywhere you turn, an ad pops up. Experts estimate **that the average person is inundated by 1,600 to 6,000 advertising messages every day.** The result? Unless you hook 'em fast, they ignore you. Is it any wonder people want information fed to them in what I call "sight bites"? Short, quick, and to the point.

How do you write in sight bites? One of the best pieces of writing advice I ever received was, "All first drafts are sh-t. But in them lies the best creative copy." So go ahead and write your first draft and don't worry about its length. Think of it as selecting the right equipment for your zipline ride. Your first draft is like going to the store, and reviewing all your options.

Then rewrite it. Seriously. Rewrite it. Rewriting is different from editing, because as you rewrite a sentence, you see ways to rephrase it to make the text more impactful. I usually rewrite a piece from two to five times. In between each rewrite, I edit, slicing off words that just fill space, and may dilute, even detract, from the content. Each rewrite and edit progressively refines your message. It's like culling through the zipline equipment options until you have exactly what you want.

Helpful writing tips: Having served as a magazine editor for seven years, let me share with you that one of the best ways to edit a piece is to read it out loud. Even better, listen to somebody else read it to you. Our tongues stumble over awkward phrases that our mental reading glosses over. And somebody else's voice places emphasis on words differently than you do. Suddenly what sounded great inside your head doesn't sound so good in another's voice.

Proofing. OK, I'm now going to climb up on my soapbox again. **Proofing is vital.** Nothing undermines your story about quality more than typos and grammaticos (those are what I call grammar errors) in your copy that you present to the audience. I have seen some royal botches. And while they may sound funny, think of what they say about your company. Here are a few rib ticklers, with a side of comment from me.

- *Salutation:* Dear fiend (I'm glad they think so highly of me).

- *Email blast:* Sneak Peak (it was supposed to be peek; maybe it's a stealth mountain?).

- *Résumé:* I'm an accurate and rabid typist (and why would I want to hire you?).

- *Letter:*…other attorneys may be 'assfisting' on behalf of… (there's a visual!).

- *Park sign:* Not a through toad (poor unwanted toads).

- *Résumé:* I have a degree in orgasmic chemistry (ooh, a new college course!).

- *Church event announcement:* The fasting and prayer conference includes meals (that's a fast fast).

- *Funeral parlor:* Please place your donation in the envelope along with the deceased person you want remembered (I'm guessing only one donation will fit per basket).

- *Bulletin:* Weight Watchers meeting: please use large double doors at the side entrance (a real 'feel good' announcement).

- *Salutation:* Dear Madman (um, are you trying to say I'm crazy?).

- *Résumé:* Received a plague for salesman of the year (not an award I would brag about).

- *Menu:* Restaurant specialty: Severing customers (get me out of here!).

Communicating effectively and accurately with your audience is a marketing essential, from writing using their phraseology, to recognizing that short and to the point is required in today's busy world. Use Tier 1 copy – say what makes your company special, and show how it offers the best solution to a customer's problems, wants, and needs. Don't treat copy and content casually, because it is often your first point of contact—and if it doesn't connect, you'll have lost a prospect to some other provider.

Chapter 9 ~ Eliminate Tree Blocks on Your Zipline to Success

Tree blocks on the zipline to success can be from outside or inside. Outside factors include changes in the market and among buyers, new competitors emerging, or a new product or service that may make what you offer obsolete or less desirable.

Those that come from within—ranging from internal processes or business philosophies that create a resistance to change and new ideas, to a belief that the company "knows what's best for the customer"—are another aspect of the "inside-out" mindset. It's important to manage your firm with an "outside-in" approach: looking at the business from the customer's point of view to reduce the risk of failure.

In addition to sharing insights on ways to spot and overcome some of your company's internal issues, which I'll expand upon in the Chapter 17, I'm going to cover how to use customer surveys to identify problems and develop a more "outside-in" approach. And as I'll be talking about surveys, I've included a detailed section on how to make them work more effectively for you as a powerful piece of zipline marketing equipment.

> ### ➤ *How to get out of your own way*

It can be hard to admit, but sometimes the biggest roadblock on the way to success is ourselves. Business owners in particular are a passionate lot. We believe strongly in our vision, and invest a lot of energy and often money. Then we become so wrapped up in the day-to-day routines that we don't realize we may actually be one of the problems. That extends into marketing, because we assume we know what's right. Now and for the future.

> **From Jug to Ultra-Premium.** During my E&J Gallo days, the wine industry was undergoing a seismic shift, spearheaded by Glen Ellen winery, which had identified a huge market opportunity. Their research revealed buyers wanted 750-mL and 1.5-L wines they could enjoy the same day of purchase, instead of having to cellar them for a length of time.

Back then, wine buyers had a firmly entrenched perception of Gallo winery as one that made inexpensive jug wines such as Carlo Rossi, even though they had a line of E&J Gallo branded 750-mL wines. Despite the company's marketing clout as one of the industry's largest players, it struggled to overcome that image.

It was not until they launched a new brand, Turning Leaf, a few years later—without any mention of it as an E&J Gallo brand—that they achieved a competitive foothold in the new wine segment, and earned a positive reputation among buyers.

Nearly 30 years later, the winery still makes jug wines. Yet it has also become a major player in the 750-mL bottled wine segment with a large and diverse spectrum of brands. And among the top? Ultra-premium award-winning E&J Gallo of Sonoma. It just took time and a willingness to evolve with the market and cater to the buyers' wants and perceptions.

Perhaps one of the biggest dangers of being too short-term focused or nearsighted is that you are actually at risk of setting your business up for failure. How's that possible? Here you are working your butt off, and you could be hurting your company? Stick with me.

Running your business day-to-day means you're down in the bushes and weeds, fighting fires, making sure products are produced, delivered, and clients made happy—just to name a few duties. You're often so busy *reacting* to situations that you don't have time to be *proactive* and periodically climb above the treetops and onto your zipline for a reality check, and to spot an oncoming branch or tree block that could knock you off your zipline until it's too late.

This is one of the most frequent issues I encounter with clients, especially when I'm summoned to help them dig out of a sales slowdown, or worse. It's not that they meant it to happen but being so inside-out focused, they "didn't see it coming." It's not unique to smaller firms—even the big players with all their resources can stumble. Consider these four instances of "not seeing it coming" and how it knocked the companies sideways, even off the zipline.

- *RIM Blackberry:* Its device was the choice of *business* customers and the leader of the emerging smart phone segment. But unlike Apple and Samsung, RIM failed to recognize that smart phones could evolve to become mobile computers, and could appeal to buyers outside the business user segment.

Even after the marketplace showed that touchscreens were more popular, RIM continued to produce phones with full keyboards. Going from market leader to market loser, the company was acquired in 2013.

- *Polaroid Corporation:* Founded in 1937, Polaroid later became known for instant photography with the One Step camera introduced in the 1970s. While today it may seem quaint, the concept of an "instant photo" spit out by a camera vs. having to take it in for film development and wait several days was revolutionary.

  Where Polaroid stumbled was a decision to prevent anyone else from having access to the instant technology and expanding the market through licensing. As 35-mm cameras gained market share in the 1980s along with one-hour photo development kiosks, the value of "instant" faded. The final straw was digital cameras. Polaroid was slow to anticipate and respond to emerging trends, and the venerable firm filed for bankruptcy in 2001.

- *Smith Corona & IBM Typewriters:* Hard to believe, but typewriters date back to the late 1800s. At one time—along with lots of secretaries—every office had multiple typewriters. Getting a typewriter as a graduation gift was standard—you needed one for college.

  As computers became increasingly powerful, versatile, and affordable during the 1990s, people substituted them for typewriters. IBM sought to adapt by getting into personal computers, but the industry had already bypassed it, and Lenovo acquired the business in 2004. Smith-Corona still makes typewriter supplies, but today focuses on thermal labels. Another example of a new technology terminating an old one.

- *F.W. Woolworth's:* Founded in 1878, Woolie's, as it was fondly called, was the quintessential department store. The place where for a nickel or a dime—hence the nickname, "The five and dime"—you could find nearly anything, stop for lunch at their famous lunch counters, browse for sewing notions, or buy clothes and shoes. Affordably priced, with stores everywhere, it was the "go-to" place to shop. But as the century advanced, the retail environment grew increasingly competitive and fragmented. By the 1980s, Woolie's was going downhill. It folded in 1997.

Each company failed to see it coming. It may have been typical "inside-out" mindsets: too much internal bureaucracy that prevented the right people from being made aware of a changing marketplace or stifled change; an unwillingness to listen to marketplace reality; a belief that as industry leaders, nobody could supplant them; or a mindset that they knew what was best for the consumer vs. the other way around. Whatever the reasons, they went from boom to bust.

Using the Zipline to Success analogy, you have to get above the trees and bushes to see what's ahead of you. So how do you accomplish this?

➤ *Course correcting for change*

If you're a smart business owner or manager—which I'm sure you are, because you're reading my book to gain insights—you should embrace the following quote by author John Wright: "Business is like riding a bicycle—either you keep moving, or you fall down." To which I add a corollary: the important part is that you're moving in the right direction, and not just pedaling like mad to stay upright.

I'm not going to deny your company may be a time or energy vampire for you. But as the person guiding your firm or department, you must climb above the "busyness" and make sure things haven't shifted, exposing your firm to impending trouble.

So what are **5 valuable steps to reduce the risk of failure** that you can put into place and develop a more "outside-in" mindset?

1. **Put on a wide angle lens.** Take off your business blinders. Don't define your company simply by your local market or industry. Look outside at firms, products, or services that your buyer could *substitute* for what you have to offer. This includes monitoring their marketing efforts and watching for ideas and concepts that may appeal to your buyers, and considering ways to incorporate them into your business. It's a cliché, but climb outside of your box and look around. Also, encourage your employees to bring ideas to you.

See a clever contest? Can you adapt it for your company? What about an interesting loyalty program, or coupon, or advertising message, or special offer? Here's a great example: My local car wash has recently placed a small digital billboard at the end of the conveyor belt, so as you're passing through the hot air blowers, you—as a very captive audience—have time to read the changing promotional messages. Clever! And I can think of a lot of ways other companies could adopt and adapt this idea.

Just like Mother Nature adapts to an evolving environment, creative marketers adapt to evolving economic, social, and industry trends.

2. Delegate the small stuff—recognize the value of your time. Yes, you're busy. But are you maximizing the value of your time?

Ask yourself, what is the value of your time per hour? For sure you're in the double or triple digits, maybe more! If your hourly rate is $100, why are you doing $10/hour work? Yes, you may feel like you're getting stuff done, but **are you working smart**? Are you focusing on the revenue-generating activities the company really needs you to be working on? It ties back to the 80/20 Rule: are you spending time on the activities of greatest value?

On my desk, I have a favorite quote from our Wellesley College president's commencement speech: "Don't confuse busyness with productivity." I think she's spot on, and it's something we're all guilty of doing.

Another problem: when you're too busy, you're more likely to default to established or easy marketing outreach activities, stuff that's been done for years. You assume they're a safe bet. But because audiences and competition evolve, what worked two, three, or five years ago likely needs revamping or replacement. That's something you can't analyze and assess if you're worrying about getting the mail stamped and out the door.

Solopreneurs and start-ups, you're probably saying, "But it's just me here!" Yes, I know. Then your challenge is to prioritize and organize your tasks, and make sure you're primarily focused on the revenue-generating efforts.

3. Quarterly reality checks. I encourage you to check the company's performance against business and marketing goals at least once a quarter, monthly is you're a start-up. Are the numbers on track? Is customer growth what you projected? Did that marketing promotion or ad campaign deliver against its objectives? If not, what caused things to miss? And what are you going to do to course correct and address the issues?

Wait until the end of the year, which is what many firms tend to do, and in most instances you'll be too late to take care of any problems. Worse yet, you may not even remember what caused them to happen!

4. Build expert relationships. Some of the best advice I've gotten over the years is, "We all need a coach." An outside expert perspective is invaluable in helping to steer the business. I'm a consultant, coach, and advisor to many firms, providing insights and advice to help guide their company. I have my own team of coaches, because I'm always looking for new ideas, better ways of doing things. We can and should always be open to learning. As world-famous

Chef Emeril Lagasse said, "If you're not learning something every day, then you're really cheating yourself."

Whether you establish a board of advisors, work with a consultant or a coach, or have a business mentor, it's important to partner with people who have expertise in business and can bring the added value of their experience and insights to help you adjust your direction as the good, bad, and the ugly situations arise.

What does establishing these internal processes add up to? It sets you up to climb above the bushes to your zipline and spot oncoming obstacles and adjust course for a smoother ride.

Now wait a minute. Didn't I say 5 valuable steps? Yes, you're right. I did. #5 is Customer Surveys. And I think they're so important for your business, I've given them their own section below.

➢ *Survey your customers wisely*

I consider customer surveys a superb marketing tool, one that is frequently underutilized by smaller businesses, but is something big companies know can be extremely valuable. Any owner or manager should add to surveys to their zipline equipment and use them on a regular basis to identify issues, problems, and opportunities.

***Zipline Essential #15.* Customer surveys can be gold mines if done properly.**

Surveys are all about measuring. Not just numbers but ideas, concepts, packaging, and more. For instance, they can:

⌘ Identify opportunities you haven't even thought about.

⌘ Red flag problem areas you need to fix.

⌘ Capture testimonials you can add to your marketing materials.

⌘ Reveal language and phrases you can use to strengthen the marketing message.

⌘ Gather research information to help refine the understanding of your buyers.

⌘ Spot emerging trends, changing preferences, or new expectations that can influence the direction and future of your company.

Some owners or managers will say they don't use surveys because they lack time to process them. I say that they're throwing away a chance to gather valuable data that could improve their company and their marketing, and alert them to oncoming tree blocks.

Even if they do surveys, the incoming data can be flabby, because they don't know how to design effective questions that really collect the valuable insights. So when they put together a survey, it uses the easy way out, with a "Yes/No, are we doing OK?" approach. Unfortunately, a poorly designed survey is GIGO—Garbage In, Garbage Out. Approaching the customer survey process with such mindset is like riding the zipline with a rusty trolley. Why bother?

Your survey data is only as good as the *way* in which you ask your questions.

There are research firms that design, administer, tally, and analyze survey data, and if you're doing a volume of surveys—hundreds or thousands—it's a very effective method. But for most small to mid-sized companies, you're collecting a lesser number of surveys, and/or the data-gathering is gradual, so tabulation can be done in-house by somebody comfortable with an Excel spreadsheet. Alternatively, online programs like Survey Monkey and Constant Contact are designed to administer digital surveys and provide instant data tabulation.

The biggest mistake I see firms make with customer surveys, besides not writing questions the right way (which we'll get into a later in the chapter), is they implement a survey without any planning. Toss something together, then have customers fill it out—paper, digital, by phone, whatever. This also is GIGO thinking, and produces data that isn't going to be as useful. There are **five key factors to doing successful customer surveys**.

1. Define the purposes of your research to ensure a well-designed survey.

2. Keep it visually simple to maintain the respondent's interest.

3. Keep it fast and easy to complete—respect people's time.

4. Develop questions that capture the data you want—avoid GIGO.

5. Use rating scales vs. yes/no questions where possible to capture more valuable data.

Let's look at how you plan and organize your survey process to optimize results.

- **Purpose.** What are you trying to measure? If you don't know, how can you write questions to gather that information? Are you trying to measure...
  - Performance?
  - Customer satisfaction?
  - Opportunities for improvement?
  - New product or service ideas?
  - Solicit testimonials?
  - Solicit ideas?
  - Gather email addresses?
  - Other?

- **Respondents.** Who do you want to complete these surveys? Choosing the right respondent is important because it impacts the results. You may want to invite people to provide feedback even if they don't make a purchase. They might be visiting your store, and you want to understand why they do or don't buy. Or you may want only people who have purchased from you in the last three months to rate their satisfaction because you implemented a new program during that period.

  For instance, my client, Sciabica's California Olive Oil, is an award-winning producer of gourmet olive oils that has been cold-pressing olive oil in California since 1936. The VP of Marketing and Sales wanted to develop new upscale packaging that communicated the products' excellent quality.

  After developing a number of design concepts, we winnowed it down to five. Next we did both in-store and online surveys. We gathered both quantitative (numeric data) and qualitative (written responses) on which concepts people liked, as well as why or why not. We collected over 700 responses, which was perfect, because the larger the number, the better you can feel about hanging your hat on the data.

  The final label selected by the buyers was actually different than expected. And Sciabica's wisely showcased the fact that it was a package selected by customers in the subsequent product restage. That cultivated a strong "feel good" response, fostering happy fans who bought more and told their friends, an ideal example of customer engagement. Today, the company continues to grow and win awards for their exceptional varietal and flavored California olive oils (SunshineInABottle.com).

- **When?** What is the time frame in which you want these completed? Will it be ongoing? One time? Morning or afternoon? Holidays? School breaks? Winter? Summer?

  Different times of day and year can actually influence whether and how many people will respond, aka response rates. Think like a customer: are you really interested in responding to a survey the week before Christmas as you run madly around shopping? Or being interrupted by the phone in the middle of dinner? OK, maybe if the surveyor offers a big incentive!

When I work with restaurants, we conduct surveys during specific times, because breakfast buyers are different than lunch buyers. This allows us to track time of purchase, food preferences, visit frequency, even test new product concepts. In every instance, the results enabled the managers to make changes that have improved the bottom line.

✂ **Type of Questions.** What type of information are you looking to collect? Different types of surveys and questions are used to capture different kinds of data. These include rating scales, rankings, yes/no, close-ended, and open-ended questions. It's essential to choose the right types of questions so as to obtain useful results to better serve customers and improve your marketing. If you'd like more details on this, check out the following box.

---

5 Ways to Write Questions to enable you to create useful surveys that meet your purpose.

1. **Close-ended:** Can be answered only using the options provided. These are best used when a question is a black or white answer: Yes or No, Did or Did Not. This allows you to zero in on specific issues you want to ferret out. For example, "From the following list, please check all the ways you heard about us," and it's a list of all your different marketing outreach efforts. Or "Did our technician arrive on time?" and it's a Yes or No option. Both of these are close-ended questions.

   Avoid Yes/No questions when what you want to learn about can have different levels. For example, take an equipment repair company who uses a Yes/No option for "Were you satisfied with our technician's service?" And 75% of surveys come back Yes, so the company should be happy, right?

   But imagine if instead they asked, "On a scale of 1 to 5, please rate how satisfied you were with our technician's service," and now it's an average rating of 3—"neither satisfied nor dissatisfied." That's not good. It's equivalent to scoring a C! As the tech supervisor, wouldn't you want to find out what's causing the low rating?

---

2. **Open-ended:** Encourages the person to answer any way they want. These questions are good for collecting interesting feedback and concepts, and often serve to generate new insights or issues, raise red flags, or identify new marketing opportunities you haven't thought about. For example, "What do you think of our new chicken sandwich?", "What do you think about our new ad campaign?"

   These are often placed at the end of a survey or a section of a survey, giving respondents a chance to express their point of view. For example, "Is there anything else you'd like to share?", "Are there any other places online you would use to find us?"

3. **Rating scale:** These are valuable when you really want to determine how *much* people do or don't like something. A person marks the number that best corresponds with how they feel. Rating scales are usually odd-numbered, in that they run 1–3, 1–5, or 1–9, with the lowest number being the "worst" rating. There is a school of thought that prefers even-numbered rating scales (e.g., 1–4, 1–8), because a respondent can't answer with a middle number, which is neutral.

   For example, "My stay at the hotel was very enjoyable," and the scale ranges from "strongly disagree" to "strongly agree." You check the corresponding box. Another example: On a scale of 1–5, how likely would you be to buy this product at $5.99?

4. **Ranking:** This is often used when you have several things you would like a person to select from, and you want to force them to prioritize what is most important. By having them rank the answers, you can see what is first, second, and so on.

   Say you're an arts & crafts store that offers classes and have some ideas about value-added services. You provide the following list and, to see what's most important, ask customers to rank order them, using a 1–5 scale.

"We continue to look for ways to serve you better. In the order of importance, please rank each of these concepts from 1 to 5."

Earlier hours of operation	_4__
Later hours of operation	_1__
Being able to make a class appointment online	_2__
Monthly specials	_3__
Free beverages in the class area	_4__

You administer the survey for a month, and get more than 50 responses. The results reveal that clients would like you to be open later, so they can come in after work, and want to have online appointments, suggesting that convenience is a big issue for them. From this data, you may decide to announce new hours, and add online appointment making, of course saying how you're doing this to make things more convenient for customers.

5. **"Wishy washy" questions.** Too often I see a survey that says, "Check all of the things on the list below you would like to see us offer/do..." This is classic GIGO because you're giving customers no restrictions. Of course they'd like to see you offer everything along with the kitchen sink. Why wouldn't they? They don't have any skin in the game.

   It's vital to attach "reality" factors to certain questions. By this I mean establish the actual context of how you would offer the product or service. For instance, when I was working with an athletics club, the owner had administered a survey asking people to check off all the different programs they would like to see offered. And in every survey, virtually all of the 15 items on the list had been checked off.

   We revised the survey and associated a price with each service. The result? With the exception of two options, most people weren't willing to pay for a majority of the proposed additional services. The two they would pay for? A 24/7 secure pass access card and on-site childcare. The club decided to introduce these value-added services, confident from the survey results that members would pay for them.

   Another version is testing pricing or other variables. Perhaps you want to offer a new menu item, product, or service. You can frame the question by describing it, giving them three price points from which to choose, and asking what price they would be willing to pay.

✂ **Survey appearance.** Have you ever been handed a survey, and it's hard to read, or been copied too many times, or difficult to follow? The design, format, and flow can have a real influence on how, or even if, people will respond to the questions. There is no one-size-fits-all format. Color, images, choice of font, and spacing are all a part of design flow. Some things to consider:

- If the survey will be completed by an older audience, you need to choose a font size that's larger and more readable; after 45, vision usually starts to change and small print is hard to read. Avoid reversed out type (light color on dark background) as it's also difficult to read. If you want to use it, your type size should be even larger.

- Headlines look better in a clean font like Tahoma or Arial, but body copy is more readable when it's a font such as Times New Roman, the typeface often used in books.

- Colors and shading help "escort the eye," an expression I use to refer to guiding a person's eyes through the survey or marketing piece. Colors should be carefully chosen because they have subliminal meanings. For example, green can imply you want money. Blue inspires trust and confidence. Red suggests innovation and creativity. It's just like designing an ad. It's not only what's being said, but what's being shown that can also influence responses.

If you'd like to see some additional sample surveys, visit ZiplinetoSuccess.com/Resources to download some helpful examples.

There is one natural weakness to the customer survey process, and you just have to accept it. Those who answer are people willing to take a survey. So you won't get the data from non-survey-taking people. That's why getting larger numbers of responses—50 or more—is preferable, because it reduces the risk of a small number of surveys producing skewed data.

What do I mean? Imagine you survey five people, and three love the new product, two not really. So off you go, invest time and money, and launch it to great fanfare... and it flops. Trying to figure out what went wrong, you survey lots more people, and discover, to your chagrin, in reality, most were actually not interested. **Small numbers of respondents risk sending you down the rabbit hole.** The same risk occurs if you survey the wrong audience. By defining the survey's purpose and respondents up front, you can feel more confident in the results.

Some more helpful survey pointers:

✂ **Branding:** Whether your survey is sent via email or is a hard copy, don't forget to always "brand" it with your company name, tagline, and contact information, because a survey is still a marketing tool. The exception is if you don't want people to know it's from your firm because that information could bias responses.

✂ **Getting testimonials:** If it is being administered to existing customers, surveys are a perfect place to ask for testimonials at the end. If you already collect testimonials via surveys, great. But have you ever noticed that the responses can be very generic, and lack those really high-powered statements you want to use on the website and in other marketing materials to impress prospects?

If you're willing to put in a little extra effort, you can boost the outcome of the testimonial requests by using what I call the Zipline Problem–Solution survey method. In the survey, three questions should be, "What problem or challenge were you facing before you decided to call XYZ company?", "Why did you choose XYZ company?", and "How did we help solve your problem?"

The responses enable *you* to write a stronger testimonial, then send it back for the client's approval. I can tell you that 9/10 times, they're delighted, and thank you for making them sound so good. They may tweak it a bit, but now you've got a powerful problem–solution testimonial that will really stand out.

Always request written permission to use the testimonials, and keep the records on file; the approval can be via email or with the person signing the survey. This is especially important with people at a company providing a testimonial; they may leave and you always want to be able to prove you had tangible approval to use that statement.

➤ *Extra hip-pocket research tools*

Research comes in a variety of shapes and sizes, and can even be a mash-up of different elements. While small to mid-sized firms often rely only on customer surveys to gather data, it's also worthwhile to consider other tools used by big companies.

✂ **Focus groups.** While some insist these are a relic of the 1990s, I disagree.

They are a very powerful research tool. An in-person discussion group made up of 8 to 12 people, a focus group enables you to probe in greater detail on issues, ideas, new products, services, and more with prospects or customers.

As a trained moderator, I have conducted over 300 focus groups for everything from video games to luxury home designs. Every time, the cumulative results of multiple focus groups have significantly influenced a client's next steps. FYI, it's a good idea to use an independent moderator rather than staff, who naturally bring a bias to the process.

Today, with digital connectivity, you can conduct a focus group online via Skype, Zoom, GoTo Meeting, and other services that allow you to gather people in "one room." I think that both in-person and online focus groups are viable, as long as you've crafted a good moderator's guide, and are recording the sessions to view or listen to later. Why record? Because there's no way to remember everything that's said, and you don't want to lose the valuable information.

Never underestimate how smart people can be! My favorite focus group story is when I was testing Atari's new Galaxians video game cartridge. The kids were in the room playing the game, with engineers watching from behind the one-way mirror. After they were done playing, several kids complained that the game felt "off." When I probed as to why, one explained that a certain character was off by at least one pixel, making it harder to "kill" that Galaxian; clearly, he was an experienced player!

Well as you can imagine, the engineer in the back was in a huff, convinced the kid hadn't a clue what he was talking about. Until he went and looked at the program code. And guess what? The kid was right!

- **Phone surveys.** Frankly, I think these are now a very weak research tool, unless it's scheduled in advance. What with caller ID, smart phones, and people understandably suspicious of spammers, unsolicited survey calls face a steep uphill battle. But a survey that you have previously scheduled means the respondent is ready to talk, and it can almost be like a one-on-one in-person interview. *Important*: Be careful about exceeding the amount of time you say it's going to take—it's guaranteed to upset the person.

- **Direct mail.** Using good ol' snail mail, these surveys are sent to customers with hopes they'll complete and return them. Like phone surveys, these have faded dramatically in popularity due to the profusion of bulk mail, and are frequently tossed.

If you do a direct mail survey, unless you're offering an incentive to respond, remember to include an SASE (self-addressed stamped envelope) or a pre-paid postage response card, otherwise you're asking the respondent to pay to do your survey. Yes, you will lose some money on postage, but you will increase the likelihood of response because you're making it easier for them.

To increase response rates, consider offering an incentive, such as a coupon, a branded giveaway item, or money. Look at how some charitable fundraising solicitations include a nickel or address labels. It encourages you to open the envelope and respond.

When it comes to surveys, companies absolutely must practice **considerate management of their respondents' valuable time.** The longer or more complex a survey, the more likely people will opt-out, unless they're passionate about the issue, or you're offering an incentive.

The Panda Express restaurant does a great job of using incentives for a basic survey. Their register receipts invite diners to do an online survey about the most recent visit, the incentive being a free third entrée on the next visit. Once you complete it, you instantly receive a code. This means you become a repeat customer, and Panda gets valuable research data. That's smart consumer research!

The power of percents I always shake my head at the manipulative power of percents when it comes to marketing, messaging, finances, and survey data. A percent can distort, understate, overstate, confuse, or exaggerate a situation, or portray it in a useful way.

- *Exaggerate:* 50% of all dentists surveyed recommend Mega-toothpaste. Hmmm, and how many dentists were surveyed? After all, if two dentists are surveyed and one loves Mega, it's still 50%. Note that this is *not* a lie—it's (ahem) creative usage of a percent.

- *Under or overstate:* Sales are up 10%! Off of what dollar base? 10% on $1,000 isn't the same as 10% on $100,000.

- *Distort:* Unemployment is just 5.7%. But 5.7% of the population of 20 years ago is a smaller number than 5.7% of today's larger population, which actually means more people are unemployed than 20 years ago.

- *Confuse:* A firm's goal is annual sales growth of 10%. For each year, the target *dollar* growth will be increasingly aggressive since the 10% increase is based on a progressively larger dollar volume. To illustrate: Base number: $100,000. Year 1, +10%: $110,000 (up $10,000). Year 2, +10%: $121,000 (up $11,000). Year 3, +10%: $133,100 (up $12,100).

- *Useful:* 75% of 500 customers surveyed gave us a 4.5/5 satisfaction rating.

  Always question a percent when you see it out of context or being used without supporting hard numbers, especially when it comes to your business. Why? Because if the percent is not presenting a complete picture, it can knock you off the zipline if you use it for decision making or planning.

Customer surveys are a powerful way to identify marketing opportunities or challenges. They can also alert you to product, service, or company issues that are putting up tree blocks along your zipline, so that you can respond and modify your course, and address the problems—*before* you lose a customer.

Part 3 – Zipline Highlights

✂ **Set your direction with tangible goals.** If you don't know where you're headed, how are you going to get there? Marketing's job is to support well-defined strategic business objectives and translate them into measurable actions.

✂ **Use pricing as a powerful marketing tool.** Pricing is not a fixed factor in marketing. Through bundles, discounts, special offers, and value-added, your price can flex to boost sale and profits. Always think with your customer's wallet. Evaluate wholesale opportunities carefully before you make any commitment.

✂ **Speak the way your customers expect.** Always present your marketing message from the buyer's point of view, and show how you solve their problems. Don't assume you "speak their language"; take time to find out. Remember in today's too-busy world, short and sweet retains a person's interest.

❋ **Get out of your own way.** Running the business day-to-day keeps you focused on the now and short-term, and risks setting you up for missed opportunities and expensive mistakes. Implement practices to climb above the bushes and onto your zipline so you can check ahead for potential problems.

❋ **Customer surveys are a data gold mine.** A variety of different survey approaches can open the door to a wealth of ideas that will help you steer and improve the business. Well-planned, well-designed customer surveys allow you to evaluate performance, test new concepts, new pricing, and a host of other marketing essentials as well as gathering valuable testimonials. Choose the right question structure to optimize results.

❋ **"Inside-out" or "outside-in" perspective.** Accept that change is permanent. The market and your customers are constantly changing and evolving, and it's vital to view your business from their perspective, not only from your own. Your customers are your best resource in figuring out where to go next.

Part 4 – Zipping for Dollars: Budget-Friendly, Proven Traditional Marketing Strategies

It's a cluttered world in the marketing arena. Everybody is waving at you for attention, hoping to interest you in their product or service, and persuade you to buy. Just like you're doing to others. The challenge is, how do you stand out? How do you get people to notice you when you have a limited budget?

Let's face it. Most of us don't have hundreds of thousands or millions of dollars to spend on marketing efforts. But that doesn't mean you should just chuck what budget you do have at the wall and hope it sticks. Instead, what you want to do is smart marketing: leveraging your dollars as cost-effectively as possible to deliver measurable results.

In Part 4, you're going to discover instant-action ideas to transform everyday business items into marketing tools, and how to convert ads, promotions, and other marketing outreach tactics into more effective sales and profit generators.

Chapter 10 ~ Stealth Marketing – Maximize the Minimal

You're about to be fascinated by everything you can do, and much of it comes at a nominal cost. When I bring it to your attention, it may suddenly seem obvious, but when we're running around, busy as all get out, sometimes the obvious slides right by and becomes a missed opportunity.

To tie back to the "budget-friendly" theme, I'm going to rate each concept on a scale of $-$$$$, just like a restaurant guide, with $ being low budget, $$$$ requiring more bucks.

Here are fifteen tried and true ideas to consider. And if you're already doing many of these, please accept my compliments, because you're ahead of many other business people!

➢ *What color is your business?*

A word before we get going. That word is **branding**. I'm often asked, what is a brand? Jeff Bezos, founder of Amazon.com says, "A brand for a company is like a reputation for a person." While we tend to think of it as a logo, it goes well beyond that. It is the message your firm presents to the world about who you are and what you stand for—your "why." It's a fusion of marketing essentials, all working synergistically to create and cultivate that "feeling" of who the company is in the mind of the buyer, and continuously reinforcing that message at each point of contact from visual images to customer interactions.

Branding can operate at several layers within a company or organization. For giants such as Nestle, Kraft, Johnson & Johnson, or General Mills, the company is the umbrella or parent brand. Each has a specific look and feel to their logos and positioning statements. Of course, they also have multiple divisions and product lines, and each has its own specific branding. Sort of like a "nested" Russian doll—a brand within a brand within a brand.

Think about your favorite brands. If the company has done its job well, whenever you see their products and logos, you "know" it's North Face, Geico, Corona. They've successfully established their brand identity and attributes in your mind. Can you imagine Tiffany Jewelers' ad looking like a Harley-Davidson ad? Nope—because that's not the brand's look or feel.

I worked in Gillette's Personal Care Division. Within that, there was the hair products group and the deodorant group. Under haircare were such brands as Silkience, Tame, Toni Silkwaves, White Rain, and more. Deodorants included Dry Idea and Soft & Dri. Each had its own distinctive brand and dedicated marketing strategy and plan.

> **Zipline Essential #16.** Your brand "look" and "message" should be consistent across all marketing materials.

A critical aspect of branding is maintaining the same look and feel across all customer points of contact. Whether I pick up your business card, look at the website, or receive a brochure or letter, everything should have a similar appearance, color scheme, fonts, etc. That's part of creating a brand look.

Branding consists of several elements. First, it's the logo, color scheme, and visual presentation of the name. Second, it's the style and tone used in communications—trendy, upbeat, thoughtful, educational, etc. Third, it's the imagery—photos, graphics, typestyle—that "fit" with the style and tone. Fourth, as we discussed in Chapter 5, it's also all the underlying zipline marketing essentials supporting "the brand" that aren't obvious to your buyer (price, product, promotion & advertising, distribution, and positioning).

Understand that establishing a brand takes time. The ubiquitous Nike swoosh did not start out on its own. It was accompanied by the Nike name for several years. Likewise, with Apple, Microsoft, North Face, and other companies, today they are able to use the standalone logo and maintain strong brand recognition. Start-ups often want an instant brand, and need to appreciate that it is equity that has to be earned with customers.

Logos and branding also evolve, responsive to changes in consumer tastes and a company's positioning and product or service mix. Logos that gradually change are known as evolutionary, in the sense that the overall brand image is preserved so it's recognizable, but it is being refreshed without sacrificing brand equity. Occasionally a company will revolutionize its logo; dumping it to create a whole new image. Some great examples:

- *Cracker Jack:* Consider the evolution of the mascots Sailor Jack and his dog Bingo. First introduced at the 1893 Chicago World's Fair, the product got its name from an enthusiastic customer who remarked "That's crackerjack," an expression meaning "first rate." Not until 1918 did the mascots appeared. Check out their evolution over a century.

Early 1900s   Mid-century   21st century

- *United Parcel Service:* Nearly 100 years later, UPS shows no resemblance to its original logo, which revolutionized itself on the first phase. From 1937 onward, it evolved.

LOGOS

1919   1937   1961   2003   2013

- *Microsoft:* Their logo has gone from funky 1980s to sharp and techno.

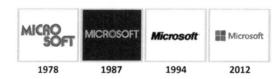

- *McDonald's:* Hard to imagine, but the Golden Arches weren't always a part of the logo.

- *AT&T:* As an example of both revolutionary and evolutionary change over a century, AT&T truly stands out. Did you know that AT&T stands for American Telephone & Telegraph Company? The original telephone ring tone was actually a ringing bell, with which AT&T's logo made a visual connection. Over the decades, as business diversified, they chose only to carry forward and evolve the lettering and circle.

Did you know that a brand itself can have monetary value? So much so that when a company is being acquired, there is actually a dollar valuation of the name—what's known as "goodwill." The acquiring firm is paying for the recognition that the well-known brand delivers in terms of customer loyalty, recognition, and future sales.

Now, as we proceed in this chapter, I'm assuming you have established some form of a brand for the company, product, or service. For most small to mid-sized firms, the company name and logo usually are the brand, unless you have categories, products, or services that have their own distinct brands.

Let's start looking at all the ways you can take your marketing efforts to the next level. I like to call this approach, **stealth marketing: maximizing the minimal.**

➢ *Un-waste your marketing real estate*

Let's begin by looking at some things you may already be doing. My first question is, are your marketing materials really working hard for you? I tell my clients that every point of contact with a customer is a potential marketing opportunity. Are you capitalizing on this?

✂ **Are you squandering your business card real estate?** Everybody has a business card; you're going to produce these no matter what. But are you treating them like a marketing tool? These are miniature billboards, yet 95% of the cards I see are only working at 50% or less of their potential. Pull out your card. Now ask yourself:

- *What's on the front?* Besides company name, title, and contact information, is the tagline there? Website? The most important selling point you want them to know?

- *What's on the back?* This has to be the most wasted real estate opportunity ever. Unless the card is embossed, the reverse is valuable space. It could be a list of services offered. The top three end-benefits about working with your firm. A loyalty rewards program, memorable quote, special offer, a testimonial, or social media sites.

  Of course you want the back to be nicely designed and readable, not a crowded cheesy-looking mess. But treat it as a billboard. Cards are fairly inexpensive to produce, allowing you to regularly revise and refresh the card's reverse.

  Helpful hint: Please don't buy 5,000 cards at a pop, unless you want to paper the office with them (exception: if you expect to meet 5,000 people in the next three months). Yes, it's more economical from a per card cost, but I can assure you—especially if you're a fairly new business—that your card will evolve and need new messaging long before using up those 5,000 cards.

- *Does it look cheap?* I've received business cards printed on very flimsy paper stock; it "feels" cheap. Others have pixilated artwork or logos that look like they were copied. Or the whole appearance is crowded, with too many fonts, or too much information. All this shouts an image of poor quality and raises doubts in your buyer's mind.

  Take the time to do it right. Collect samples of cards you really like for ideas. Many print shops have in-house design teams that can help. Most online printers offer business card templates. If you can't afford a designer, then do some research online about effective business card design. Don't waste this valuable piece of real estate.

  √ **Budget friendly rating: $**

✂ **Are you hiding inside your vehicle?** If you have a vehicle you use for business, what marketing has it done for you lately? Once again, this is a traveling billboard.

Usually when I spot a company vehicle, what I see is the name, phone number, and maybe a website. Sometimes a list of services, even a logo.

Here's what I don't often see:

- The tagline, or what makes them unique and sets them apart from the competition.

- The end-benefits of their services—what makes them relevant to me.

- Special points highlighted to engage my interest—such as free on-site estimates.

- The back panel of the van or truck being used! I mean, seriously. What part are people most likely to see when they're sitting in traffic or on the highway?

Yes, you have limited available surface area. So cherry-pick the most important communication points and work with those. Your goal is that when people see the vehicle, it's memorable. Think of vehicle wraps. Aren't those eye-catching?

And by the way, even if you don't have a formal business vehicle, you can employ low-cost tactics such as static interior-window clings or exterior magnetic signs to make your car or truck serve as a billboard in selected situations. Think of Mary Kay Cosmetics. Every car has the pink logo and slogan tastefully placed on the rear window using vinyl lettering.

Helpful hint: We're a web-fueled world. It's better to put a website than a phone number if you have to choose between the two. First, it's easier to remember. Second, they get to learn about all you have to offer when they go to your site. Also, the world wide web has been around over 20 years, so ditch the www. It's a dated look.

√ **Budget friendly rating: $-$$$$** (car wraps can be expensive.)

�֎ **Are your windows nude?** Office windows are another latent billboard that can be used very tastefully to showcase your business and services.

A local architect's office exchanged the clear window glass for a pale eye-catching aquamarine. Prominent white lettering features the name, logo, a short list of services, and a website. They've made "dead" space useful—and conveyed their great style.

Restaurants and coffee shops are often set back from the street. Brightly colored banners that fit within the windows are inexpensive (try HalfPriceBanners.com) and can be hung from inside using suction cups, as can signs. Interior vinyl lettering can also be applied. I suggest interior application because it reduces wear and tear on the letters, or vandals attempting to scratch them off.

Helpful hints: Important things to consider for window banners: KIS!

- Their job is get people's attention. Keep them clean, easy to read, with a short message. Special offer! Now Serving Breakfast! Sale! Special Event!

- The most powerful visual color combinations are bright red on canary yellow followed by black on canary yellow. Especially for people driving past, because bright colors draw attention—subdued colors don't. If people are walking by, you have more flexibility on choice of colors as there is more viewing time.

- Keep fonts simple. Block type is best, such as Arial, Tahoma, or Verdana. Fancy cursive fonts or funky letters can be hard to read, especially at a distance.

√ **Budget friendly rating: $-$$**

✂ **Are you signing wherever possible?** Companies tend to focus on their big exterior sign, and often forget all the other potential signage opportunities they have. Some of which are actually often more noticeable!

- **Sidewalk signs:** From a basic A-frame to creative cutout, these attract the attention of passersby. In fact, they may be the only thing people see, because your building's sign is literally overhead and out of sight. The best ones use bright colors, or are clever, such as the cutout chef figures you sometimes see in front of restaurants. My favorite street sign is "Mr. Mechanic," a robot-like figure made from a muffler and other random car parts that stands in front of a (surprise) automotive repair shop.

  How effective can a well-designed sign be? A high-end shoe store located on a side street had a sidewalk sign with white background, black border, and black lettering. Not only was it invisible from down the street, it stood at such a low level, it "hid" behind parked cars so people driving by couldn't see it. I suggested they repaint the sign frame a cheerful canary yellow with gold trim, and raise it from two feet to four feet high—and people started coming in, resulting in the first profitable month.

  A restaurant on a main street downtown struggled to get new customers. I had the owner put up bright red and white window lettering listing yummy menu items—above the height of parked cars—and a tall pedestal sign with the day's specials and metallic balloons. Business turned around, and five years later, profits keep growing.

Helpful hints:

- *Color and movement:* If it "fits" with your brand, feel free to "bling it up." People's eyes are naturally drawn to shiny and moving objects, such as balloons, pinwheels, and streamers.

- *Versatile A-frames:* For the budget-conscious, I advise buying a basic A-frame and inexpensive, colorful 2- by 3-foot vinyl banners to attach to each side. You can produce different banners and rotate messages and promotions on the same frame.

- *Be different.* Look for ways to be noticed. Inflatable "air dancers" come in many styles. Easy-to-stick-in-the-ground feather flags exist in stock and custom options; flags are perfect attention-getters because they flap. A nearby bench is an ideal place for your logo and message; find out if you can rent it. Remember wooden Indians? Consider a carved or cutout character in front of your place. See something clever while traveling?

Snap a photo, and ask the business owner where they bought it. Conduct an Internet search for "unusual sidewalks signs" for more inspiration. Do check in advance to ensure your ideas comply with any city ordinances or landlord restrictions on sidewalk or other forms of signage.

√ **Budget friendly rating: $$-$$$.** A-frames and flags can be $50-$200+ apiece.

- **Neon signs.** Neon was once the king of signage. Times Square used to be aglow with amazing animated neon signs. People actually visited the Square just to see these works of art. Las Vegas and Reno were filled with legendary neon signs.

   While digital sign boards have replaced much of this, neon can still be used as an effective and distinctive marketing tool. But take it up a notch. Instead of the everyday boring "open" sign, be more creative. Can it have movement—blinking or random sequences? Or a mix of colors? Can you find neon signs that tie back to what you sell? Yes, it may cost a little extra, but it will also stand out more. Plus, there are companies that make custom neon if you really want to go all out.

   A few creative neon signs I've seen: a colorful ice cream cone beside the "open" sign at an ice cream shop; a rainbow "open" sign blinking in different color sequences; a 57' Chevy for a classic car repair shop.

   √ **Budget friendly rating: $$-$$$.** Stock neon signs are less expensive.

- **Human signs.** Poised on busy intersections, today's human signs have come a long way from the days of the sandwich board. The best are the "spinners" who spin the signs to draw your attention while perched at the traffic light.

   A simple rule for these signs is to make them eye-catching: very short text, three to five words. Clean bold type. Bright colors. Also, make sure the person is presentable and reflects well on your business. A grubby guy in torn jeans, unless you're selling torn jeans, just doesn't send the proper message. Again, check city regulations.

   √ **Budget friendly rating: $-$$.** The cost of the sign and the person's hourly rate.

✄ **Are you stuck on me?** Don't omit the versatile sticker. From oval to die-cut, plain to embossed, one color to metallic, stickers are only limited by your budget and creativity. Not only can you design one with your logo and website in company colors for strong branding, you can create others for special promotions, as giveaways (kids love stickers), and more.

Rather than spend money on customized shopping bags that require a large volume order, sticker plain bags instead. Use stickers on your products. Put one on a shipping box when sending out packages—think of how many people handle them and can be introduced to your brand. Why do you think Amazon has its logo on every box?

Some companies produce stickers or static clings that retailers can use in their windows, doors, or at the shelf to increase visibility. It's known as POS (point of sale).

√ **Budget friendly rating: $$.** The cost of design and quantity printed.

Is your building bare? Many moons ago, long before billboards cluttered nonexistent freeways, there was... the exposed side of a building! Look at building walls in old New York or San Francisco, and you'll see faded ads promoting girdles, electric shavers, shirtwaists, and whatnot. Today, smart firms are waking up to the fact they have empty exposed wall space that can be used for advertising. If your walls can be seen by people driving or walking by, why not use them for advertising? Do check city ordinances and the landlord's policies first.

Such ads can be done conservative or crazy, as suits the buyer audience. I've seen something as simple as a large company logo, tagline, and website. Some really creative companies have invited local artists to do a mural that showcases their products or services in action, or a scene that features their products—and generates stories in the local paper. If you have an awning, remember that can be used as well.

Of course, some landlords won't want the building exterior painted, but they may be willing to allow you to hang a large sign or banner that can achieve similar purposes. Always get permission in writing.

Helpful hints: A few extra words on exterior signs. Some sign makers are experts, others are not. Ultimately, you're in charge of what is designed and put up. Your first concern is readability. Don't get caught up in an elaborate design with lots of text that nobody can read from a distance. Why waste the money?

Please, maintain your sign. It represents the company. Faded or peeling lettering, lights out inside the sign, or the material on which the letters are mounted being cracked or yellowing can all send the message that you don't care about your business. It's like a typo on a résumé. If you don't care about that first impression, what does it say to a buyer regarding what to expect from the rest of the customer experience?

√ **Budget friendly rating: $$-$$$$**

✂ **Are you going out bare-chested and bare-backed?** Staff is another marketing billboard, giving you a chance to reinforce the brand at every point of contact. Are they wearing company-branded clothing? It might only be a hat, but as they interface with customers, this is a commonly missed opportunity. While attire can vary by industry and situation, you should make an intentional decision on this, rather than it being haphazard.

When I worked at Evans Communications, all repair techs had logoed shirts and wore specific attire. The company paid for dry cleaning and replaced worn items. This delivered multiple benefits: clients trusted the technicians because they appeared professional; it impressed them because it said Evans was willing to invest in its employees; and wherever the technicians went, their clothing marketed the company.

Helpful hints: If your budget doesn't allow for embroidered or printed shirts, then invest in quality engraved plastic name tags with a company logo that staff can wear if they work with clients. Also, consider doing the tags with magnetic backs vs. pins, so as not to be poking holes in employees' clothing.

Establish a uniform of a certain colored shirt and slacks/skirts. Some big companies have done this so successfully that it's become a part of their brand identity, such as Target with its red shirts and khaki pants.

√ **Budget friendly rating: $-$$$**

Dear Mr. Company President: Please remind your employees that when they are driving a company vehicle or wearing company clothing, they represent your brand. I have called business owners multiple times after dangerous encounters with "their" trucks speeding or weaving in and out of traffic to remind them of this.

Likewise I have sometimes witnessed a group of employees at lunch cursing or drinking booze while wearing company shirts. Employees are a marketing billboard too. What message is your staff sending?

✂ **Do you have the right stuff?** Sometimes I'm convinced we are all packrats. Go to a convention, event, or trade show and what does everybody go hunting for? The free giveaways. So what do you offer?

Often referred to as "premiums" or "advertising specialties," these free items are imprinted with your brand and other information. The free factor makes them an ideal marketing tool. And if you do them correctly, people hang onto them, creating constant visual reminders of your firm. Call it "feel good" marketing; you're being generous by giving away stuff, and people feel good about your company for doing it.

Unfortunately, most firms give away the same old stuff. Pens. Notepads. Post-it notes. Ya-awn-nnn! What do you think happens? It's not memorable. It all fuses into a heap of pens, notepads… you get my point. Choose items that are different, not something you see every day. How do you go about giving the right stuff? There are two methods I like to use.

- **"Fit to message"** means selecting a premium that ties back to and reinforces your overall brand message and what the company does. For example, a travel business I work with uses keychain flashlights as giveaways. This ties back to the concept of going on an adventure and exploring, for which you often need a flashlight. Here are some other creative giveaways where something distinctive was selected to reinforce each company's marketing message:
    - Agricultural lending bank: branded flower seed packets.
    - CPA firm: cellophane-wrapped chocolate calculators.
    - Gourmet olive oil maker: branded recyclable shopping bags.
    - Art supply business: fun and funky glitter pens.
    - Software firm: a bobble-head stylus for touchpads.
    - AAA: keychains with a 'reward for return' tag
      so the owner will get their keys back.
    - Shipping supply store: small pocketknife
      to open letters and packages.

- **"Fit to audience"** aims at choosing a premium that will impress and/or connect with an event's attendees. For instance, at a B2B trade show, Intuit gave away mobile phone battery chargers—perfect for the on-the-go business audience. At a cycling contest, a bottled water company gave away over-the-shoulder water bottle holders. At a California home expo, a landscaper handed out drought-tolerant succulents. In each instance, the companies are choosing something **memorable**. The right stuff.

√ **Budget friendly rating: $-$$$$** depending on how creative you want to be.

Be carefully clever. I'm a noisy advocate for looking at other industries and adopting new ideas for promotional giveaways, but it's best to stick to items that are durable, long lasting, and fit with the image your company wants to present. Sometimes, what you think is a clever approach falls flat. Worse yet, it can boomerang and offend. Here are some things to avoid.

- *Stay out of the bathroom.* It may sound obvious, but while toothbrushes and hairbrushes may be acceptable if that's what you sell, most bathroom hygiene products are not. Bathroom humor may be fine in movies or on stage, but not in your business.

- *Avoid political items.* Just like the sensible advice to avoid discussing politics and religion with people you don't know, politics are polarizing and often divisive. While some clients may be in your political camp, others aren't, and you risk alienating them.

- *Break out the magnifying glass.* Please avoid tiny items that make it a struggle to read your name and logo because people won't bother. Readability should always trump cleverness.

- *Totally disposable.* I confess to being puzzled about using disposable promotional items. Why bother? If something is going to be tossed, it means your name and message are going to be forgotten. And isn't that contrary to the purpose of giving them?

✄ **Sampling works.** Consider sampling as a form of a giveaway. What do people love about going to Costco? Sampling all the food freebies. Think about cosmetic firms. They routinely offer samples with product purchase. My concrete manufacturing client, Bertelson Precast, gives away a free jump drive with his catalog of products loaded on it. Sleep Number gave me a free travel pillow so I could test its comfort.

Sampling can range from small portions of food products, to a small bottle of a beverage, to a CD music selection. You can even sample services, offering a free small job within your profession of landscaping, window-washing, or housecleaning, so a prospect can experience your quality of work. Even I do sampling—I offer prospects free downloadable information that can help their business as an example of my expertise.

Remember that you don't have to give premiums to everyone, as that can get expensive. Use a tiered approach where you have low cost items anyone can take, and then selectively give away more pricey items to prospects, key clients, etc.

√ **Budget friendly rating: $-$$** depending on how creative you get.

✤ **What does your phone have to say about you?** Here's another great piece of wasted real estate: your phone! As in your phone message. Huh? Stick with me on this, because it happens all the time.

Here I am, calling in, and your phone message says I have to briefly wait. And then it goes to silence or music, maybe interrupted by a tinny voice apologizing for the wait. So I'm sitting here, a captive audience, waiting for you to pick up. And waiting, and waiting....

Why on earth would you waste that air time?

Smart marketers take advantage of their on-hold message to promote a product or service, interspersed with interesting educational information that portrays them as knowledgeable experts, with very brief spaces in between of music or even silence. They are retaining a listener's interest without inundating them with promotional messages. It's a respectful, balanced communication to the customer.

In fact, some companies deliberately route incoming calls to go through the voice message sequence *before* they pick up to ensure that it's listened to by the caller. It may be a 10-, 15-, or 30-second message, but it connects.

For instance, say you're a dentist. Your on-hold message can open with a thank you for calling (pause), office hours and address (pause), then announce a new service or a special offer (pause), then briefly discuss the risks of bleaching to enamel. Length of time: 30 seconds to 1 minute.

If you anticipate longer hold times, do longer voice messages. Depending on how frequently your customers call in, remember to refresh the message at least once a quarter, preferably once a month. Otherwise the message gets stale.

Have somebody with a pleasant voice do the message. For both a man's and a woman's voice, use one that's deeper—it connects more strongly because it comes across as authoritative. Enunciate clearly, speak naturally, and don't drone in a monotone. There are agencies that do professional voice messages, if you can spend a little money.

Be sensitive to the fact that there are cultural variations. If you've ever been to Disneyland, you'll notice that different language announcements vary between male and female voices, because Disney has researched what each audience responds to.

Important tip: Always call in from an outside line to listen to the voice message and make sure it comes across as professional. Is it clear and easy to understand? I don't know about you, but I simply despise worn out voice messages with a scratchy voice, stuttering music, and hard-to-understand instructions. Right out of the gate, it tells me a lot about the company, and none of it is good.

√ **Budget friendly rating: $-$$** depending on if you do it in-house, or hire talent.

✂ **Are you a smart snail-mailer?** The demise of snail-mail, as many derisively call the stuff that arrives in the mail box, is grossly overstated—if you use it wisely. Is it true that the majority of what falls through a mail slot is junk mail or bills? Sure. While I'll be talking more about direct mail in Chapter 12, here are a couple of effective low-budget marketing tactics that go far in building customer relationships.

• *Thank you cards:* We receive so little genuine mail these days that an old-fashioned hand-written (<u>not</u> preprinted) thank you card absolutely surprises and delights. It may be a simple expression of appreciation for their being loyal or becoming a new customer. You may choose to include a thank you token such as a discount or some form of a freebie. But the fact you have taken the time to do this speaks volumes to clients.

Some folks will argue with me saying, "just use email." Except everybody else is doing that, so if you want to stand out, why not do it different? Some more smart tips:

  o Don't use black ink when you write the cards. It triggers a perception of "form letter" and "preprinted." Colorful ink, such as blue, including on the envelope, reaffirms that it's handwritten.

  o Use a real stamp. This helps signal it's genuine vs. junk mail. There are fun and colorful stamps available at the U.S. postal office. Or, if you really want to zip wild, consider having a customized postage stamp designed by the various online providers with your logo, a special image, etc. Now *that's* branding!

    ◦ Like any marketing tool, overuse creates a wear-out factor, so don't overdo these.

- *Other cards:* Building on this value of personalized cards, consider other holiday card options that fit well with your business. For example, if your target audience is mothers, then Mother's Day is a good fit. If your company specializes in party supplies, can you tie into major party holidays, such July 4th or Halloween?

  One of my favorite tactics is sending Thanksgiving cards. Think about it. Everybody sends Christmas cards, which means yours gets lost in a veritable paper deluge. Almost nobody sends Thanksgiving cards out, which means your card will get noticed. Once again, it's about standing out from the crowd.

   √ **Budget friendly rating: $**

✂ **Odds 'n Ends.** I'm often asked my thoughts on brochures, flyers, and other printed items. Thanks to websites and the Internet, many such materials have become much less important. Plus, you usually have to print several thousand to make it cost-effective.

The real issue is that printed materials are "static," meaning you can't update the information quickly when needed. What happens if you have 5,000 brochures, and you discontinue an item, or add a service? Ooops. Yes, there are ways around this, but as a zipline marketer, shouldn't you plan instead of react? Here are some things to consider when evaluating whether or not to produce these items.

- *Brochure:* Does your buyer prefer a brochure? For example, 55-plus audiences often do. Like all marketing materials, a brochure should serve a purpose. Is it to repeat the same information as on the website? Highlight key services? Feature hyper-targeted information? Have something to hand out at events? If you're just doing a brochure because you think you're supposed to, rethink yourself.

- *Flyers:* Best used for promotions or to highlight a specific message, these usually have a short shelf life. Design it as appropriate for both your product (or service) and the expectations of the buyer. Don't go cheap and junky-looking if you're a high-end business. Even on a flyer, how you present your business tells your prospect a lot.

  Helpful hint: Avoid the "stick it under the windshield wiper" distribution tactic. Many towns forbid this. More importantly, people can be irritated that you touched their car and may have damaged the wiper. Definitely the opposite of your intention!

- *Door hangers:* While once used extensively, door hangers have down-shifted to being associated with inexpensive products and services, such as pizza promotions. You can navigate this by doing a better quality piece, such as using a stiffer paper stock. They are labor intensive, because you need to hire somebody to hang them.

  √ **Budget friendly rating: $-$$**

A word about Public Relations: PR always seems like an easy freebie, and many of my clients will ask me, how do they get more PR? It ain't that easy.

When print media such as newspapers and magazines were king, many reporters eagerly monitored PR announcements that could lead to an interesting article. Those days are gone. And even then, a strong headline, story, and topic were needed to get attention.

Today, it's actually about **marketing your PR message** to cut through the blizzard of "look at me" clutter that inundates reporters. View it from a zipline marketing perspective. If the media organization is the buyer of your PR, what are you going to offer as a "reason why" to pick up the story? The answer comes from having information about their publication—their reading/viewing audience, common topics or themes, etc. How will your topic connect with their readers/viewers? Simply sending out a PR announcement that you're having a Mother's Day brunch—unless you're in a small town with a very local newspaper—probably isn't going to get a pick up.

PR is a definitely a useful part of your zipline marketing equipment, but has to be properly packaged to boost the chance of attracting media interest.

✂ **"Do it different" ideas.** I'm a cheering squad for firms that seek ways to use a different spin when it comes to connecting with buyers and developing loyalty. Don't forget the value of having loyal customers: they aren't easily seduced by competitors because price is no longer their sole decision factor in buying from you—it's the relationship you have built with them. Here are some more ideas for you to percolate on. And for even more "different" ideas, check out Zip Wild in Part 6.

- *Give away balloons at events:* Balloons always create smiles, and are not just for kids. Buy custom balloons printed with the business name, rent a helium tank, and enjoy a large flock of people walking around with your brand floating over their heads.

- *Magnetize it:* Clever and/or useful magnets with a company name and logo are a great way to keep in front of a customer's face. But be creative. Don't just go for the over-used calendar magnet. Can you do something that ties back to the business? Or has high usefulness? A favorite of mine is a compass from a hiking supply store that I can stick on my bike's handle bars.

- *Bumper stickers anyone?* Depending on your buyers, bumper stickers with fun images, creative quotes, or kooky statements do double duty. One, the buyer gets a laugh plus a reminder each time they see it. Two, their car is now a billboard for your business.

- *Sponsor a local event or contest:* While you may not have the big bucks to be a key sponsor for a local contest or event, consider donating a product or service as a prize. Most events will list all supporters in their marketing materials, which is a good way to get your company's name out. If you're donating products, make sure they are branded.

√ **Budget friendly ratings**: $-$$

➤ *Avoid the 3 Bs: Boring, Basic, Been Done*

I know you're busy and probably meeting three of you coming around corners. But don't let that be an excuse for falling into a rut and doing the same premiums, advertising, and promotions year after year, or that everybody else is doing. If you do, it becomes stale and disappears into the crowd. That's what you want to avoid, isn't it?

What are the warning signs that you've fallen into the 3 Bs trap? Here are ways to spot the yawn or invisibility factor.

❋ Boring. *Alert:* Gets a yawnnnn….

- No longer delivers sales bumps—because you've done it so often, it's expected.

- Customers don't remember seeing the current ad or promotion because it's the same or similar to the one they've seen for years.

- Fails to attract new buyers because your existing clients don't remember to tell people about it.

- You don't remember when you last did it because you've done it so many times.

- Your eyes glaze over when you resurrect it for another use.

❋ Basic. *Alert:* Appears invisible

- Doesn't capture attention, so people don't take action.

- Too bland. The appearance, offer, or message doesn't interest or engage your buyers.

- Lacks creativity. With all the design options out there, there's no excuse for a visually uninteresting piece. I'm not saying it should be crammed and jammed. But does it garner interest?

❋ Been Done. *Alert:* Falls flat

- Looks like everybody else's ad, promotion, etc., sometimes dubbed as copycat. Think car commercials. If you turn off the volume, can you tell the difference between them?

- So many people have done the concept so many times that it's threadbare. Remember ad jingles from the 1990s (McDonald's – 2 whole beef patties; Almond Joy – sometimes you feel like a nut; Budweiser frogs – Bud… weis…er). It wasn't that they weren't clever, but after a while, because everybody was doing them, they became dull.

Smart marketing is leveraging your dollars as creatively and cost-effectively as possible to deliver measurable results. Make sure that all your marketing real estate is communicating and reinforcing the company's key marketing messages. And don't get stuck in a rut of doing the same thing over and over again, because it will dramatically increase the risk of dropping off your customer's radar screen—and maybe even letting a competitor attract their interest!

Next, let's zero in on advertising and promotions, which, as you now know, are only a part of the marketing zipline.

Chapter 11 ~ Marketing Outreach: Should You Advertise or Promote?

While many companies insist they are "doing marketing," in reality what they're doing is advertising and promotion—frequently without any strategy or planning behind either one. The end result often is frustration and disappointment in the results. But this doesn't have to be the outcome.

As you know from our marketing zipline model in Chapter 5, ads and promotions are key pieces of equipment in the zipline marketing system. Both are part of what's known as marketing communications or what I refer to as marketing outreach. Marcom, as it's sometimes called, also includes PR, webinars, sponsorships—all the efforts to connect with customers.

Big companies know that in order to deliver results, marketing outreach efforts need to be structured in a manner that supports the business and marketing strategies.

So, what's the difference?

✖ *Advertising* has one primary job: to persuade people to buy now or later.

✖ *Promotions* are designed to generate sales within a specific period of time.

Although they are technically different, they can often overlap: companies develop ads that include a promotion, and well-developed promotions use smart advertising principles.

Let's first take a look at how you can develop ads and promotions with clearly defined purposes and select the right media to optimize results. Note that many of the core principles of developing effective advertising also apply to promotions, so I address both as we go along in this chapter. We'll focus on promotions in greater depth in Chapter 12.

➢ *Best ways to advertise cost-effectively*

There are two main advertising categories: image and brand. Image is the domain of giants like Chevrolet, Visa, or Anheuser-Busch, because they spend the money without the intention of generating immediate sales. You'll often see these types of ads during the Olympics and Super Bowl. Designed to reinforce image and positioning, they make you feel good about the company and its products. Think Budweiser's "Lost Puppy" ads or Coca Cola's "Polar Bears" series.

Brand advertising is aimed at generating sales; it's designed to motivate you to purchase that product or service. These ads focus on product specifics, end-benefits, and solutions. Denny's meals will fill you up without emptying your wallet. Red Bull will boost your energy for a busy day. Cheetos will satisfy your snack craving. The majority of advertising falls in this category. You see it, and it (hopefully) makes you want to buy.

Clients often tell me, "I need to do more advertising. I'm not getting the results I want yet, so more has to be better." Or they grumble at me, "Advertising is a waste of money—it never does anything for our bottom line." To the first I'll say, probably not. The second, yes, you're right… if you aren't using a strategy and plan.

> **Zipline Essential #17.** Advertising and promotions can be big financial drains when done without purpose.

Let me ask you a question. **What is the *purpose* of your ad campaign or your promotion?** The understandable response is, "Well, d-uh, to generate sales." To which I will reply, what kind of sales? New business? Profitable? New customer? More sales per customer? Inventory liquidation?

As with everything in zipline marketing, marketing outreach efforts such as advertising and promotion are driven by setting specific goals, followed by the steps needed to get there. The more you have *not* defined what you're trying to achieve, the more likely the outcome will fail to meet your expectations. For example, are your ads or promotions supposed to:

- Create excitement and get people talking about you?

- Stimulate trial of a product or service?

- Be a Loss Leader Lure to get customers into the store for multiple purchases?

- Generate inventory clearance to make way for new inventory?

- Quickly generate revenues and profits?

Let's set the stage by zooming in on a couple of client experiences. See if you've ever been in either of the following two situations.

What would you do? **Buy bundles and leave it to us.**

A retailer decided to do TV ads because they knew their prospects watched TV. So the retailer chose "bundles" of shows on the regional cable provider. A bundle means the ads would be on a pre-determined group of shows. There would be a discount for buying the bundle instead of individual air time on specific shows. By buying in bulk, the retailer figured it would be more cost-effective. Any idea how this could misfire?

Jot your answer down: _____

_____

_____

Answer: When we did research for the client, we discovered that most of the shows in the bundle weren't ones being watched by the prospects! So the presumed "savings" actually resulted in wasted spending. Yes, the client was able to run more ads, but so what? It would have been better to spend that money on the right shows, even if it meant fewer ads. Volume is *not* a substitute for focus.

Beware the easy way out when it comes to buying media! OK, let's try another one.

What would you do? **Being everywhere is vital.**

It was the beginning of the 2007 housing foreclosure crisis. A bankruptcy specialist was advertising everywhere in the regional market—every newspaper, radio channel, and magazine. Although he was spending over $10,000 a month, clients were just trickling in and he was puzzled as to why. Why do you think his advertising might not have been working? [If you've read the whole book so far, I *know* you know the answer.]

✏️ *Jot your answer down:*_____

_____

_____

Answer: For one month, we had him implement a simple tracking system. Beside every office phone was a sheet with a list of all the media channels being used. Every time a new prospect called, the first question was, "How did you hear about us?" A tick mark was placed next to the caller's response. Within one month, data showed that over 90% of calls were coming in from one radio station, and 10% from one newspaper. The attorney rerouted all his ad dollars into those two media channels, and in less than a year he jumped from a staff of three to 30. He had learned to focus his spending where it would work the most productively.

What I call splatter advertising, which is what both clients originally did, is one of the most common mistakes. Running ads everywhere in hopes that they connect, and not planning or targeting advertising efforts in a way to maximize results with minimal spending.

How often do sales reps contact you to place an ad in their publication, on the radio, put a coupon in their booklet, or an ad on a shopping cart basket? It's their job to persuade you to advertise, and there's nothing wrong with what they're offering. But you need to be able to answer, **"Is this the right media for my business?"** so you can make an informed decision and cost-effectively manage ad and promotional expenditures. How do you go about doing this? Read on!

➤ *Essential media rules you need to know to choose wisely*

It's important to be aware that both ads and promotions are broken into two distinct components: Creative and Media.

✂ *Creative* is the message, copy, and images laid out in a design that inspires buyers to think and act.

✂ *Media* refers to the different communication channels where you choose to place your ad or promotion.

> **Zipline Essential #18.** Do not buy any media without a plan in place.

With both ads and promotions, you absolutely need to map out the process to manage them effectively. Let's start with the **6 steps to results-driven media buying.** Because, after all, isn't it ultimately about the outcomes?

1. Define your goals and objectives
2. Determine and plan your budget
3. Identify the focus, message, and/or offer
4. Select the correct media channels
5. Produce well-crafted content that connects with your buyers
6. Evaluate results

Now you'll see how this method reduces risk and can dramatically increase your chances of success. We'll use a real time example as we go through each step.

1. Define the goals and objectives. What is the purpose or goal of the ad or promo? Clearly state the objectives in as much detail as possible, as these are integral to selecting media and how much to spend. Would you spend $50,000 on an ad if your goal is to generate $25,000 in sales? I sure hope not!

Next, ask yourself, is the purpose poorly focused (PF) or well-focused (WF)? Here are some PF client examples, and the WF alternatives we developed. Note that I'm assuming that as you go through this process, you have already defined your target buyers and prospects, why they buy from you, and what buttons to push (if not, see Chapters 2 and 5).

- **PF:** Our ad campaign needs to attract affluent buyers in our town.
  - *WF:* Our ad campaign will be aimed at people in the XYZ zip codes where affluent buyers live, and needs to deliver 50 new customers in 30 days.
- **PF:** We want people to know we're here, so we're going to advertise.
  - *WF:* To create awareness of our business and generate $2,000 in weekly sales, we're going to focus our ad campaign on the three

key reasons customers buy from us, and feature some sort of special—event, offer, giveaway—to attract them.

- **PF:** Our promotion needs to generate more sales.

  ○ *WF:* We want to increase average per customer sales by $5, and increase our total sales by $1,000 per week within two months.

- **PF:** We're going to promote our barbecues.

  ○ *WF:* Our goal is to sell 50 BBQ units. Since male homeowners are the primary BBQ buyers, we'll develop an ad and promo combo that will launch one month prior to Father's Day, and position this as a great gift idea. We'll evaluate giving away a BBQ tool kit with every sale, a $50 retail value.

See how the WF zooms in on detailed specifics, such as sales goals and time periods? In other words, being well-focused defines the direction in which to go, and what you want to achieve, and helps aim the zipline. Let's work on an example for a new company about to open.

- *Company:* Holistic Wellness

- *Products/Services:* Therapeutic massage

- *Target audience:* Young mothers and businesswomen who are stressed out and need an escape to recharge.

- *Objective:* Introduce our business to the target audience within a 30-minute drive radius and get prospects in the door to try us out.

2. **Determine and plan your budget.** How much do you plan to spend on this specific effort? Over what length of time? If you only have a $2,000 budget, and a full-size print ad in a desirable magazine costs $4,000, time to look elsewhere. Likewise, if you have only $2,000 for an entire year, you want to choose the hardest working options possible.

At big companies, a marketing outreach budget is usually planned in advance for the entire year, with portions allocated to specific efforts. People often ask how much to budget. A quick rule of thumb is 3% to 5% of gross revenue. Use this as a starting point, but it is by no means a hard and fast rule. It really depends on your industry, strategic business goals, financial resources, and your buyers' location.

Now, in today's increasingly digitally-driven advertising and promotion arena, there appear to be a lot of "free" advertising options. **Remember there's**

no such thing as free. There are costs, either obvious or hidden. If it takes several hours each week to administer Facebook and prepare ads, that's a cost—time is money. If you're paying per click for Google Ads, there's a cost. If you're on Pinterest posting product shots... you get my drift. The good news is that these can be very low cost options, and may be a perfect fit to reach your buyers. We'll talk more about zipline digital marketing options in Part 5.

Note that during budgeting's initial phase, costs are estimated. Then there's a feedback loop cycle during which things such as actual media costs are determined, as well as quantifying the costs associated with any promotional offers. This data enables the budget to be revised and fine-tuned. We'll delve into this in the next section. So, let's say that Holistic Wellness sets a budget of $3,000.

3. Identify the focus and offer. Once you define the goals and initial budget, next comes deciding on what the ad's focus and, if relevant, the promotional offer is going to be. Note that an offer doesn't always have to be an incentive to buy. It could be an open house, an event, a charity fundraiser.

Your message is dictated by knowledge of your buyers, and what has to be said and offered to make them want to take action. In other words, **what is your CAT (call to action) going to be**? (Yes, I know the proper acronym is CTA, but CAT is more memorable and fun.)

The more focused on the buyer's wants, needs, and expectations, the better the chance of developing an ad or promotion that will connect. Knowing this, Holistic Wellness decides to offer a trial massage coupon for $25 off the regular $75 price.

4. Select the advertising media based on the proper "fit" for *your* business. There are a lot of media options out there. Having a budget and CAT, the next step is to identify the media channel that will cost-effectively reach your desired audience. How do you do that? Start by asking the ad sales representative for a media kit. Most reputable companies will have one.

What's a media kit? It provides audience demographics on who and how many people read/watch/listen; where the media can be found/seen/listened to; and the rationale as to why you should elect this option for your business. Some will also include rate cards—how much it costs to advertise—or provide one upon request.

Your goal is to ascertain if their readers, viewers, or listeners and your buyers are the same or closely aligned. You might love country music, and the local country music radio station's rates are cheap. But if your target audience listens to classical, your ads won't reach them. You may read a newspaper, but if your buyers are Millennials, guess what they're not reading? An ad on a TV station may seem a great idea, but if your business serves only a small geographic footprint, and the station covers a big market, it could be a waste of dollars.

Case in point: A spa I worked with asked my opinion on a radio station's pitch to sponsor a popular DJ's show. At first blush, it seemed like an ideal opportunity. But a little bit of probing with the sales rep about the listeners revealed the audience was mostly football enthusiasts who enjoyed the DJ's Saturday morning sports show—blue collar males ages 18–40. The spa targets women 30–55 who are middle to upper income. Simply put, not a good fit.

If you don't choose media channels that are a good fit with your buyers, you risk frittering away your ad budget and having weak results. Sometimes it seems easier to advertise everywhere. Please don't. Get the media kit.

What does Holistic Wellness decide to do? After reviewing the media kits of several area publications and radio stations, they choose the local lifestyle magazine with 40,000 circulation, and decide to run a full page ad on the back cover, featuring the offer.

Helpful hint: The Media Schedule. Big companies actually develop what's known as a media schedule, often drawn up by their ad agency. It's basically a full-year calendar that maps out when all the ads and promos are being run, via what media channels. It's also used to plan for anticipated sales surges and establish lead times with manufacturing to ensure adequate inventory, and with customer service for sales support coverage. At a glance, the marketing executive can see what's coming up and make sure all necessary pieces are in place.

You can do a simplified version of this with a wall calendar or an excel spreadsheet for both upcoming advertising and promotions. It's a helpful visual reference chart to stay on track and allow adequate time to plan ahead, book media, and more. Remember, your zipline marketing goal is to be proactive and plan, not react and hope for the best.

See the following example.

Sample Media Schedule

Simplified Media Schedule

	January	February	March	April	May	June	July	August	September	October	November	December
Magazines												
A	Full page $2000	Full page $2000	Full page $2000						Full page $2000	Full page $2000	Full page $2000	
B				1/2 page $700	1/2 page $700	1/2 page $700						
C										1/4 page $1000	1/4 page $1000	1/4 page $1000
Newspaper	1/4 page $1500 - mid-month, Sunday, Local	1/4 page $1500 - mid-month, Sunday, Local	1/4 page $1500 - mid-month, Sunday, Local	1/4 page $1500 - mid-month, Sunday, Local	1/4 page $1500 - mid-month, Sunday, Local	1/4 page $1500 - mid-month, Sunday, Local	1/4 page $1500 - mid-month, Sunday, Local	1/4 page $1500 - mid-month, Sunday, Local	1/4 page $1500 - mid-month, Sunday, Local	1/4 page $1500 - mid-month, Sunday, Local	1/4 page $1500 - mid-month, Sunday, Local	1/4 page $1500 - mid-month, Sunday, Local
Radio												
KMMM				15: sec spot, traffic, 5-9AM, 4-7PM $500/week		15: sec spot, traffic, 5-9AM, 4-7PM $500/week			15: sec spot, traffic, 5-9AM, 4-7PM $500/week		15: sec spot, traffic, 5-9AM, 4-7PM $500/week	15: sec spot, traffic, 5-9AM, 4-7PM $500/week

5. **Assemble key content that connects with your buyers.** What are you going to show and tell? An effective ad is when all elements work together to communicate and reinforce your message and better capture a buyer's interest. There's the obvious: the copy and offer. The subliminal: the image, fonts, colors. And the voice or tone.

What images are you choosing, what copy and message? Don't just leave this up to the sales rep at the media channel. I've seen too many mediocre ads produced when firms take this route. Even if you're not a copywriter, you need to be prepared to give specific directions on the style and tone, so the person creating the ad or radio spot knows your expectations.

Is the copy to be upbeat or serious? Should there be a lot of copy, or just a headline, key end-benefits, and a link back to the website? Is the image going to be a photo or a graphic? Is it a focal point or the background? Will the ad be in color or black and white? How should the offer be presented, what level of detail is necessary, and are there any disclaimers needed?

If it's radio, a man or woman's voice? Music in the background or not? And what kind of music? Funky? Hip-hop? New-age?

Now, let's summarize how Holistic Wellness completes the entire planning process.

- *Objective:* Introduce our business to the target audience community within a 30-minute drive radius and get customers in the door to try us out.

- *Budget:* $3,000

- *Focus & offer:* Offer a trial massage coupon for $25 off the regular $75 price.

- *Media:* Local magazine with 40,000 circulation. One-time full page ad on the back cover, featuring the offer.

- *Key content:* Image: relaxed looking woman enjoying a massage; style & tone: upbeat, bright, fresh, inviting—clean colors, light or white background. Message: focus on escape and relief, with our three top end-benefits they will enjoy plus offer.

In my workshops, I always recommend participants create a Zipline Idea Inspiration folder as an inspiration resource to refer to when it comes time to design an ad campaign. Collect ads, images, and headlines that engage and interest you. See something cool online? Do a screenshot and save it in a digital folder. Take a quick smart phone shot of the TV ad.

Don't just monitor your own industry for ideas. Look *outside* your industry's borders because it's too easy to get stuck in a rut when it comes to ads and promos, and keep doing the same thing year after year, or worse yet, do the same thing as everybody else.

Urban legend has it that Sam Walton, founder of Wal-Mart, was an advocate of searching for new ideas from any source. He urged employees to be on the lookout for great marketing, advertising, and promotional ideas, no matter what industry or business, and report them back to the main office. If an idea was used, the employee received a big bonus. Whether true or not, it's a great story and shows an intelligent business philosophy of being ready to adapt to change—an essential ingredient in today's rapidly evolving marketplace.

6. **Evaluate and measure results.** This is where 93% of firms I work with frequently tumble off the zipline. They plan the ad and/or promotion, do all the steps—and then never check to see if it delivered any results! If you don't know how well it did or didn't work, how can you determine whether to repeat it, or how much it actually cost the company? Chapter 12, which concludes the section on promotions, will walk you through the smart ways to evaluate and measure your advertising and promotional results.

Now, an **"opportunity arises"** disclaimer. Sometimes advertising, promotional, charitable, and/or community support opportunities arise that you didn't know about during the planning phase and that you feel are a good fit for your business. So, when preparing the marketing outreach budget, define the *types* of opportunity activities you are willing to spend on, establish a budget, and stick to it. If they flop, because you've planned for it, you won't be wringing your hands at the "wasted" money. Too often firms dribble away funds on unanticipated marketing opportunities and then later wonder where the leak in their budget is.

➢ *Be a smart media negotiator*

You've established your objective and budget, and selected media based on it being a good fit with buyers and prospects. Now you have to be ready to negotiate for the best deal. And an important part of this is by having a basic knowledge of some key terms and how they apply to your decision-making process.

No surprise, like most industries, media providers have their own jargon. The two most important ones **you need to know are Reach and Frequency.**

✂ **Reach** is the number of people exposed to an ad at least once during a specific time period. For example, say you run a full-page newspaper ad with a 200,000 circulation in Wednesday's food section; the ad is *potentially* exposed to 200,000 people. It is never guaranteed—people could skip over your ad, not read the paper that day, etc.

✂ **Frequency** is the number of times a person or household is exposed to an ad. Take the same ad above, run once a week for a month. That's a frequency of four, because the potential audience may see your ad four times.

✂ **Gross Rating Points (GRPs):** Defined as Reach × Frequency, this is probably one of the most confusing measures in advertising. Contrary to what the formula implies, GRPs don't measure the actual size of the audience reached, but the number of potential impressions as a percentage of a target population.

GRPs are preferred by broadcast and outdoor media because they focus on what percentage of all households in a market the media reaches. For instance, if a TV station reaches an average of 25% of total TV homes in your county six times over one week, it would deliver 150 GRPs for that period (25% Reach × 6 Frequency). Raise the reach and/or frequency, and the GRPs increase. GRPs enable media buyers to have a common measurement to compare different media options and test different reach and/or frequency combinations.

As a small to mid-sized business, you're likely more concerned with how many people you're reaching and how often. So I prefer to use Reach and Frequency as the primary planning tools. How do these two factors play out in your decision making?

> ### Zipline Essential #19.
> ### Reach without Frequency = wasted $$
> ### Frequency without targeting = wasted $$

Your goal is to select the right mix of targeted reach and frequency at the best price to optimize your outcomes. Let's say your community's population is 250,000 people. You've designed a postcard to promote the business. For maximum reach, you'd send it out to everyone. But is that smart? No, because not all 250,000 fit your buyer profile! Of that 250,000, maybe 50,000 are potential buyers. So instead, you could send a postcard out to the 50,000, once a month for six months—a six times frequency.

Now that you know all this, let's get down to some smart negotiating tactics. While most firms have a limited budget, the good news is that in many instances, **media sellers are often slugging it out for a share of your advertising dollars.**

Your buying clout arises from two factors. First, the media available in your target market(s). If there are lots of media options from which to choose—meaning lots of competition for your ad dollars—you usually have more negotiating power. This is amplified if there are several magazines or newspapers or radio stations vs. just one of each. The caveat is a very successful media channel who dominates the market often doesn't "need" your ad dollars, so you'll have less leverage. *The New York Times* is the grand dame of newspapers, and doesn't have to go hunting for advertisers, but many newspapers are struggling for ads.

Second, manage your budget to get the most bang for the buck. This is where selecting media that's the right fit is so essential. So you can concentrate ads where they're most likely to be seen or heard. You leverage your budget by translating it into frequency, because the more times you buy a particular firm's media, the greater the discount. If you look at the rate card, you'll see things like 1-time rate (1×), 3×, and so on. By committing to multiple buys, you get a progressively higher discount off the 1× price.

Important: You get bored with your ads far faster than the buyer does.

Research indicates that it can take a prospect six times before the ad registers in their head, longer if they're not in the market for your product or service. So, if you can't run an ad or promotion frequently, then it should be designed to work even harder to connect with buyers.

That's the basics. Now, some more **smart negotiating tips.**

❀ **New can be good!** Being a new advertiser can get you discounts. Many media providers are eager for your business and, if you ask, will give you first time customer discounts, sometimes for several months.

❀ **Old can be good.** Most media providers' prices increase annually, often as much as 5%. But if you will commit to media buys *before* year end with them, you will often get to keep your current rate, or get a discount off the upcoming rate increase.

❀ **Location, location.** In print, you can select from ROP (run of press) or Preferred Placement. In ROP, an ad is placed at the publication's discretion, wherever there's free space, and is usually the least expensive option. For Preferred Placement, you pay a premium for prime locations, such as back cover, in the food section, etc. If you don't have a specific spot you want your ad to be, choose ROP. However, be careful. A colleague told me they went ROP in a newspaper with an ad for baby products… and it wound up on the obituary page! The outcome? Zero response. Young parents aren't looking at the obits.

Radio has largely the same approach, and goes by time slots and shows. Want to be anchored to a specific show, or around traffic or weather? Those premium positions cost more. If you're willing to run any time during the morning, the cost per spot is lower.

Now, a few more things to know about media buying.

❀ **Be careful about trading visibility for volume.** It's a common mindset to think frequency is the top priority; you now know that's not true. It's about being visible to your buyers.

A business card-sized ad in a newspaper could run every week, but it has a very low chance of being seen. A larger ad run less frequently is a better choice. I knew a retailer who for years ran a quarter-page newspaper ad once a week for three weeks before a sale. Recently, they instead ran a full-page ad one time and couldn't believe the response—more people saw the ad. Going forward, they plan to run only that one full page ad.

A radio spot can sound like a good idea, but *when* it runs is a factor.

Ask yourself, when do people listen most closely to the radio, especially if they're driving? During weather and traffic reports. So it may cost more to be there, and you can't run the spot as frequently, but it increases the chance of being heard.

✂ **Know about "Make Goods."** Sometimes mistakes happen. An ad doesn't get run. The radio spot runs on the wrong day or time. Or the spot sounds lousy, or the ad looks awful because it was blurred due to a printing problem. Whatever.

Media providers want you to be happy, and the standard policy is to offer a "make good"—literally, making good *their* mistake. In most instances they will offer to run the ad or spot again at no charge. This doesn't apply if you send a poor quality ad that doesn't meet their specifications, or a shoddy radio spot that you produce. Only if it is their error.

Most of us don't have the creative, design, or vocal talent to come up with advertising that engages or connects with our customers. So, some options to consider.

✂ **Use the media provider's design group.** Different media providers may offer ad design, or voiceover for radio, either at no charge or a discounted rate. If you don't have an agency or an in-house person doing this work, consider taking advantage of the offer—but make sure to give explicit directions, and review and sign off before release.

✂ **Consider working with an agency.** Agencies establish relationships with the media, and because they do buys for multiple clients, can often negotiate and pass along discounted rates. The agency usually earns a commission for a media buy, commonly 15%. If a radio station charges $100 per spot, you'll be billed $100 by the agency, who in turn will pay the radio station $85. If the station direct bills you $100, they will pay the agency $15. Sorry, with few exceptions, if you choose to buy direct, it doesn't mean you'll save the $15.

Have you ever looked at an ad and it's really gotten your attention, while others are just a mishmash? That's another advantage to working with a *well-qualified* ad design group or agency, particularly for visual ads. They understand design and layout. Effective ad design, copywriting, use of colors, fonts, etc. requires knowledge and skill. There are methods to improve response and increase viewer interest. Headlines, subheads, graphics… they have to work together for optimum response. You want your company's ad to be the one that gets the audience's attention.

Marketing outreach efforts such as advertising and promotion are more cost-effective and likely to deliver desired results when done with a clearly defined purpose and a detailed plan. Always select media based on how well it aligns with your target audience. When buying media, develop a balanced strategy of reach and frequency to get in front of your prospects, and to maximize outcomes. Zipline marketers know that it's all about planning and implementing with a clear purpose to create a more enjoyable ride with a good payout.

Chapter 12 ~ How Not to Throw Money Away on Promotions

Promotions are a very powerful marketing outreach tool—when done right. They can drive sales, create awareness of your product and service, trigger trial, even build business through word of mouth and referrals. Done poorly, not only do they fail to deliver desired results, they can actually have a negative impact on a company's image, and are just money being tossed into the breeze.

Here are some of the core purposes of smart promotions.

- High speed hit to generate business
- Create buzz and get people to take action
- Cultivate customer loyalty
- Stand out from the competition and get noticed
- Create a branding concept or character
- Cross-promote with other businesses or products
- Cost-share with other companies

Successful promotions use zipline marketing strategy and planning to play the price–promotion–value game in order to inspire buyers to take action. Let's look at ways to add value to your promotions, and avoid doing ones that not only fail to deliver results, but can chew away at your bottom line.

➢ Best ways to promote cost-effectively

As discussed in the advertising section in Chapter 11, promotions are designed to produce sales within a specific time period. Now I am often asked, aren't promotions, sales, and ads the same? The answer is, it depends on the content.

Used in its broadest sense, a promotion presents a call to action. Promotions can be designed to appear like an ad in publications or other media, but their job is to emphasize a time-sensitive offer: "Today and today only! 25% off!" They are perishable and end by a certain date. Sales are a type of a promotion, and are usually tied to some sort of announced offer, although they don't have to be; think of an exclusive in-store discount. By contrast, a "pure" ad does not have a promotion in it—it informs, but there is no concrete call to action.

As we covered with advertising in the previous chapter, first you have to decide on the promotion's purpose, goals, and budget prior to choosing the marketing outreach method. What's its purpose; what does it have to achieve? Announce a sale? Motivate people to try a new service? Generate cash flow? Attract new customers? If you don't define a promotion's purpose, then selecting the offer, coming up with creative, choosing the delivery method or media, figuring out a budget, and measuring outcomes is going to be sheer guesswork.

Next, develop the details. If you want to attract more customers, how many? If you need a cash flow boost, how much and how many sales are needed? If you want to sell more dinners in your restaurant, how many and at what cost? If you want to encourage existing customers to bring a friend, how many? Do I sound like a broken record? Yes, because **a promotion's goals are primarily number-driven.**

After you determine the target body count and financial objectives, you're ready to develop the promotion, cost it out, and decide on the media vehicle. A little later in this chapter, we'll do a cost–benefit analysis that will show how to avoid losing money on a promotion. Or if it's going to lose money, it's done intentionally (which can be OK).

Finally, you can decide on your media channels. The same advertising rules from Chapter 11 apply regarding Reach and Frequency, and selecting media that your buyers read, watch, or listen to. Here are some extra helpful pointers in evaluating different media when you're doing a promotion.

Media able to reach a larger audience includes newspapers, radio, TV, magazines, and the Internet. Each has different frequency and reach, depending on the markets they serve and their audience.

- *Newspapers* – low frequency, large reach, one-time read. They're good for special offers.

- *Radio* – higher frequency and large reach. Scheduling is key, because you want a spot to run when *your* target audience listens. Radio is ideal for "exciting" promotions with energy that can be communicated via music and voiceover so they audibly stand out.

- *Magazines* – low frequency, with variable reach depending on their markets. Usually a one-time read. Because they sit around, they are best for pure advertising, unless the promotion has no expiration date.

- *Internet* – mixed frequency, large reach, *if* they find you. Very cluttered and competitive, lots of choices. Check out Part 5: Zipping the Digital Divide, for more details.

- *Local media* – targeted at specific regions, markets, even zip codes, and includes door hangers, direct mail, human signs, postcards, flyers, and neighborhood coupon books.

- *Phone book yellow pages* – published once a year, they are kept on hand for reference, particularly among an older audience. Some communities have local phone books, which can be useful if you serve a limited geographic area. *Helpful hint:* as a low cost high impact option, instead of a standalone ad, evaluate doing an "in column" ad using color, your tagline, and one to two key selling points, plus the website. In-columns refer to the actual columns in which the company names and phone numbers are listed in the directories.

> **Direct mail is not dead!** There's an improved way to use direct mail to connect with your buyers using zip code targeting. The U.S. Postal Service introduced a powerful tool that has rejuvenated direct mail as a viable marketing option. It's called Every Door Direct Mail and, in a nutshell, it enables you to target potential customers who fit your buyer profile. Using a mapping tool, you can select postal routes based on demographics; then USPS delivers to every address on those routes. No need to purchase mailing lists, and prices are under 20 cents per piece. Learn more at www.USPS.com/business/every-door-direct-mail.htm.

➤ *How to play the price–promotion–value strategy game*

The two easiest ways to make sure a promotion flops or doesn't deliver desired results? By not looking at it from the buyer's point of view, and not creating the right value.

Case in point: I was working with home décor retailer who did monthly promotions on their high-end gas fireplaces. But they just didn't seem to produce sales. Why? Because from the buyer's point of view, the offer wasn't worth responding to—it was too low relative to the high price of the product.

What do I mean by value? From your buyer's perspective, whatever you're offering has to be of enough perceived value, enough importance, that they want to take the action you're asking them to take.

Ever seen a 25-cent coupon for a $6.99 product? It's probably not enough to inspire you to clip it, head to the store, and make the purchase. Why? Because your time is more valuable, and the coupon's discount isn't enough to motivate you. Yet you would likely hustle out the door for a 50% off sale at a favorite clothing store, because you can see the savings.

A promotional offer has to be "worth it" for a buyer to take action. Just as with your overall pricing strategy, it's about the perceived value in your buyer's mind. It's the psychology of effectively fusing price and value, and it comes in three primary forms.

✂ *"Such a deal!":* The promotional offer is seen as a great savings or value as compared to the regular price, or the scarcity factor makes the offer more valuable.

- Think of how people will line up, even camp out, on the chance of getting one of a limited number of available promotional items. The 1990s Ty Beanie Babies mania is an example. Or the recent run on the metal alloy Chase Sapphire Reserve Credit card. Despite the $450 annual fee, there's a waiting list. There's also status with successfully buying hard-to-find items on sale, such as big screen TVs, the newest Xbox game, etc.

✂ *"Bundles":* All the elements included in the offer create a high perceived value. In other words, the buyer is paying less for more. Costco is a master of this technique. Think of their bundled or large-pack products.

- Infomercials personify this tactic. "You receive all this for only...!" The seller assembles a slew of value-added benefits worth such and such a price, and then you discover how much you "save" with the special offer if you make a purchase in the next few minutes. As an example, when I managed the FoodSaver vacuum packaging line of products, we would bundle the unit with canisters, free special bags, and other goodies at a price exclusive to the infomercial.

- BOGOs (buy one, get one free), discounted packages—buy three, get the fourth free; buy three and save $X—all these leverage bundling in a way that shouts, "look at all you're going to save!"

✂ *"Extras for Nothing":* These are promotional add-ons that make a buyer feel they're getting more for less. They're also very effective in creating trial of new products.

- They're usually free or deeply discounted. A trial-size bottle of Listerine shrink-wrapped to the big bottle. Clinique cosmetics often offers a trial size with purchase. A free dessert with purchase of two entrées. Buy 2, get the 3rd one free. Spend $200 on housekeeping services, and get one extra room free.

Value also is associated with knowledge. Think of high-powered motivational speakers such as Jack Canfield, Steve Harrison, Louise Hay, and Tony Robinson. Because people perceive significant value in their expertise, they're willing to pay more to attend their events. Why do experienced or well-known lawyers command a higher fee? Or doctors? Because the buyer believes this experience equates to significant value from which they will benefit.

> *Zipline Essential #20.* **Create added value from the buyer's perspective to motivate them to take action.**

So when evaluating promotions, ask yourself, what added value can be put on a product or service to make it seem more valuable from a buyer's or prospect's viewpoint? Can you add something that amps it up with minimal impact on cost, but creates lots of perceived value? Or highlight something that you do anyway, but can call out as a special service?

Let's say you run a jewelry store, and Valentine's Day is near… marriage proposals are in the air! You offer an engagement set at $999. But to distinguish it from all the other jewelers promoting the same thing, you include lifetime cleaning, a free written appraisal for insurance purposes, and say what the full *retail* value is for all those extra goodies—$500. To your buyer, you're *giving* them $500. We'll talk more about cost–value analysis in the next section, but see how you can create perceived value and differentiate yourself from competitors?

Here's another. You have an oil change center, and do changes for $39.95, just like your competitors. To add value, you call out everything the service includes: "Free 10-point safety inspection, wiper blades, air filter, tire pressure check, coolant, window-washer fluid…." Now a buyer reacts with, "Wow, I get all that for *just* $39.95? Great deal!" Plus, the message of "safety inspection" also adds value because it says your company cares about their personal safety.

Now, let's talk about coupons. Did you know that an effective coupon promotion can generate a lot of very useful customer information? Here's a client case history to illustrate.

***What would you do?* Which promotion is doing what?**

A garden nursery has gotten involved with Internet marketing. It has been doing a solid job with traditional advertising, newspaper, yellow pages, and the like, and is able to track how effective these channels have been. But its new focus is on the Internet.

The nursery retooled its website; is on Yelp, Twitter, and Facebook; and regularly sends out promotional emails. All outreach efforts are designed to drive traffic to a current promotion on the website. Sounds efficient, right?

But there's a problem. The nursery is struggling with how to correlate which Internet marketing efforts are delivering results. It's the right question to be asking. Got any ideas where the problem lies?

Jot down your answer. _____

_____

_____

Answer: The retailer is using a one-coupon-fits-all strategy. In other words, no matter what marketing channel a buyer comes in from, each one is receiving the same coupon. So there's no way to tell which channel is delivering what.

The good news? There is a solution. Have you ever observed how big companies assign a code to both print and digital coupons? Print coupons usually have it tucked away in a corner. As retailers send their collected coupons to a redemption firm, those codes are used to track the coupon's source. Very often, different codes are assigned to different markets to refine the data being captured, such as by state or region. Digital coupons usually have a specific redemption code you input, or a prominent bar code that needs to be scanned if it's printed and used at a store. Designating a specific code to a coupon is the trick to tracking its origin.

Now, you might argue with me that really doesn't work for a smaller company. Sorry, but size doesn't matter if you have a website. A website is capable of having hidden pages that are not visible to the entire public. Different pages can be set up so that a person linking from Yelp will land on one page, whereas a person responding to an email will land on another.

You can offer the same or different promotions on each web page, and even test different offers to see which generates more results with each channels' respective audience. For instance, the Yelp person gets Offer A, and the Facebook person gets Offer C. The coupons on each respective page have their own code.

To the customer, it's seamless. They print the coupon, and/or go elsewhere on the site to redeem it. Yes, it may cost you a little to have the unique web pages and coupon codes, but you will quickly find out where people are coming from.

Expiration dates can be marketing tools! Did you know that expiration dates are often used by big companies as a marketing tactic?

For example, different expiration dates can be tested to see if short redemption periods do or do not generate a faster response. You may have noticed that most coupons have a much shorter life cycle than they did 10 years ago. Back then 3-, 6-, even 9-month expiration dates were commonplace. Today I usually see expiration periods within 30 days, forcing people to "act now." CVS drug stores email out coupons with a 3-day expiration date!

Of course, a later expiration date may be featured if an item is bought infrequently and has a longer gap between buying cycles such as deodorant, oil changes, or restaurant offers.

The net takeaway is that you're capable of managing your customers' redemption habits in the same way the big companies do with a little bit of extra effort, and minimal extra cost. At the end of a promotion, tally the physical coupons brought in, and look at the analytics for the online coupons redeemed to get a clear picture of what is working from where. The goal of all this is to find out what traditional and digital media channels work hardest for you, and where to concentrate your spending—the proverbial biggest bang for the buck.

If this approach is outside your budget or you don't have the staff to manage it, no problem. You can offer a one-size-fits-all promotional coupon. If you run your offer simultaneously across multiple media channels, then the best way to track results is to ask buyers how they heard about the offer and keep a record.

Now, on to determining what a promotion will cost you, and if it's worth doing it.

Believe it or not: a promotion can be rigged to *not* generate sales

Have you ever eye-balled a promotional flyer or ad with a coupon or discount offer, but not acted on it because the amount was not worth it to you? This can be *intentional*. The goal is to get you to *look* at the piece and read about the product, but not motivate you to use the offer. The piece is actually doing double duty as an ad, with the promotion used to hook your attention, where a plain ad might not have done that.

Another coupon tactic is to create "barriers to redemption," a fancy way of saying putting up roadblocks to make it more complex to redeem a coupon or take advantage of a promotion. For example, in order to be eligible to win a prize, you have to go to a website, enter a special code, complete a survey, and then be added to a list to be entered into a drawing. Marketers know that the more steps a person has to take to get something, the more likely they will be to drop out along the way.

The company still achieves advertising visibility, but the promotion doesn't cost them as much as if it took only a single step to redeem. Basically, to a certain extent, you can actually control how many people are likely to respond to a promotion.

For example, when I was working on the Silkience Hair Care brand at Gillette, we designed an offer where you had to submit a proof of purchase with an entry form to receive $2 back on your next bottle of shampoo. Consumers had to buy the shampoo, cut off the POP, fill in an entry form, and mail it in (four steps). We calculated that under 10% would redeem the offer, and based our projected promotional costs on that.

➤ *The smart way to not lose money on promotions*

When it comes to promotions, companies often just "run a promotion." And where this can really clobber them is when they fail to do an upfront cost–benefit analysis.

> *Zipline Essential #21.* Avoid ready, fire, aim. Cost
> out a promotion *before* you do it.

A cost–benefit analysis is about crunching the numbers first to estimate the promotion's cost vs. the benefits or outcomes it will deliver. FYI, there's nothing wrong with losing money on a promotion—as long as you *know* that's going to happen *before* you start.

Say, you're the owner of Reno's Best Body Wrap, and you've decided the promotion's purpose is to attract new customers to try your new raindrop therapy using a trial offer. The goal is to get 90 new clients in the door in one month. So you assemble an offer of $25 off the regularly priced $75 service for the month of May, and run an ad with a coupon in a coupon booklet, which is mailed to 60,000 homes. At the end of May, you tally the results, and you had 100 people who redeemed the coupon. You congratulate yourself, and feel you planned the promotion effectively. Well, yes—and no.

How much did your promotion make? $5,000 bucks, right? Wrong! You actually lost money. Check out how to misfire on calculating the cost and benefits of a promotion.

- 60,000 coupons featuring a $25 discount off regular $75 price

- One-time cost of advertising: $3,000

- Number of coupons redeemed: 100 [under
  1% redemption; (100/60,000)]

- Total cost: $3,000 for ad + $2,500 [$25 × 100,
  cost per coupon in lost revenue] = $5,500

- Actual revenue generated: 100 coupons × $50 per massage = $5,000

- Net gain or loss: –$500 (loss)

- *Strategic outcome assessment:* However, although you lost money on the offer, 45 of the people redeeming the coupon signed up for a massage bundle, so **the lifetime value of the customer**—all the additional income from multiple visits—outweighs the loss and made this a successful effort.

The promotion's cost is both the media cost and the amount you "lost" off the full price of the service. A buyer would have paid $75 at full price. You gave away $25 to motivate them to try the service. That is a real cost.

However, since many became repeat customers, the promotion delivered. But what if it were a different offer and you expected them to only buy once; are you willing to lose $500? That's a strategic decision you should make up front.

Let's say you want to run an ad with a coupon that offers a free flashlight to everyone who comes into your hardware store. Go through the above steps, but when calculating the cost, it's the lost revenue from the flashlight. If it's not a product you normally sell, and have purchased specifically as a free giveaway, then it's the cost of the flashlight.

One thing I also encourage clients to do is play with different redemption numbers to see if you can handle a big response. Imagine if instead of 100 people, 1,000 people redeemed the offer! This often happens where a company underestimates redemption and the promotion's cost actually hurts their bottom line. Not only that, but they may have had a huge out-of-stock, buyers waiting in long lines, and the outcome is not only a financial loss, but a customer relationship mess.

Another example. Say you're a high-end restaurant. Your goal is to attract both new and repeat customers. You give away a free dessert with every two entrées purchased. The dessert costs you $3.50; you sell it for $6.75. You print 100 coupons and hand them out with each check. Fifty people redeem them.

- Coupon cost: 50 × $6.75 (because you "lose" the full value of the dessert): $337.50

- Average profit per entree: $9.25; × 2 entrees: $18.50; × 50 redemptions: $925

- Net gain/loss per redemption: $925–$337.50 = $587.50

Let's look at a more complex promotion.

> **What would you do? Hot stone!**
>
> We'll use our Holistic Wellness spa again. It wants to drum up new customers quickly. They plan to offer a hot stone therapy session, and decide to run an ad with a coupon in a promotional circular that is delivered to 80,000 households (cost: $350). The offer is a BOGO (buy one, get one free) presented as "Bring a friend, and the second Hot Stone session is free." The regular price is $45. The spa receives 100 calls, 80 book an appointment, 60 show, and 40 schedule for another session, resulting in 20 regulars a month. Did they make or lose money?

✎ *Jot down your answer:* _____

_____

_____

Answer: Let's do the math.

- Cost of advertising: $350

- Coupon cost: $45 [It's a 2 for 1, so one service is free]

- Number of people who redeemed coupon: 60 [under 1% redemption (60/80,000)]

- Cost of redemptions: 60 × $45 = $2,700

- Actual revenue from promotion: 60 × $45 = $2,700

- Net gain or loss: –$350 (loss)

- *Strategic outcome assessment:* However, the spa also was able to persuade 40 of these new customers to book another appointment. So even if they only came back one more time, that's 40 × $45 = $1,800 in revenue. Subtract the $350 loss of the original promotion, and Holistic Wellness spa actually had a net gain of $1,450!

The variables in the equation may change, but it's essential that whenever you are *planning* a promotion, do a cost–benefit analysis to avoid unpleasant sticker shock. Test the concept before you implement it. Be smart! Why run promotions that cost you money over and over again? This analysis is how the big companies do it, and you should too.

> ➢ **Warning: what a promotion can say about your business!**

How you package a promotion can send positive, or negative, messages about the company. A promotion is a combination of the offer itself, how it impacts revenues, plus the media you use to get it into the hands of the target audience. It's how you put this all together that's an important part of your zipline marketing plan.

Too often, I will see a company have a hodgepodge of marketing outreach approaches. **Inconsistent images and copy, fractured messages, or a confusing mix of media can do damage to your brand and business.** Earlier, in Chapter 5, I talked about how all the zipline marketing essentials have to be integrated and work together to support the company's positioning. That applies to promotions as well. How you present the firm says so much.

Imagine your favorite meal. Maybe it's grilled fresh salmon with rice pilaf. Or a charbroiled steak with fresh mashed potatoes. Or a delicious vegetarian burger and fries. Got the visual? Can you almost smell and taste it? Now, take a dirty plate and serve the meal on it. Didn't that just ruin it for you? That's the risk of doing a badly crafted promotion or ad.

How you deliver your promotion to people in itself tells a story. Ever seen any of these situations happen?

- An ad for a beautiful dress in a ratty tabloid newspaper? I'll doubt the quality because I question the company's media choice.

- A poorly copied menu insert that fell out of the newspaper? If you care that little about your advertising, maybe I should be worried about your restaurant's quality.

- A postcard with tiny unreadable print because there's too much information on it? I'm not going to waste my time because you're not considerate of me as a buyer.

- A billboard with a toilet on it (I'm not making this up) and 20 lines of text that you can't read within three seconds as you drive by? I can't receive the message. And, given that billboards tend to be pricey, that's money down the toilet.

Call it subliminal advertising, but the method you use to deliver the promotion is just as important as the content.

As with ads, there are professionals who can design promotions. But if you do it in-house, think about your target audience. Use images that appeal to them, the words, colors, and typestyles that fit with your positioning. Whether sophisticated or snazzy, funky or elegant, send a visual and/or audio message that presents your product or service in the best light possible.

➢ *Turn your customers into ambassadors*

There is no more powerful—or more dangerous—marketing resource than your customers. Call it "word of mouth" or "buzz." Your buyers can have a lot to say about your company—good, bad, or indifferent. And in today's social media environment, they're able to reach a far greater audience than ever before.

Your goal is to convert them into ambassadors, to create such a strong and loyal relationship that not only do they tell people about your company, but when a competitor tries to lure them away, they're not interested. When this happens, you have cemented a bond based not on price but value. And that kind of cement is pretty hard to dynamite loose!

People love to share experiences. When you're looking for a gentle dentist, expert lawyer, good restaurant, trendy bar… what do you usually do? Ask a friend, a coworker, a family member, right? It's been that way probably forever. Can't you just imagine George Washington asking Thomas Jefferson, "And who is your tailor, my good man?"

We put more trust in what others say than anything else. Which is what makes quality customer testimonials so valuable. After getting a recommendation, you may do an online search, study reviews, and so on. Look at how Amazon actively solicits buyers' feedback on every purchase— they're collecting reviews. And, consider how if you read a negative review, you could have second thoughts about the product, service, or company.

Customer dissatisfaction is nothing to scoff at, although some firms who believe they have a captive audience erroneously assume it doesn't matter. So, before you shrug and say it's not that important, check out these eye-opening research facts about unhappy customers.

- ☒ Customers tell twice as many people about poor experiences than about positive ones.
- ☒ 91% will not do business again with a brand that failed to meet their expectations.
- ☒ 86% of people won't purchase from a company that has negative online reviews.
- ☒ 85% of people share *any* customer experience stories in person.
- ☒ 81% of consumers who switched loyalties say the company could have done something differently to keep them as customers.
- ☒ For every one customer complaint received by your company, 26 other customers do not tell you—but they sure tell others!

In his excellent book *Word of Mouth Marketing,* Andy Sernovitz says, "Word of mouth marketing is for any size business. You don't need to have a hot website, to be in a sexy industry, or to have a cool, innovative new technology.... You just have to give people something to talk about."

When you think on it, there's a powerful feedback loop that can be triggered by your ads and promotions if they're set up correctly. Buyers who feel they receive a great value, have good experiences, who enjoy shopping from or working with you, are going to tell others. If you have a fun or exciting promotion (more on this in Part 6), you can really get them talking, sharing, and making noise. Free positive PR by any name is wonderful!

Now, you have the option of being passive and just smiling when this happens. Me, I think you should develop a plan that's a part of your zipline marketing strategy for turning your happiest customers into active ambassadors, because they are truly pearls without price. Why? They provide free advertising (*that's* what I call cost-effective!), valuable testimonials, and help drive new clients to your business. They become your advocates, sometimes for free.

A great example is the success of GoPro cameras. In its early years, the firm strategically focused on ego-crazy extreme athletes, notably the weekend warriors who wanted video proof of their exploits that they could upload to YouTube. As a result, with every GoPro video upload, the proud athlete became a product ambassador.

Sometimes an incentive can be offered—and it doesn't have to be money. My luxury homes client, Trilogy at the Vineyards, is wonderful at turning their homeowners into active ambassadors. They coach them on the "company story" and have them take prospective buyers on tours. During new model showcase events, ambassadors are recruited to drive shuttle carts and transport visitors, and answer any questions. Each receives stylish company-branded clothing and name tags to make them feel a part of the team, and are recognized and thanked for their assistance via newsletters and emails sent to all community members.

Why all this bother? Because home buyer prospects are skeptical of sales pitches. They would listen, but wanted to speak with real homeowners who could offer trustworthy insights about the homes' quality and what living in the community was really like. The outcome? Increased sales and satisfied new buyers, who in turn became ambassadors.

Promotions are an essential piece of your zipline marketing equipment. Leveraging well-planned and cost-effective promotions to create awareness, boost sales and profits, generate trial, and develop a flock of happy customers who will promote you to others is smart marketing. Use them wisely.

Part 4 – Zipline Highlights

✄ **Budget-friendly marketing opportunities.** From the wasted real estate on the back of your business card to nude windows, bare-chested staff, and a mute phone, you have lots of marketing outreach opportunities you may be missing.

✄ **Develop advertising smarts.** If you're going to play the advertising game, you need to know the rules. Leverage Reach and Frequency the right way, and know how to assess, select, and negotiate media buys that will deliver the best results for your business.

✄ **Don't let promotions cost you money.** Don't "just run a promotion" and hope for the best. Determine the purpose, offer, and media vehicle, and do an upfront cost–benefit analysis to make sure the company can afford it. Afterward, measure the results and why it did—or did not—achieve your goals.

✄ **Create word of mouth and customer ambassadors.** Today's digital world demands you use word of mouth as a marketing tactic more than ever. Your customers are a powerful marketing outreach tool that you can leverage to your advantage.

Part 5 – Zipping the Digital Divide

Digital marketing is top of mind these days. Websites. Social media. Facebook. Instagram. Twitter. The options keep proliferating. And evolving. What was valid a year ago may have shifted gears today. What was hot has gone obsolete... Myspace anyone? I will tell you right up front, there is no fixed answer to digital marketing. It's a challenge to keep up, and even more confusing to decide where to put your energy.

From your view up on the zipline, there are three drivers in your digital marketing: website, social media, and email lists. Each plays a role in your marketing strategy and plan.

- **Website:** answers what is this product or service, what can I do here, why should I be here and not on some other site, and what do I do next?
- **Social Media:** is about listening, connecting with your customers, and building relationships, *not* about using it primarily as an advertising and promotion platform.
- **Email lists:** are people who have agreed to hear from you, and where it's perfectly acceptable to make offers and deliver value.

Depending on your industry and buyers, the weight of these digital tactics in your zipline marketing mix may vary. A company targeting Baby Boomers may lean more heavily on the website. A restaurant reaching out to foodies will more likely emphasize social media, while a motivational training company may focus on email lists.

I'd like to give a special shout out here to Eric Spellmann, Owner of Spellmann & Associates, for contributing to this chapter with his exceptional digital expertise. I highly recommend you check out his insightful digital business video series at EricSpellmann.com/videos.html.

So how do you determine the right digital media options for your business, judge your website's effectiveness, build social media currency and visitor traffic, and manage reviews? Read on to learn more.

Chapter 13 ~ Smart Digital Tools to Help Grow Your Business

As with all forms of media—and digital is a form of media—the same rules apply that we discussed in Chapters 5, 6, and 11 of first defining the goals and objectives, budget, and how digital fits into your overall marketing plan.

But there's a critical difference in digital marketing that creates a major stumbling block for many companies. It's all about...

➤ *Relationships vs. Advertising*

You may have heard this before, but it bears repeating. Digital marketing is fundamentally about first building relationships with prospects and buyers. This is a concept that virtually all firms initially struggle with because it's not about using the traditional hard sell of ads or promotions. What frustrates managers is that not only is there rarely any immediate measurable return on efforts, but sometimes there's not even a direct correlation between sales and social media investment.

The sales pitch should only emerge when the relationship is established because **it's about building trust.** Scams. Spam. Hackers. Security breaches. All this and more are the dark side of the digital marketing sphere. Each time people visit a website, they may wonder, is there a risk of my personal information being stolen? A Trojan or worm infiltrating my computer? Malware being downloaded? Being barraged by nonstop spam because my email was sold?

We cruise the Internet hoping for the best, but often suffer the consequences. And so we are, presumably, more cautious about what we respond to. If a friend or colleague recommends a website, we begin with a much higher level of trust—a classic word-of-mouth referral. If it's a familiar company or brand name, we are likewise more open-minded.

But for most smaller companies lost in the wilderness of literally millions of websites and Facebook pages, the chances of being found by accident are infinitesimally small. And if your website or Facebook page does not effectively engage visitors or persuade them it's a worthwhile site to trust and explore further, the chances of their returning are even tinier. I tell my clients that

consumers today have the attention span of a gnat. Three to five seconds, and zap, they're gone—you've lost them.

One reason Facebook became popular in its early days was that people enjoyed the advertising-free environment. Then Facebook had its IPO, and it had to worry about profits and the bottom line. "Suddenly" advertising appeared, and now, companies have to pay to boost posts to reach more of their followers. But they can now also design and send out their own targeted ads to attract new followers.

Fact: advertising chases buyers. Where ever they go, it's just a matter of when, not if, before ads begin to appear. Remember when sports stadiums had names, like San Francisco's Candlestick Park? The new sports arena is named Levi Stadium. It's all because big companies want to take advantage of the huge branding visibility to both existing and prospective buyers.

Your goal is to develop a digital marketing outreach approach that is not an in-your-face shout, but a "we're glad to meet you, let us know if we can help you" handshake.

➤ How to choose what's digitally right for your business

With all the available options in the digital marketing arena, we often feel pressured to be everywhere at once because if we're not, we're worried that we must be falling behind. Let me start by saying, "not true!" Do you need a digital marketing presence? Absolutely. But selecting which ones is like choosing any other form of media.

> *Zipline Essential #22.* **Digital marketing must target where *your* buyers are.**

First, identify which digital platforms are capturing a "share of eyeballs" from *your* target audience. Where do they spend a majority of time? Second, determine if that digital media channel is the right fit for your business.

For instance, the digital photo sharing site Pinterest is a great forum for recipes, wedding topics, fashion, etc. Typical user profile: 87% female; primary age range of 35–44 (29%) followed by ages 25–34 (27%); average income of $25,000–$49,999 (37%) followed by $50,000–$74,999 (33%). If these don't match the buyer demographics you identified in Chapter 2, then a social media strategy using Pinterest isn't a good fit.

Here are three steps I recommend. One, there's a vast amount of data on who is using the different forms of social media, and it's constantly evolving. Do an Internet search for the most current audience demographic profile on each digital media option you're considering.

Two, survey customers and ask them, where would they go to find a product or service like yours? If you're a new firm, survey prospective buyers, and ask the same question. It might be Yelp or the online Yellow Pages. Or neither. Invariably, each time I have my clients do this, they're startled at how differently their buyers "shop" vs. what they assumed. Don't presume you have to be everywhere—**you only need to be where your audience goes online.**

For example, when I conducted a survey among age 55+ prospects for my luxury homes client, we discovered that 75% were using smart phone and tablets. They were heavy users of Facebook because they wanted to stay in touch with the grandkids. A small percentage of the women were using Pinterest. But only a tiny smattering used LinkedIn or Instagram.

Three, scope out what competitors are doing online. Are they on Pinterest? What's their Facebook page like? Are they doing Instagram videos? And look not only at your direct competitors but also the big players. Remember, large companies are spending big bucks on research to track and connect with their buyers. Learn from them.

We're going to zero in on core digital topics to help you decide on next steps and make informed marketing decisions. Don't try to implement all of these steps at once, because you'll run screeching from the room. Instead, take one step at a time, adding as you go.

➢ *Is your website really doing its job?*

A website remains the heart of your digital marketing empire, and as such it needs to always present your company the way buyers and prospects expect to see it. Think of it as your storefront. It must attract people and make them want to return. For the do-it-yourselfer, WordPress, Wix, and Weebly offer the ability to economically design your own website.

The big headache about websites is that what people want to see is constantly evolving, meaning your website has to be regularly refreshed, even revised. Seven years ago, it was all about animation and eye candy. Then came the scrolling banner. Followed by the multi-box template. Now it's single page design with a scroll-down format. And next year? Who knows?

When you're a smaller company, website maintenance seems more of a pain in the you-know-what than anything else. Yet it's essential. Here are **8 Key Website Checkpoints** to consider as you review your current site. As part of the review, I encourage you to invite some buyers—both existing and prospective—to critique the site. It's a great form of customer engagement, and is usually a real eye-opener as to how they really see the business.

1. **Where do the eyes go first?** A site has to hook visitors in three to five seconds. Make sure the first thing they see is interesting enough to stay. *Helpful hint:* Check out the website on different browsers, such as Mozilla/Firefox, Internet Explorer, and Chrome, to make sure its appearance is consistent everywhere, and images, objects, or formatting are not getting lost or rearranged.

2. **Do they immediately know what the site is about?** Present your key message right up front. Too many distractions, and they may not even know what is being offered.

3. **Is the key info "above the fold"?** This phrase is used in web design to refer to the portions of a page that are initially visible without having to scroll (it's a term borrowed from newspapers that refers to articles that appear "above the fold" of the paper—the most prominent spot). Don't make visitors search. If they have to scroll down to find the main idea, you risk their leaving before reaching it.

Remember that websites today are often viewed on mobile devices. Review how your website appears on these and make sure key information appears quickly. Also, verify that your site has a mobile responsive design that can adapt and reconfigure its appearance so that it looks good on any type of device.

4. **What's the CAT (call to action)?** Email addresses are one of your most valuable digital marketing currencies because visitors have given you permission to contact and pitch to them. Your site should offer a sign-up web form with an incentive to spark visitors' interest and persuade them to provide their email. This web form is the heart of building an email list, which can be used for future digital marketing outreach efforts.

It could be to start a free trial, download a freebie, learn more, etc. Choose something that will provide the most perceived value: useful tips, actionable advice, or special deals that will immediately benefit prospects, such as 10% off their first purchase, or free shipping. Also, make the CAT web form visible above the fold to immediately engage them. An alternate option is to make it a pop up window.

Be sure that you clearly state you will respect their privacy and not sell their contact information. This way, visitors will be more willing to provide it.

Important: **Don't leave money on the table.** Make sure to manage any leads, and respond promptly. Whether you use programs like Wufoo.com or Emailmeform.com, an autoresponder option as with Constant Contact, or manually respond when using a free service like Mail Chimp, your visitors expect action when they sign up.

Helpful hint: Avoid using the dated "Click here" phrase in links and text. Instead, select more powerful action verbs, such as Shop, Buy, Discover, or Learn more.

5. Is it easy to find the benefits? Visitors want to learn as much as possible about how your product or service will make a positive impact on their life. Focus not just on its features, but on its benefits and how it solves their problems or satisfies their wants.

Helpful hint: If your product or service is one that comes with a lot of possible questions from prospects, include an FAQ tab on the navigation bar.

6. Is the design welcoming or irritating? Ever visit a website that rubs you the wrong way? Make sure your site isn't doing the same thing. Consider that people are familiar with a layout with the logo in the upper left and horizontal navigation across the top; they will often abandon more innovative designs.

Choose complimentary colors and quality images that tie back to your brand and positioning. Make the site easy to navigate. Design it to be easy to view. Stick with a simple clean font, large enough to read without having to be enlarged. To optimize readability, avoid light letters on a dark background except for call out boxes. Don't use long, text-heavy paragraphs that are likely to get skipped. Instead, break copy into smaller sections that are easy to scan, and get the points across. Bullet points can be very effective.

7. Are you static or kinetic? YouTube, Instagram, and other video-based sites have fueled demand for multimedia on websites. You can boost appeal and the time people stay on your site with videos, podcasts, tutorials, and other multimedia options to present your message.

Helpful hint: Video doesn't have to be this huge scripted process as if you're producing a TV commercial. In fact, research reports that visitors often respond more strongly to casual videos, even those taken with smart phones, because it seems more believable. Even if you don't have a lot of money to spend, there's no reason to not have video on the website.

8. **Do you connect?** A website is not a billboard. It's an opportunity for visitors to get to know what the business is all about. If they feel a connection with what they're seeing and reading, there's a better chance they will become a customer. Tell your story using an engaging and conversational writing style, and explain why you are the best choice. And don't forget links to all your social media sites, such as Facebook, Twitter, and Instagram.

Let's discuss how to assess a website's effectiveness. Unlike a brochure, the website is a *dynamic* marketing tool, capable of being changed as often as you choose. And like any marketing tool, you want to know how it's working for you. Make sure to **incorporate website analytics,** which reveal how visitors move around the site. How long do they stay? What pages are they going to? Google Analytics is a free solution to tracking site traffic and statistics. Visit Google.com/analytics to add this function.

What should you also look for once the analytics are set up? Evaluate how much traffic you are getting and where it's coming from, such as your blog, social media posts, affiliates, or from organic traffic (searches for the company or other phrases and keywords). Ideally, when you do any form of traditional or digital marketing, you should see a spike in online activity.

SEO (search engine optimization) rankings are about getting seen by more people because ideally you appear earlier in the search results. Including keywords and inbound links from your other social media sites are important factors in improving SEO. However, be advised that **keywords are no longer the only thing that dictates SEO.** In 2014, Google revised its search algorithm to look at relevancy, in other words, matching search *phrases* people use vs. just keywords. This means quality written content is vital. And that you should avoid "keyword stuffing" where you stick or repeat lots of keywords in a sentence or on the page. It reads badly, is dated, and is a turnoff.

Helpful hint: Search engines crawl websites about once every two weeks, looking for fresh content and updates, which is why blogs, articles, and adding testimonials can be so useful. The more dormant your website is— say, you haven't done anything in the past several months (or years)—the lower its SEO potential. Google Analytics has a companion tool called Search Console that gives website owners access to lots of data about how Google Search is interacting with their site (Google.com/Webmaster/tools). Another powerful tool is Google Trends (Google.com/Trends) which allows you to find information on search rankings and trending topics, so you can hook people by engaging their interest with contemporary issues.

A quick sidebar: Dormant social media suffers from a different malady than a dormant website. Recent data says that if you can't maintain an active Facebook business page with a post at least once a week, it may be better not to have one. Inactive pages lose visitors' interest, and they may disconnect for good.

And a final note: where is your email coming from? Are you still doing Sam@yahoo.com or Kenisha@aol.com? That instantly shouts, "I'm not a serious business!" If your company name is Fuzzy Graphics, then email should be coming from Lois@FuzzyGraphics.com. Not only does it reinforce the business name, but it also helps create trust, because it's coming from a genuine company.

What would you do? **So much to say on our website…**

Kidpower International is a global nonprofit leader dedicated to providing both empowering and effective child protection, positive communication, and personal safety skills for all ages and abilities. Their original website featured multiple services, programs, and courses, as well as extensive resources and research data. Every page presented informative content and dozens of links. But Executive Director & Founder Irene van der Zande was concerned it was being pre-empted by competitors' websites, and no longer performing as strongly as it once did. She wanted to identify what had to be changed. Any ideas of what steps Kidpower needed to take to assess the situation?

✍ *Jot down your answer.*_____

_____

_____

Answer: As part of an all-day *Zipline Marketing Blueprint* workshop I conducted for Irene and her Kidpower team of staff and board members, we scrutinized the website. Prior to our meeting, I had assessed their top five competitors, and observed that Kidpower's site was dated looking. Virtually everyone else was using photos and short content to visually engage visitors. Some included a web form offer; several used video. Strong branding (logo, tagline) was prominent on every page, and the navigation bars made it easy to find more information.

But among one of the most important "finds" was how competitors were labeling their pages to increase SEO. As we clicked to different pages, and studied each page's URL in the search bar, rather than just repeating the domain name, providers were labeling pages with strong keywords and phrases that people would use in a Google search. For example, Bullying and Harassment Prevention, Child Abuse Prevention.

Kidpower completely revamped their website (Kidpower. org) and their International Child Protection Month website (ChildProtectionMonth.org). Essential information was put above the fold, every page was branded, more photos and videos were added to "connect" with the audience, and navigation was streamlined. Every page's URL was labeled to optimize search. Now visitors can more easily find and see all the organization has to offer.

The most important takeaway to remember is a well-designed, visitor-friendly website is the anchor to your digital marketing outreach efforts, and has to be managed on an ongoing basis. Review, refresh, and revise to remain interesting and relevant to your ever-evolving customer base.

Chapter 14 ~ Leveraging Social Media and Building Social Media Currency

From an owner or manager's perspective, social media's marketing value is ultimately about persuading buyers and prospects to come back to your website and buy. It's as simple as that. However, unlike traditional advertising, social media cannot be an "in your face" approach, where each contact is some form of a promotion, sale, or offer to buy. That actually antagonizes visitors; if you do it, you won't be liked or followed by many people, and social media marketing is all about the volume of people you reach.

> ***Zipline Essential #23.* Don't treat social media primarily as a sales platform.**

Social media's success is based on the *gradual process* of developing social currency through the building of trust-based relationships over time that cultivates awareness of your firm, with minimal direct selling. The gradual part is what frustrates so many companies—but relationships take time to build.

If you want to argue that social media is a waste of time since it shouldn't be used to sell, let me ask, can you afford not to be using it as a part of your marketing strategy? Think about it from a target audience perspective. Gen Z, Millennials, and Gen X are heavy users of social media and it's a critical factor in their decision-making process. You have to be there.

➢ *Four key pieces of zipline equipment for social media*

There are a variety of resources to launch or enhance social media activities. The following four are essentials.

1. Get your social media footprint in place. At minimum, set up a Facebook business page and LinkedIn account. Depending on the business and where your customers spend their social media time, you may want to be on Instagram, which is ideal for photo- and video-based postings, and Twitter. Each increases your firm's exposure and allows you to communicate with prospects and buyers. They also help improve your SEO.

Once you set up the accounts, get active! Start posting links to your blog, website, or to other interesting material that you come across.

What about content? Social media is about educating and informing your readers by sharing insights, articles, advice, and more, and over time persuading people that your company is an expert and somebody they can trust, and one they may buy from when the want or need arises. When it comes to promotions and sales, a useful rule of thumb is no more than one out of every four posts should be selling. Use a delicate touch!

"I just got a friend request from someone in the castle."

Clients often complain they don't have enough time to manage all this. There are two solutions. If you'd like to consolidate your social media dashboard to one hub, consider using a service like Hootsuite (HootSuite.com) which acts like social media command central. You can manage all your accounts, schedule updates ahead of time, and even monitor conversations about the firm. Alternatively, depending on the company's social media marketing outreach goals, you can hire a part- or full-time person to manage this for you.

Important: Be careful about sending the exact same content to all social media platforms. Tweak it enough so that a person who is following your company on more than one social media channel isn't seeing the same thing everywhere.

2. **Should you blog?** Blogs are a popular social media tool, but more people are shifting to doing short-form version blogs on high-traffic sites such as Facebook and LinkedIn vs. one exclusively on their website. A common practice is to showcase a part of a blog on Facebook and then link it back to the website, giving people the chance to read in greater depth—and see all the firm has to offer.

Note that as with all social media, blogs are not focused on promoting the business. Don't go overboard on blogging, and feel you have to send a blurb out every day unless that's what the audience expects. Why? First, we're drowning in over-communication, and if you overdo it, they'll tune you out, or worse, just delete you. Case in point: in one group I joined, a member sends out four blog posts a day! I not only ignore them, but I'm irritated because it's inconsiderate of my time. *Helpful hint:* I actually have set up a specific email account dedicated for receiving Facebook posts, blogs, etc., so it doesn't clutter my primary business email.

Second, it will devour your time. Producing that much content is labor intensive. While viewpoints vary on frequency, depending on your audience and industry, posting one to two times a week is a safe guideline. This ensures fresh content that keeps visitors coming back.

Some suggestions for blog posts include industry-specific tips; book and article reviews; tutorials and how-to's; interviews with employees, customers, or partners; and, as a gentle way to promote your business, occasional giveaways, contests, and surveys.

Important: Blogs, Facebook, and other social media sites are designed for comments and sharing. By being on them, you invite people to engage and interact. It's important to monitor the dialogue and comments, and respond to questions within one to three business days because people like to feel connected. **Don't be passive when it comes to social media.** It's a dynamic and interactive environment, and lack of response on the company's part signals that the firm is not as customer-centric as it should be.

3. **Are email newsletters dead?** No, they're not. But they have changed! Five years ago, I would see elaborate newsletters designed and sent out as attachments, complete with mastheads, images, and running one to four pages in length—basically a digital version of a print newsletter. But like all digital marketing methods, they've evolved into shorter, more condensed almost blog-like emails that link back to longer content.

Parsed out into short paragraphs, with attention-grabbing colored subheads, they're designed to enable the recipient to scan content quickly, see if anything sparks their interest, read a summary blurb, then click through to learn more. The most effective newsletters are a blend of information and education, sometimes with an offer or promotion included.

4. **Subject lines that sell:** You want to write email subject headers to get better open rates. This is a hot topic among marketers because emails are the best tool for business-building offers. What steps should you take to get the audience to open your email?

Ask yourself: where do most folks read their emails today? You guessed it… on their smart phones, which have seriously impacted "best practices" for email marketing outreach. And they actually don't read—they scan, scrolling quickly through emails to determine which to open. And what optimizes getting people to read emails today may surprise you.

The first thing they look at is not the subject header, but the "From Name" source. This is why having a branded vs. generic email is even more important today than two years ago—it's about branding, trust, and credibility. If the email address is one they know and recognize, or appears to be coming from a reputable sender, they're more likely to open it. If you sign up for my emails, and see an email from Claudia@ZiplineToSuccess.com, you would be more likely to read it, vs. Claudia@yahoo.com, right?

Next comes the subject header. Effective subject headers use psychology. To be noticed and cause the person scanning their emails to slow down, **write them to pique interest, curiosity, or concern.** Because today we read in short visual "sight bites," it must instantly hook them. A strong subject header has to answer the reader's one question: "Why should I read this?" Note that the subject header shouldn't be more than five to six words or 40 characters in length to capture interest, and the first three words are the most important part of the hook. After six, the subject header can bleed off the screen and the words are lost.

Helpful hints: Use strong commands, dangling phrases, intriguing questions, and sharing news. One of the most effective is a call to action, either implicit or inferred. Use "you" and "your" to make it feel more personal (two of the most powerful words in marketing outreach!). Use numbers written out—but no greater than 9, because a higher number makes people assume it's going to take too long to read, and not open it. A few examples:

- Write winning email headers
- Don't miss this!
- Reserve your spot
- Early bird special
- Open late. Just in time
- Do you have the perfect gift?
- You coming? Just 3 seats left!
- You can't miss this Sunday's show

- Essential oils. See what they can do
- Three mistakes marketers make

And a few things to avoid: All capitals. Excessive punctuation (???, !!!). The words *spam, credit card,* or *weight loss,* and $$$ and other symbols. These all boost the likelihood that spam filters will block your email.

Seeking subject header inspiration? Check out online news headlines; most are written to snag attention. Start paying close attention to the emails you receive and you'll quickly spot the best ways to bait the hook and get buyers interested.

Important: The Federal Trade Commission's CAN-SPAM Act makes it illegal to email promotional messages to people without their permission. Penalties range up to $16,000. And it applies to all forms of commercial messages, not just bulk mail. To ensure you're in compliance, learn more at FTC.gov/tips-advice/business-center/guidance/can-spam-act-compliance-guide-business.

➢ *Bring on the traffic!*

Once you've set up and started participating on social media, the next goal is to connect with customers and prospects and keep them coming back. One of the most valuable ways to do that is by making it easy for them to move between all your social and digital spaces.

Create links from all your social media sites—blog, Facebook pages, Twitter accounts, any social media outlets—back to the website and vice versa. Not only does it improve SEO, but when others retweet or share these links, you get exponential exposure. This is free advertising, and it's essential you take advantage of it.

Making your business more visible online can be done through a variety of other methods some of which are free. Use these zipline digital marketing tactics to boost visibility.

- **Claim your online business listings.** If you haven't already, please, please, please, claim your online business listings. I'm permanently amazed by how many firms just don't do this. And it's free!

  Yelp, Yahoo, Bing, and other search engines automatically post your business listing online based on the company's phone number. But it's your responsibility to go to that listing, claim it by verifying you're the owner, and then add photos, a company description, and links to your website and social media sites. Plus, notice how when you're searching for a service or company, the search engine presents online yellow pages to look at? You can and should be there too. A good place to start this entire process is at Google.com/business.

✕ **Use your web form for targeted marketing.** You're collecting emails through your web form offer. What are you going to do with them? Send out targeted messages such as events, coupons, incentives, webinars, etc. that will encourage people to take action and use your product or service.

✕ **Leverage LinkedIn.** LinkedIn tends to be underutilized when it comes to social media marketing. Don't just add network connections and sign out. Look at ways to join relevant groups where your buyers or prospects are, enter into dialogues, even share your blog posts. There's lots of activity on LinkedIn, and it can be a great place to promote content, share ideas, and build the brand.

✕ **Are Google AdWords a good option?** Google is the best known Pay-Per-Click (PPC) ad platform. Those short ads that you see at the top of the search results? Those are courtesy of Google AdWords.

The basic premise is that you bid on keywords that are most relevant to your business, and then pay Google a certain amount for each time someone clicks on your ad. Within nanoseconds, Google enters thousands of keywords and ads into an "auction" to determine which ones are most relevant to the search query, and the winning ads are presented at the top of the results. Visit to Google.com/AdWords to learn the details. As with any media option, there are pros and cons. Some considerations:

Pros

- There's the chance to appear on the first page of the search for maximum exposure.

- You can be up on AdWords relatively fast.

- AdWords ads can help to drive traffic to your site quickly.

- You control your budget. You can specify spending, set a maximum cost per click for keywords, and then only pay for clicks.

- You can stop AdWords at any time.

- It's a great way to test different keywords to better understand how prospects search for your company, and then incorporate what you learn into the SEO practices.

Cons

- You pay for clicks, whether or not a visitor buys the product or service.
- Competition keeps increasing, and the cost per click keeps going up.
- AdWords have a short shelf life. Once your budget is spent, ads stop.
- Characters are limited to 25 in the headline, 35 each in the two lines of text, and 35 in the display URL. Within those parameters, you need to include an attention-grabbing headline, benefits, keywords, and a call to action.

Are Facebook ads a good option? While boosting ads on Facebook used to be a popular way to increase visibility, today, it's nearly impossible to achieve significant reach to *new* prospects without buying ads. The good news is that Facebook has really amped up its advertising options, and improved tools are making them an effective choice. You now have the ability to hyper-target prospects, zeroing in on demographics, location, and other buyer characteristics at an in-depth level. Of course, you need to know your customers' characteristics in the first place (see Chapter 2 for more about this).

Facebook offers a comprehensive guideline for how to set up ads at www.Facebook.com/business. Once you're satisfied with the way the ad looks, you then choose the target demographic and see the ad's estimated reach.

There are some additional things to consider. A powerful attribute of Facebook is that you can quickly test different headlines, copy, and images to see what generates response. We work in a visual world and photos attract more attention than plain copy. Because of the ability to tinker with the ad, you can test different photos to see which produces a better response. Or copy. Or headline. But don't mess with all three at once; otherwise, you won't know which changes are impacting the results.

Where you send people when they click on the ad is an important part of your strategy. Different destinations can produce different outcomes. Do they go to your Facebook business page? Your website? Whatever page you're sending them to must be engaging and give them a reason to stay longer.

When I used Facebook ads to generate book sales, I initially sent them to my book's website to learn more, and sales were minimal. Instead, I now send people directly to my Amazon page, and sales have jumped because people can take action and make a purchase.

The key thing to remember when comparing Facebook vs. Google ad options is that with Google, you choose *words* that people will be searching for. With Facebook, you choose what *type of people* the ad will be sent to. Facebook more closely aligns with the traditional concept of advertising to a specific target audience.

➢ *What's in your digital marketing wallet?*

A pillar of social media is the building social currency. In its broadest sense, it means establishing a trustworthy and reliable reputation in the digital world—what I like to call your digital marketing wallet. You see social currency in the online merchant or eBay seller who receives 97% to 100% buyer approval ratings. Or the website that passes your antivirus software's inspection. And in the reviews and feedback you receive as to the quality of a buyer's experience with your company. If I Google your business, what can I find out?

> *Zipline Essential #24.* **Online reviews are critical influencers in how people shop.**

Customer testimonials are valuable currency in your social media wallet. Yet so often companies post any old testimonial on their site, or put the entire testimonial up. Please, don't post B-grade testimonials unless that's all you have; and as soon as you get an A-grade, switch them out!

To leverage testimonials online, it's vital to think like a zipline marketer—they must connect with the prospect and validate your company. Rather than necessarily use the whole testimonial, identify and consolidate the strongest points so it's short and hard-hitting. In other words, edit! There's two ways to do this. One, edit the testimonial, and send it back to the client for approval. The alternate is to do what newspapers do. Use ellipses (the… you see in text) to indicate the copy has been edited.

"Please visit our website and tell us about your experience with this sale. You can win a gift card good for a free glass of lemonade."

Reviews are important coinage in social currency, and the digital form of both word-of-mouth and public relations. According to Entrepreneur.com, 72% of people indicate that "positive reviews make me trust a business more."

The younger your audience (under age 50), the more likely they are going to check out reviews about your company, service, or product. It may be on Trip Advisor, Yelp, Amazon, or eBay. What they read can strongly influence their buying decisions.

According to ReviewTrackers.com, reviews have a measurable impact on a firm's revenue. For example, there can be as much as a 9% increase in revenue with each additional star rating on Yelp. Unlike testimonials you post on your website, reviews are pure unedited feedback, and therefore seen as theoretically more trustworthy. And, unlike your website, they can go viral for better or for worse. Here are two legendary whoppers.

- **"United Breaks Guitar" YouTube Video:** In 2009, musician Dave Carroll and his band were flying on United Airlines. Their baggage handlers damaged his $3,500 Taylor guitar. While trying to file a complaint, Carroll reported he encountered rudeness, avoidance, and a lot of red tape. So he posted a "United Breaks Guitars" video on YouTube. It went viral. Some feel the video contributed to the airline's stock value dropping, costing shareholders millions. Needless to say, United contacted him to resolve the problem.

- **Southwest Airlines "Too Fat to Fly."** Passenger and film director Kevin Smith had just boarded a flight when he was told he was "too fat to fly." The Southwest captain felt he was a "safety risk" and ordered him off the plane. Smith tweeted the whole incident. It was picked up by major media outlets, including *USA Today* and ABC. Southwest promptly issued apologies on its website and through Twitter and presumably gave him a make good.

> *Zipline Essential #25*. **Do not succumb to snarling in negative social currency situations.**

It's not all wine and roses in the digital marketing arena. As you just saw, sometimes you merit a lousy review if you have done a poor job. But how you react can influence your social currency. Why? Because not only do people check reviews, they check out how you *respond* to negative reviews.

The first rule of dealing with negative reviews is to not take them personally. They happen. When a justifiable negative review occurs, acknowledge it, be polite and constructive, apologize, and try to address the concern. If appropriate, offer some form of reparation.

If the customer is in the wrong—and this does happen—remain courteous and acknowledge the comment. You may need to cite company policy or offer an additional perspective on the situation so that readers get both points of view. But in no instance should you ever "attack" the reviewer.

Think of negative reviews in context of public relations. In crisis situations, PR experts use the Three R's Strategy: Regret—show sincere regret that it has happened. Reason—clarify the situation's causes and understand the reasons it occurred. Remedy—offer a solution.

What's truly irritating is when people give poor reviews who have never been to your business or used your product or service! I've had many clients report this occurring. I even had one tell me that a competitor was paying people to post negative reviews in hopes of damaging this particular business! As another example, I know a coffee shop owner who had a fellow give her a one star on Yelp. Except he had never even visited because what he described didn't match what her shop offered. Even though she knew this, she responded by saying she was sorry he had a bad experience, and hoped he would return and enjoy a free coffee.

The same previous rules about what to do when dealing with a customer in the wrong apply. Be gracious and professional. Note that you can sometimes file a complaint with the online review site, if you feel the review is inapproproate and needs to be removed, but there is no guarantee they will take any action.

While you may fume and fret at negative reviews, your replies, including whether or not you responded, are an important part of your firm's social currency. The good news is that over time, these reviews "wear out." If there's a bad review that's two years old, and there are no subsequent bad reviews, then it loses its social currency from the reader's viewpoint.

➤ *Three more useful digital marketing pointers*

✺ **It's all about content:** There's TMI on the Internet (too much information). And since you're going to be adding to it, make sure your content isn't just gas, but something of value from the buyer or prospect's perspective.

Practice EIAI. Educate, inform, amuse, inspire.... There's a variety of ways to come up with topics, even short blurbs, that will keep you top of mind. Try creating Top 10 lists, helpful tips, or best practices in your industry. Don't feel you need to restrict content solely to your business or profession; sometimes the unexpected and unusual is a good way to "startle" your readers and get them re-engaged.

Content can be repurposed. Don't just post and forget. Look at ways to turn a series of blog posts or articles into an e-book. Or refresh as new data or ideas come along. Or convert it into a webinar, video tutorial, podcast, or teleseminar.

✺ **Repurpose "lost" data.** Building on the idea of repurposing, there are cartloads of data, studies, and statistics available online through news and industry reports. And many don't get much coverage. It's a good method to use to educate and inform readers—and reinforce that you are the expert they want to work with now or in the future.

If you're part of an association, or good at research, or have a staffer or intern who likes digging for this sort of stuff, seek out these studies and data and then repurpose them into blogs or articles. Highlight the important or interesting parts of the study, add images or charts, and personalize it by adding your own thoughts or predictions based on your interpretation of the data.

✺ <u>Ask</u> **for reviews and testimonials.** Many companies take a passive approach to collecting reviews and testimonials. Don't! Be proactive. Ask your best customers to post positive reviews about their experiences. Some companies offer various $5 merchant reward cards as a thank you to customers who post a genuine review on Yelp. I routinely ask for reviews as part of the performance evaluation surveys I send out to my clients after completing a workshop, speaking engagement, or consulting project.

If somebody demurs because they feel they're "not a good writer," offer to draft a review for their approval. I know a freelancer who sends people a pre-written "testimonial" and asks, "Would you agree with this statement? May I post this with your name associated?" Sometimes saving them the time of writing encourages them to say yes.

As a courtesy, always ask how they want their name or company cited, for example: Carl Knox, Peoria, Illinois; C. Knox, IL, or CK, IL. Sometimes individuals and companies don't want their name mentioned; in those cases, simply mention the town, state, or nothing.

An added advantage of reviews is that larger numbers can improve your SEO. They can also help balance ratings. By this, I mean that a higher number of reviews reduces the impact an individual review has on the total rating. Say you have two reviews, and a one-star and a five-star; that's a mediocre 2.5-star average. But with 20 reviews, two one-stars, and 18 five-stars, that averages a 4.6-star rating. Simply put, review volume is good—as long as they're overall favorable.

✂ **Create your own videos.** I mentioned it earlier when talking about websites, but it bears repeating. Video is hot. Even mini 30-second to one minute videos. While it can cost serious dollars to get professional videos produced, there's nothing wrong with trying it yourself or hiring a film student from your local college.

YouTube is where videos go to be seen (YouTube.com). It's the best place to put your videos, and the channels are free. You can link from the company's website to its video channel, rather than having to embed a video in the website, which can slow loading time.

Part 5 – Zipline Highlights

✂ **Work your website.** Just because your company puts up a website doesn't mean it's working hard. Take a look at it from the customer's perspective. Is it contemporary? Does it connect with them immediately? Is there a call to action? If the website is just a static online brochure, it's time to move into the 21st century.

✂ **You don't have to be everywhere on social media.** Don't succumb to the idea that you have to be on every social media platform available. As with any form of media, whether your firm is on Facebook, Instagram, or LinkedIn, each has different, sometimes overlapping, target audiences. Select the platforms that your buyers are using, and become an expert in connecting with them there.

�֎ **Dealing with reviews and comments.** Online reviews are today's testimonials. You want great reviews—and you need to ask for them. At the same time, turn negative reviews into a constructive opportunity to improve your standing with subsequent site visitors.

✖ **Traffic doesn't "just happen."** There are millions of sites online. You need to constantly look for ways—social media, blogs, and online articles—to connect with your audience, and draw them back to the website. Make sure you've claimed your business listings and are listed on other major sites where your buyers go to check out reviews.

Part 6 – Zip Wild! 7 Creative, Innovative, and Eye-Catching Marketing Ideas to Set You Apart from the Crowd

It's time for a section that's more fun and frothy! I guess I should begin by saying there are way more than seven ideas here. But it helped make the title sound intriguing and it hooked you, right? That's marketing! And, for even more added value, these ideas can be tied into your digital marketing efforts, even if it's only sharing photos or video.

You now know that marketing as a whole is about the integration of all the zipline marketing essentials in such a way that your product or service isn't a commodity, but is something unique and different. Marketing outreach is about winning the contest for people's attention. At its heart, it's about separating your company from competitors in ways that make prospects, customers, and maybe even the world take notice. And part of this process is being creative and having some fun.

Very often, when I'm invited to speak or teach workshops, I'll be asked to talk about creative marketing ideas and unusual ways companies can set themselves apart. So let's do it! From customer of the month, to creative loyalty programs, to the unexpectedly wacky, I believe you'll find ideas that inspire you—and that you can adapt to your own business.

Chapter 15 ~ Taking Spins on the Zipline Ride

The first time you ride a zipline (at least in my case), you hang on for dear life. Feet pointed straight ahead, clinging to the harness, seeing the landing platform hurtling toward you as the world blurs by. And wondering how hard the stop will be. The second time is totally different. You know the routine, and now you begin looking around and testing what happens when you move arms or legs, causing you to twist about, providing new perspectives and adding to the fun. And then you consider what else you can try.

The same applies to marketing. You may be a bit conservative when you begin, figuring just how to ride the marketing zipline. Then, you start looking for ways to do it differently. Admittedly most companies don't have blank checkbooks, so you have to "create smarter," not harder. Using imagination is one example of being a smart zipline marketer.

In 1971, Rollin King and Herb Kelleher started Southwest Airlines with one notion: "If you get your passengers to their destinations when they want to get there, on time, at the lowest possible fares, and make darn sure they have a good time doing it, people will fly your airline." When Southwest first took off, many were sure it would fail because the market was saturated with established competitors. But Southwest did things differently. From birthday parties, to dressing flight hostesses in colorful hot pants and white knee-high boots (it *was* the 70s!), to giving passengers free alcoholic beverages during daytime flights, Southwest made traveling different and fun. Sales took off and the new airline never looked back.

Keeping an eye open for different approaches is at the heart of zipping wild.

✂ **Be alert and be adaptable.** Anytime you see a great idea, in this book, online, in a store, or anywhere else, ask yourself, "Can I adapt that for my business?" What things can you do to put your own "spin" on it? Remember the Wal-Mart story I shared in Chapter 11?

✂ **Strive to stand out.** Permit yourself to be creative and have fun. Truly stand-out marketing involves a willingness to be sassy, different, and tongue-in-cheek to get attention. Think about Geico. Mispronunciation of the company's name led the now-familiar gecko, and the bizarre situations in which he finds himself are amusing and memorable. Or think of Flo in the Progressive Car Insurance campaign. The firm created a unique character and built a humorous expertise-based campaign.

✂ **Make it memorable.** Doing things differently—either slightly or dramatically—is important. Things go viral because they're memorable. But whatever you do, make sure it ties back to and positively reinforces your brand and story. After all, this *is* about marketing.

Now, two important notes. Good marketing is like a good recipe; it's about balance. Go overboard with a spice or flavoring, and it can overwhelm the person eating it. **A smart zipline marketing strategy blends the attention-grabbers with the tried and true,** creating excitement among your buyers without wearing them out. It encourages you to test innovative approaches without short-circuiting marketing efforts you've previously done that you know produce good results because you've measured them.

> *Zipline Essential #26.* **Don't sacrifice sales on the altar of creativity.**

When you're coming up with new ideas, don't forget what motivates your buyers to make purchases. You don't want to spend money getting the attention of people who won't buy. Unfortunately, sometimes agencies and companies get so caught up in the creative, they forget that the ultimate goal of marketing is generating sales.

David Ogilvy, often considered the father of modern advertising, once famously noted that when you're watching a TV commercial, turn off the sound. If you don't know what the product or service is, then the commercial is a waste of money. Remember: the main purpose of marketing outreach, whether crazy, cool, or common, is to capture the attention of potential customers and motivate them to purchase the product or service.

➤ *Zipline above the crowd with unusual, even "crazy" ideas*

Some of the following ideas may seem off the wall, others not so much. But my goal is to inspire you to think of new ways to apply them or derivations of them to your business. If you're already doing any of these, hurrah for you! Let's start with people-focused ideas.

✂ **Create your own "celebrity" brand ambassador:** Run a brand ambassador competition. This person can serve as your spokesperson, and become the face of the business for a period of time. Invite customers to become your ambassador by pitching you on why they're the right person, and what they're going to do to help create awareness.

Think about it like this. Beauty pageants create a contest to hire a pitchwoman for a year. While you may want a famous celebrity as your pitch person, most firms can't afford that. Can you find somebody local or less known, and create excitement in the process?

For example, if you're a sporting goods or an outdoor adventure company, wouldn't you have liked to have had Kevin Jorgenson and Tommy Caldwell, who made the historic free climb of Yosemite National Park's El Capitan in 2015, as brand ambassadors?

❆ **Create a customer of the month (CoM):** It's fun to spotlight customers. Not only does it create goodwill, very often they will share and forward such announcements to friends and colleagues, fostering more awareness of your company. Call it free PR. Tie it back to a theme so people understand what defines a CoM. Is it how long they've been a customer? Because they performed an exceptional community effort? What sets them apart?

Defining the parameters helps encourage customers to see if they are eligible, or even better, want to become eligible. Make sure you announce and promote this via both social media and your website, as well as at the counter or reception area, and have staff talk it up. If you have the budget, consider doing some print or radio.

❆ **Feature specialty clubs.** Clubs make customers feel a part of your firm, give them a sense of exclusivity, and foster loyalty because they return to take advantage of club benefits. The fancy marketing lingo for this is "customer retention." Specialty clubs are a variant of a loyalty program, such as frequent flyer miles, but the goal is to make these even more distinctive so that they're memorable as well as worth the customer's time.

You've seen birthday and VIP clubs; do you have one? An automotive repair service client launched a 500,000-mile club for clients who have that much mileage on their cars! They get free tune-ups and a chance to share their stories in online monthly emails.

I know salons that have "most unusual hairstyle" clubs. A pet store promotes its "best dressed pooch" club. A photo studio that has a "cutest baby photo" contest and gets its customers involved in the voting process each month to keep them engaged. The essential ingredient in all this is the interaction with buyers because it creates added value, and makes it harder for a competitor to steal them.

Look at your products and services, and ask, what can we do, what themes can we come up with for clubs to engage our customers and keep them coming back?

❆ **Zipline your prizes & points:** Especially creative loyalty programs bestow points and rewards in ways that are unexpected. Why? Because it's different, gets customers jazzed, and stirs things up. And, most importantly, it gets them talking and coming back.

Now before you argue that point-based loyalty programs are only doable by the big companies, let me share a new perspective. Digital loyalty rewards services provided by third-party companies such as Belly (BellyCard.com) and Perka (Perka.com) offer creative solutions that make it easier for smaller firms to implement such programs.

So how can you zipline a loyalty program to new heights? Check out the ways a simple twist can jazz up your efforts.

- *Basic coupon:* 10% off coupon for being a long-term customer.
   - *Zipline it:* One-minute shopping spree to grab as many goodies as possible for just $XYZ. Choose the right length of time so they can feel they received a wonderful opportunity. Videotape it with a smart phone and post it online. For extra spin and increased PR, tie it back into a charity your company supports, where a portion or all of the proceeds go to that charity.

- *Basic reward:* Earn so many points, get something for it.
   - *Zipline it:* Give a reward for no reason. Review your preferred customer and/or new buyer lists, and send an email saying how glad you are that they're a part of the customer family, and surprise! Here's a free something. One of my fine-dining restaurant clients sends an email for a free dessert, no purchase required. In other words, no strings attached.

- *Basic prize redemption:* Redeem your points at your store or online.
   - *Zipline it:* Let customers redeem points for exclusive products or services they can't buy on your site or in store, making it something that not everyone can get.

      USA Today reported two extreme examples of this: Alley Cat Comics in Chicago let customers punch the owner in the stomach after 50 visits (ouch!). Bagelsmith in New York let customers who collected 7,500 points arm wrestle the owner for equity in the store.

      Makeup retailer Sephora's VIP program amps up loyalty rewards by offering surprise treats as well as discounts to clients spending a certain amount within a calendar year. In what's known as a tiered incentive program (the more you spend, the more you receive), shoppers are awarded VIB status when they spend $350 in a calendar year, and VIB ROUGE when they spend $1,000.

      Another way to be creative with prizes without breaking the

bank is to partner with other firms who will sell, maybe even donate, their products or services at a deep discount in exchange for the free publicity and awareness. Think a trip, dinner at a restaurant, a cruise, a new bike... the list is endless. I know a travel company that contacted all the region's historic hotels, and gives away free hotel stays as part of a package, promoting those hotels on the website. It's a win–win for everyone.

- *Basic loyalty program sign up:* Sign up and get points and discounts.

  o *Zipline it:* Support a cause. Research reveals that 83% of Americans want more companies to support causes. This is especially true for Millennials. Capitalize on it! For every 1,000 points a buyer earns, you'll donate $X to a specific cause. Note that your choice of charity also tells people a lot about the company.

     I was at an event where the speaker offered attendees an option that if they made a donation to a specific charity he supports, and sent him proof of the donation, he would critique their books. It created a tremendous "feel good" among the audience, and they were lining up after his presentation.

✂ **Wacky and/or creative contests.** People enjoy the excitement of a contest and a chance to win. Even though they know the probabilities are low, why shouldn't they give it a whirl? So, have fun and be creative. Think of Nathan's Hot Dog eating contest—it's become legendary. So has Duck Tape's "Stuck at Prom" Scholarship contest where imaginative teens create attire using the sticky tape for a chance to win $50,000 in cash scholarship prizes. An awesome "feel good" contest!

Could you develop a treasure or scavenger hunt? Maybe something with geo-caching? What about an innovative way to use your product or service? Brainstorm with staff and clients, and you're guaranteed to come up with something creative. Contests can be fun, wacky, and imaginative: a messy desk contest, ugly sweater contest, pet/owner look-alike contest, etc.

It's important to check what the contest rules are in your state, because regulations vary. For example, it may not be permitted to require a purchase to enter, or you may have to specify that it's not for people under a certain age, or there may be restrictions on the type of prizes that can be offered. Try searching under "Rules for Operations of Contests and Sweepstakes" to find out your state's rules.

I believe that **contests with perceived high value prizes are especially strong**. In other words, what counts is what people *think* it's worth. You've seen the cars given away. But did you know that the firm has negotiated a special deal with the auto seller? To the contest participants, that car is worth a lot more than what the company actually paid for it.

Have multiple winners to delight multiple customers, and give people the hope that they have a better chance at winning something. Try offering more than one prize, with several low-cost items as a third prize, and progressively higher value items up to the grand prize. Give other firms a chance to get in on the contest. Contact them and ask if you can offer their product or service as a prize at no or low cost in exchange for promoting their company to your clients, which exposes them to a whole new prospective audience.

On a budget? Give away what you can afford—maybe a dinner for two, a 10-minute shopping spree, or a backpack filled with school supplies. You can even bundle your products or services as a prize. My salon offers a Day of Beauty contest twice a year, where winners receive a massage, facial, haircut, manicure, and pedicure, along with lunch. A transmission repair shop I work with bought a discount bundle of coupons to a next-door restaurant, and gives one to every client who decides to wait.

✂ **Fun & funky visual contests.** In case you're off the grid, we've become a very visually-driven world. At a recent business conference, it was intriguing to hear a Facebook expert talk about adding photos to posts if you really want people to read them. Look at the explosion of YouTube videos… need I say more? So how can you leverage this to the company's advantage? For starters, consider that photos and videos are a great form of user-generated content that can be reused elsewhere online, as well as for promoting and creating awareness. Always have a contest runner up or two, so that multiple people have a chance to "win"—it expands the feel good and the talk-about-it factors.

Too often a photo or video contest is basic and blah; take a shot of such-and-such and submit. Can you spell y-a-w-n? It's the contests that are unusual and eye-catching that get folks talking, sharing links, and actually motivate people to submit. Think how *America's Funniest Home Videos* utterly relies on folks submitting home-brewed video clips.

Really want to get noticed? Go for a "record breaker" contest, where you're trying to do something that gets you into the *Guinness Book of*

World Records, or by breaking some other record (industry, local, regional, state, national, etc.). The media often covers these events, many people get involved, and it's both fun and utterly photogenic.

Some examples of other video contests: unusual selfies; dizzy dances; crazy cleaning confessions... you get the idea. For fun and to provide inspiration, I tracked down a few really different visual contests.

- How about Green Care's "most unusual place to recharge an electric car"? The winning photo was a car recharging on the surface of a lake. The prize? A brand-new $649 AeroVironment TurboCord combined 120-Volt/240-Volt portable charging cord.

- Photo Contest Insider challenged people to find the unusual in what might seem everyday situations. Prize: a free one-year subscription; the winner could choose from several photography magazines.

- Stormtrack asked people to submit all the weird things they see while on the road throughout the season. Odd signs or crazy people; basically anything that makes you think, "what on Earth?"

A note about leveraging contests online. Promote them on all your social media. If you're running a photo contest via Facebook, make sure it's still promoted on Instagram, Pinterest, Twitter, etc. Announce it to all your email subscribers. They are already interested in what you have to offer, and are more apt to let others know.

Make contests sharable; add "share this contest" buttons if you have an entry form on a website, or simply encourage social sharing in general. The more folks who know about your contest, the better. Consider offering bonus points for sharing.

For purely online contests, check out Rafflecopter.com as a possible resource. The company can help to set up a contest and place an entry form on your website.

➤ *Get noticed with the unexpected or unusual*

Now that we've looked at a series of creative approaches that invite customers to take action, let's look at the many other ways to be different, even edgy in your campaign to break away from the herd.

✄ **Do more business card drawings.** Companies tend to only do these at events. Why not elsewhere? Put a raffle jar or basket on the counter or reception desk with a sign asking visitors to drop cards in for a chance to win something. You might offer a free product sample or something fun.

Or cross-promote with other businesses, offer their products as rewards, and have them do the same for you. Then you both reach a broader customer base. Once a month, do a drawing, and start again.

Meanwhile, you've collected lots of email addresses. At the month's end, use the emails to let folks know that although they didn't win this time, they're welcome to join your emailing list to be kept informed of future giveaways and special offers. This way, it's an opt-in email, expands your list, and creates opportunities for future sales.

❀ Get noticed with food. Most things involving food attract attention. Look for ways to partner up with local businesses and a restaurant to host or sponsor a special event or activity, complete with food. By partnering with other firms that have their own customer databases, you will all have exposure to new prospects for a nominal cost.

Food can be used for PR activities as well. I read about how one company sent s'mores kits to local TV newsrooms to help promote a camper and RV show, and got great results.

❀ Host an event or class. A powerful way to connect is by hosting an event or class, which gives the opportunity to present your business without blatantly selling it. Showcase the firm's expertise while educating guests; impress people by bringing in a keynote speaker; present a forum with guest panelists to educate attendees about important issues and topics related to your industry or business; and more. By establishing your firm as being willing to educate and inform, it brings added value to client relationships. Plus, the media is more apt to cover these events, giving you free PR.

❀ Create a funky holiday. Today is "Purple Hair Day," or "Wear Army Boots Day," or "Give Ice Cream to a Friend Day." A funky holiday that catches buyers' interest and promotes the business, service, or products is only restricted by your imagination. Make sure to publicize and promote it. Not only will you get noticed, but if you make it a recurring holiday, people will look forward and plan for it. FYI, you can have more than one a year.

❀ Mad Hatter Gifting: In the book, *Alice in Wonderland,* the Mad Hatter notes that there are 364 "un-birthdays" to celebrate. Too often we focus on key holidays and birthdays to send client gifts. Just like everybody else who is doing the same thing at the same time, which makes yours much less memorable. Consider sending a gift to your most valuable customers when nobody else is likely to be doing it.

✂ **Go 3D:** Can your marketing materials be more visually engaging using 3D? You've seen pop-up birthday cards, and they really stand out—or should I say up? You're not limited to birthday cards. Pop-ups can be designed in a wide assortment of products to create clever advertising and branded items. For example: pencil cups, mailers, point of sale, and more. Just Google "pop up promotional items," and you'll find multiple firms that do this.

✂ **Defy gravity.** Instead of always designing your window displays, lettering, signs, or banners in the same old way, how can you break out and try something different? Can you animate with lights or other components? Think how Lionel trains in toy stores enliven holiday displays. The Gap clothing stores literally turned window displays upside down to grab attention, proving gravity should not always be a limiting factor if you think you can make visuals more intriguing or exciting.

✂ **Apply online for business awards.** Many industries have business awards, and it's worth applying, because you can win and receive a badge to use on all marketing materials. Badges boost credibility and sales because they independently validate your quality.

If there aren't any awards for your industry, create your own. It's a great way to get attention from other companies that want to apply, which can in turn translate into networking opportunities.

✂ **Trade show showmanship:** Companies participate in trade shows as an efficient way to get the word out to lots of prospects. But how can you get noticed in a sea of booths? If you're just putting out some pens, notepads, and a candy dish, you're making yourself less memorable. Do you really want to be invisible?

In Chapter 10, I shared how to ensure your giveaway goodies (advertising specialty items) tie back to your business and are memorable. Make them stand out from what everybody else has so people will want to hang onto and use them. Some more ideas:

Since you're there to be noticed, why not start the day or night before the event by providing some special attention to trade-show attendees? Could you host an event in a hotel conference room and invite target prospects and clients? For added interest, can you have a speaker do a mini talk and provide extra value and a reason to come?

Door hangers are a creative option. The evening before the event, hang them on select guests' hotel room doors, with a special offer and your booth name and number. Or bump it to the next level by hanging a logoed bag with nibbles, company information, and a call to action. Folks can then use this convenient bag in which to collect trade show info and goodies, and meanwhile they become your mobile billboards. You should see a bump in booth traffic.

✄ **Be where others are not:** It's hard to cut through all the advertising clutter, especially if you're relying on traditional channels, such a radio, print, and such. So, consider putting ads in unexpected places where your target audience is likely to be, visit, or see.

- o *Rent ad space on the side of a rock climbing wall.* It's one way to be "in your face." Look for unusual places to rent space—sports centers, bounce houses, parachutes, airplane banners, and event booths. Be where others are not.

- o *Rent ad space on the side of a truck or bus.* This takes a traveling billboard to a whole new level.

- o *Rent ad space on a mobile billboard.* Some smart entrepreneurs have created mobile billboard platforms on trailers and drive around towns showcasing your ad. How about an airplane towing your banner along a beach or over a big event, or a hot air balloon with your banner hanging on it?

- o *Incorporate your ad design around or right above a door handle.* Where does a person's hand go to open a door? Put an ad cling or sticker there. Keep it short and to the point.

- o *Use your shipper for advertising.* Many smaller companies miss a marketing opportunity that big companies use all the time. If you can afford to, create branded shippers; think of how Zulily, Nature's Sunshine, and FedEx boxes prominently feature their logos. If you can't afford to preprint your boxes, then have logo labels made and stick them on every package you send. And don't forget to put your website on the labels, enabling people to check out your company.

○ *Don't forget your envelopes.* While the U.S. Postal Service has strict rules about where advertising info can go on the envelope's front because of how the automated readers operate, the reverse side is open to creativity. Each person who handles that envelope can see the ad or promotion. Check with the USPS office for current regulations.

Meanwhile, don't just use a ho-hum return name and address on the front. You can make that area interesting through use of your logo, tagline, and website.

○ *Include flyers in your shipping boxes* that tell about products, upcoming specials, sales, events, and places to connect with your company on social media. Cross promote with other companies and include their flyers if they'll include yours.

○ *Use your bill or invoice to promote and educate.* Think about the invoices your firm sends out. Everybody opens them. So, why not include promotional flyers or marketing information along with the bill, or even printed on the invoice?

When I managed marketing at a telephone company, we put our newsletter in with the monthly bills, and also printed the most important special offers right on the invoice, so people couldn't miss them.

And now, to wind down this chapter—and show how you can get really wild and crazy—here's a short list of truly "out of the box" creative marketing outreach efforts that went viral, and impressed even me, a seasoned marketing consultant. I've provided the links to where you can check them out. FYI, I really did want to include the images in this book, but respecting others' copyrights is an integral part of being a good marketer.

• *Nestlé gets benched.* Famous for chocolate, the Nestlé campaign transformed slatted park benches into open Kit Kat Bars. Beautifully designed with a 3D effect, these eye-catching benches are a great example of putting creative advertising in unexpected places. http://adsoftheworld. com/media/ambient/kit_kat_bench

- *McDonald's in a crosswalk.* McDonald's employed chalk artists to convert the yellow lines in a crosswalk into an enormous package French fries. Talk about not-so-subliminal advertising! Makes you wonder how many of the pedestrians suddenly had a craving for French fries. http://adsoftheworld. com/media/ambient/mcdonalds_macfries_pedestrian_crossing

- *Putting the squeeze on.* To showcase its reptile exhibit, the Copenhagen Zoo ad designed a stunning visual mobile ad where a python appears to "squeeze" an actual commuter bus as it's driving along. The crushing effect is so realistic, that you can't help but do a double take... and worry about the passengers! http://adsoftheworld.com/media/ambient/ copenhagen_zoo_snake_bus

- *A Nike ball takes a wrong turn.* Creative design and assembly made it appear as if a huge Nike ball had smashed into an older building, dislodging the bricks that looked ready to fall. Talk about high impact! And while you're visiting this site, check out some other highly creative campaigns. http://www.creativeguerrillamarketing.com/guerrilla-marketing/18-of- the-most-memorable-guerrilla-marketing-campaigns/

- *Cingular takes dropped calls to an extreme.* From a tall screaming orange vertical billboard, a chunk actually had "dropped" off, and was sitting on the sidewalk. It's a great visual portrayal of the impact of dropped calls. Scroll down, because this site features not only Cingular, but a host of outrageous ad concepts. http://notaniche.com/outrageous-ads/698/

Part 6 – Zipline Highlights

✂ **Make your business memorable by standing out.** Truly "be noticed" marketing involves a willingness to be different and have fun as a way to attract attention. Whatever you do, make sure it ties back to and reinforces your brand.

✂ **Balance attention-grabbing marketing activities with the tried and true.** Use creative ideas in conjunction with ones that are proven to work for your company for a balanced marketing strategy and plan.

- **Ideas are everywhere.** Anytime you see a great idea, think if there are ways it can be adapted for your business, and put your own spin on it. Whether it's an unusual contest, cross-promotional prize offers, loyalty programs that keep your customers coming back and make it hard for competitors to butt in, or by surprising and delighting your buyers with the unexpected, look for ways to set your company apart from the crowd.

Part 7 – Keeping on Course – Maintain Your Momentum for a Smooth Landing

Now that you've learned how to ride the marketing Zipline to Success, and acquired the zipline marketing essentials and tactics, as well as new ideas for ways to do things, I want to close with a few important steps you should take to maintain the momentum and reap the benefit of all your efforts.

After reading my book, one of the comments I hear is that people are all fired up, and then day-to-day business drags them off the zipline and back down into the bushes. So let's address ways you can help reduce that risk by putting into place FOHRM business anchors, establishing systems to measure results and adjust your zipline course for improved outcomes, and creating your own zipline marketing strategy and plan.

Chapter 16 ~ So How Do You Know It's Really Working?

Do you set your company up for falling off the marketing zipline? Unfortunately, more often than not, the answer is "yes," unintentional although it may be.

When marketing efforts fail to deliver, it produces frustration, confusion, even irritation. How often have you said, "Well, we launched a new product/ service, but nobody bought it," or "We ran an ad or promotion, and nothing happened!"? And if that aggravation isn't enough, it costs you in both dollars and time. Let's review ways can you avoid this.

➤ *Simple ways to measure results*

Think back to riding a zipline. You measure its success by the speed, smoothness, and how much you enjoy it. Simple and straightforward, right? Successful zipline marketing is the same. As I've highlighted throughout the book, it's measured by whether or not your efforts have achieved the goals you set forth at the beginning, including how it benefits the bottom line, if that is among your goals.

Of course, measuring the impact on the bottom line means you have to have good financial reporting processes in place. As you saw in Chapter 5, it's essential to know your product or service's costs to be able to accurately calculate profits, and conduct a monthly review of revenues and profits.

> *Zipline Essential #27.* **You can't manage it if you can't measure it.**

Results not only enable you to assess outcomes, but also establish vital parameters so you can manage a program and make course corrections, improvements, and more. After reading this book, you now know that just winging it and hoping for the best rarely works. Effective zipline marketing is a balanced fusion of developing and offering a product or service that fits the customers' wants and needs, at the right price, and is available where they expect to buy it, supported with strong marketing outreach efforts, all wrapped up in positioning that communicates what makes the company, product, or service unique.

In Chapter 11, we discussed that an essential part of measuring is tracking buyers' responses by using the "how did you hear about us" approach. Here's a recap on that, as well as additional tools to measure marketing outreach results.

1. **Phone & Email tracking:** To gather detailed information on what results a specific effort is delivering, I've suggested you have the "how did you hear about us?" tracking sheet beside every phone, and on the website contact form.

Remember, however, that marketing does not operate in a void. Successful marketing motivates buyers to connect with your company, but it's the product or service quality, caliber of customer service, and the actual sales process, including the website, that determines whether or not they buy. Put another way, the job of marketing outreach is to get customers in the door. Don't blame the marketing department if the in-store, over-the-phone or online customer experience drives them away.

Helpful hint: Educate your personnel about the importance of this process. If they don't understand the data's value, they may be lax about collecting it.

2. **Sales bumps:** Did sales increase during and shortly after the period of the ad or promotion? By how much? As compared to the same period last year? Were there any other things going on that could have influenced outcomes?

For example, if you have a bicycle sales and service shop, and Amgen's Tour of California goes through town, it will probably affect sales results.

Helpful hint: Try not to run several different promotions and ads simultaneously on one product or service if you want a clean performance measurement for each one. When too many offers are flying around, it can clutter the buyer's mind, and they won't remember which marketing effort influenced their decision. Give each tactic its own test period so you can truly measure results.

One exception would be if it's a "buy more, get more" promotion. For instance, if you're running a progressive savings of $15 off of $50 or $30 off of $100, your customer instantly understands it. But if you simultaneously offer $15 off in the newspaper, $20 off online, and $10 off in a magazine, and your buyer has access to all three, which offer do you think they're going to use? It will skew results. Don't mess with the data. The KIS rule is always good to follow so as to get clean reads on your marketing efforts.

3. **Coupon redemptions:** If you provide a coupon (digital or print), collect them as they come in and/or track usage of the code online, and then tally how many were received vs. how many were sent out, aka the actual redemption rates. (See Chapter 12 for details.)

These allow you to evaluate which coupons prove most successful at generating sales and more money to the bottom line. From the data, you can zero in on which offers to reuse, with tweaks or the same, for the best return on investment.

4. **Speed of response/redemption:** Most people redeem a coupon within a fairly short time window, while it's on their minds. You can force the issue by adding the phrase *expires by, limited supplies,* or *limited time offer.*

Track how quickly people respond to an offer by noting when they come in or click through the email promotion. Offers with high perceived values usually trigger faster responses, which translates to faster cash flow. (See Chapter 12 for details.)

5. **Cost of promotion:** What did the promotion actually cost you and did it result in net positive or negative sales? Read Chapter 12 for an in-depth explanation about this.

6. **Performance vs. goals:** How did the promotion go vs. the goals you set for it? If you wanted 20 new customers, did it deliver? If you wanted to increase sales revenue by 10%, did it achieve that? Why or why not? If you don't know

what a promotion delivered in context of whatever goals were set at the start, how can you determine how well it performed?

As part of this evaluation, also assess your conversion rate, as we discussed in Chapter 6. If necessary, try to assess why people didn't redeem an offer or coupon; maybe they came to the store or website, but didn't buy. Is there something that you could have done differently to trigger a purchase?

7. **Postmortem:** *Always* conduct a post-marketing outreach evaluation by doing the above six steps, and then deciding, "Would we do this again? Why or why not?"

Also look at beyond the numbers. After all, your buyers are humans. Did they enjoy the buying experience? Did they vent any frustrations? Did the lines get too long because enough registers weren't open? Did they feel welcome? As you now know, emotions are a critical ingredient of the customer experience—their "happiness" factor will influence how they respond to your marketing activities.

If the effort flubbed, try to ascertain the source of the problems. Were they of your making or outside variables over which you had no control, such as the stock market plunged, there was a flood, or a competitor ran a better offer at the same time.

If the postmortem answer is yes, you would do it again, what could you do differently, if anything, to improve it? Different time of day, better graphics, different offer? Make notes of your decisions, because I guarantee that five months down the line, or next year, nobody is going to remember the details. That way you all have a reference point when you start the next strategic zipline marketing planning cycle.

If you're a start-up company, you may need to test different marketing outreach offers to find out what works best. One shortcut is to look at what other successful companies in your industry are doing. Another is to be very customer-centric and ask prospects what would get them interested in making a purchase. Dig beyond the obvious answer of "lower prices" because it's a common and easy response. Could it be follow-up customer service, free extended warranty, a VIP program?

The trick to using marketing outreach efforts, including advertising and promotions, is to recognize that like every other part of your zipline marketing equipment, they require smart planning, follow through, and evaluation. If you just fling it at the wall and hope it sticks, chances are it's going to ooze down. Yuck!

A word on seasonality, culture, and location. When I lived in Mexico, and Christmas came around, what with all the palm trees and warm weather, it was hard to feel any sense of the holiday. Why? Because I'd lived for a long time in Boston, and the holiday was snow, lights, and brrrrrr! But to the locals, it was colorful decorations and the arrival of special baked goods, and parties.

No matter where your company is based, when you're planning marketing outreach efforts, remember where your buyers live, especially if there is a seasonality or a cultural factor, and make sure your images, copy, and message fit with it. Christmas in the northern hemisphere is summer time in the southern hemisphere!

Because your company has set strategic business goals, a postmortem reaches beyond measuring marketing outreach efforts to the whole marketing strategy and plan. A comprehensive evaluation of each of the marketing plan's steps and outcomes is a vital part of the performance review process. Was a new product or service launched as planned? Did the revamped customer service strategy increase the number of repeat customers? Did increasing distribution to a wider geographic area deliver projected sales outcomes?

In my corporate days, we had to take all these performance evaluation steps, and then prove to our managers why we would, or would not, recommend repeating a marketing effort, ad campaign, or promotion. By using this data, it was about facts, not just our opinions.

An unusual way of measuring results—testing deodorants: Here's an off-the-wall bit of business trivia. Have you ever wondered how the efficacy of a deodorant is measured? In my Gillette days, it was by professional "pit-sniffers." Different deodorants blends would be sent home with human guinea pigs, who would then come back to the lab to have their armpits sniffed by lab personnel to test the odor blocking efficacy. No, I am not inventing this! I'm sure there was a formal name for the people doing this job, but we always knew them as the pit-sniffers. Puts a whole new spin on the concept of measuring results!

➢ ***"Please, tell me what you think"***

Don't omit the power of customer surveys (Chapter 9). Finding out what people think about different products, services, and customer service, as well as ads or promotions, is another perfect survey opportunity. When they redeem an offer, a quick online or in-store postcard survey asking them to rate how much they liked the promotion gives you instant data. Or hand a survey out at the register so as to get more feedback on various topics that you want to know about, and tell them if they'll complete it immediately and stick it in a specially marked box, you'll give them XYZ. I like to say that everybody loves being asked for their opinion, so don't be shy about getting it from them.

Marketing activities that do not have clearly defined goals are difficult to measure. And if you can't measure them, how do you know they flourished or flopped? Part of your zipline marketing strategy and plan should always include measuring of outcomes so that you can plan the best course to improve future results.

Chapter 17 ~ Optimizing Your Zipline Strategy for Success

It's an understatement to say that business owners and managers are typically being pulled in a dozen directions daily. You have to wear way too many hats, and deal with everything from accounting and customers, as well as overseeing product sales or the providing of services. And everything in between.

All this can easily become a dangerous kink in your zipline. Why? Because no matter how capable you are, **nobody is good at every aspect of business.** I'm not saying you don't understand the concepts, and you may be strong in several areas. But everything? Nope, not even if you have an MBA. Acknowledging this fact is the hallmark of a smart business person.

Venture capitalists and bank loan officers know this—it's why they require the management team's resumes. As one of my MBA professors once said, an investor is more willing to take on a B idea with an A team than an A idea with a B team, because the investor knows that missing skillsets among owners and managers can torpedo a company.

➢ *Are your FOHRM critical anchors secure?*

As part of identifying where possible expertise gaps may exist in their firms, I ask clients three key questions. What are your and the company's strengths? What are your and the company's weaknesses? And what is the value of your time?

You may have heard of doing a SWOT analysis for your firm (you can do it for individuals as well): Strengths, Weaknesses, Opportunities, and Threats. It's a very useful tool, and can help identify functionality gaps or zipline kinks that can jeopardize the business. While I won't go into depth here, I'll briefly skim the surface.

Most people are eager to talk about strengths. When we do a SWOT as a part of a business assessment, there's always a list of a company's strengths. Yet what's also important is recognizing weaknesses. Almost invariably, that list is quite short, sometimes nonexistent, or it declares that lack of marketing is the greatest weakness. Often, it's not.

"It's time once again for the morning motivational roar."

I advise my clients that every business needs to have the FOHRM key infrastructure pillars in place that will support business growth: Finance, Operations, and Human Resources, and Marketing.

1. **Finance**. Do you have solid financial and accounting systems in place to track what a product or service really costs, ensure the right pricing structure is developed, know actual revenues and profits, and determine the capital resources available to invest back into the business? If not, then like the Gizmo story at the beginning of this book, your marketing efforts could do more harm than good.

2. **Operations.** Do you have good operational systems in place? This includes customer service procedures, response policies, contracts, production practices and systems, and inventory management and control procedures. Not having efficient and cost-effective operational systems in place can swiftly undermine a company's financial well-being.

When I teach *Zipline for Success* workshops, I will often ask the entrepreneurs, what are your planned hours of operation? Who is going to handle the phones or the reception area? Who is ordering parts and managing inventory? This is all part of operations. Not only the systems, but how the business functions. Entrepreneurs often assume that every hour is a revenue-producing hour, and have not yet realized that huge chunks of the day can be consumed by operational issues. Which is why they often wind up working crazy-long hours.

3. **Human Resources.** If you're a company of more than one, you need HR. First, it dramatically reduces your risk of legal exposure. For example, are you compliant with state OSHA regulations? Are you working with subcontractors to minimize employee costs and taxes—which may expose the company to state and federal law violations?

Second, HR also establishes well-defined policies and procedures so that employees know the rules and job duties. Do you have job descriptions, performance objectives, disciplinary practices, and an employee handbook? If not, how can you discipline an employee for failing to do their job, when you didn't clearly define their duties?

Do you have proper hiring practices in place for your state? The phrase "terminate at will" does not necessarily mean you have free rein with firing employees; they may still pursue unemployment or legal recourse. HR is about the effective management of human capital.

4. **Marketing strategies and plan.** Have you established a business strategy that outlines where you want your business to go, and have you figured out the steps necessary to get there? Without these, a marketing strategy and plan are operating in a void—which increases the risk of wasted time and money, and disappointing outcomes. With them, marketing can develop a well-crafted strategy and plan designed to deliver against those objectives.

A marketing zipline relies on sound business infrastructure—the pylons on which it runs and the wires on which you zip. Do you have a good zipline business infrastructure in place?

Your answers to all these questions and more will likely reveal weaknesses. But recognize that the flipside of a weakness is an opportunity for improvement. Be honest about the gaps in your business as well as your own and your management team's capabilities. If you're great at strategy, but so-so on execution, what steps will you take to resolve it? If you're ramping up for production, but aren't familiar with manufacturing processes, shouldn't you work with somebody who can provide guidance as to cost-effective practices? If you need marketing materials, but don't have the time or in-house expertise to do design, can you outsource? If you hate bookkeeping, but aren't in a position to add staff, could you hire a bookkeeper to do the books once a month?

Here are two excellent resources to help your company on its journey. For several years, I have donated consulting time to our local SBDC chapter (Small Business Development Center). A part of the Small Business Administration (SBA), these centers are located around the country and provide an array of affordable consulting resources to companies of all sizes (SBA.gov/offices/headquarters/osbdc). Another excellent resource is SCORE, a volunteer-based organization with chapters nationwide that connects firms with experienced mentors (Score.org).

Finally, ask yourself this: **what is the value of your time?** Are you worth $75, $100, or $200 an hour? Think about what your peers are paid in the same industry. Too often I see owners and managers trying to do everything because they think they're saving money. In reality, they're taking themselves away from zipline-level management practices, business-building efforts, and revenue-generating activities, which is where they need to focus. Hire. Outsource. Delegate. Stop trying to do it all.

➤ *Get above the weeds and bushes*

The day-to-day nature of running a small or leanly staffed business carries a danger of being devoured by details. **Owners and managers are at risk of constantly just reacting to situations**. Worse yet, they're too busy to become proactive, as in planning ahead. In Chapter 9, we talked about getting out of your own way. Some more pointers.

Companies face never-ending challenges. The smart ones realize the need to keep reinventing themselves, especially to attract each subsequent wave of prospective buyers that enter the consumer pipeline. Think of the current generations. According to Pew Research, at nearly 77 million strong, Baby Boomers were the dominant players for decades. Gen X, sometimes nicknamed the Echo Boom generation, is much smaller at 68 million. Today, at a projected 83 million strong, Millennials are taking over the stage, busy redefining the playing field at every level. And Gen Z is coming up behind them.

Most big companies know that periodic "coming up for air" is an essential part of strategically redirecting to respond to changing markets. So once or twice a year, they do a market analysis. They scope out new and existing competitors, reexamine pricing, evaluate new products or services. They assess things that may erode market share, maybe even derail their business, if they don't start preparing for those changes. And then they start planning—which means looking ahead—for what strategic steps they have to take to respond.

Unfortunately, many firms become mired in too many layers of bureaucracy, or too comfortable in the way they've been doing things for years or decades, or too busy with an overloaded plate, and don't see the danger until they smash into a tree. We constantly read about their bankruptcies and failures among both industry leaders and local businesses.

As a business owner or manager, you *must* budget time to come up for air, to climb up on the zipline and see what lies ahead. Whether it's a management retreat, calendaring time to do your market analysis, or tasking somebody else to do the research and then you review and interpret it. Whatever it takes, your company has to keep its fingers on the pulse of a constantly evolving market environment. If you can, hiring an outside firm to help with this can be valuable since it brings an independent perspective and fresh insights that could make a huge difference in the company's future.

➢ *Get your Zipline sequenced for best results*

Let's zero in on the marketing aspect, since that's been our focus. I've talked about the importance of strategy—the overview of what your marketing goals and objectives are, in context of how they are going to support the company's business goals. Simply put, if the company wants to grow to revenues of $1 million dollars, what is marketing's strategy to contribute to that happening? If you have a sales team, they will set their goals and objectives based on the marketing strategy and plan, which is based on the firm's business strategy.

As we talked about in Part 3, the Zipline Marketing Plan is the detailed month-by-month roadmap for a full year of how you're going to deliver against those goals. What new products or services are you going to introduce to what audiences and at what price points? What advertising and promotions are you going to do, what media channels are you going to use, when are you going to do it, what components, what offers, what do they cost, and what is the impact on your marketing budget? What marketing outreach efforts? What sponsorships? And how will these activities impact the company's overall operations? And how does it need to gear up for all this? For a free downloadable sample marketing plan, go to ZiplinetoSuccess/Resources.

A good example is a client company that does a huge anniversary sale. Strategic planning starts months in advance. Marketing essentials are reviewed and detailed out—new products, timing, offers, projected sales units and volume, media, PR, and other factors. The sales projections are then translated into production planning; how much additional inventory needs to be produced to ensure no out-of-stocks? What glassware, ingredients, and packaging components need to be ordered to support production? Are there any storage capacity issues? What additional staffing needs to be in place to support the sale? And so on.

Organizing the zipline marketing steps you are going to take for the full year in detail, projecting and planning for the outcomes, and then measuring results is essential to accelerating your sales and profits. Big companies usually do this at least three months ahead of the upcoming calendar year, and sometimes up to a year or more in advance, depending on the production

221

lead times. In my Gillette days, we started planning four months ahead, and would develop a marketing plan that ran out 18 months.

Look at it this way. Does a general charge into a field of battle? No. They strategize and plan. Do you hop on a zipline and hope for the best? No. You determine where you want to go, get set up, and ride the zipline that's best for your business. Be a smart zipline marketer: plan, estimate, and measure.

> ## Putting it all together: Creating Your Own Your Zipline Strategy for Success Plan

There you have it. The essential zipline marketing equipment, strategies, essentials, and tactics that the big companies use, and you can now use to plan your own Zipline to Success. These "big company secrets" are now yours!

One of the most effective tools I use in my different marketing workshops is building a marketing strategy from concept through plan. We may use an imaginary company or participants' current business situations. Our goal is to go through the actual process of not just learning about but practicing the concepts, because I'm a big believer in hands-on doing. It's the best way to learn, and has made all the difference for my hundreds of clients. Give a person a fish vs. teach a person to fish…. You can learn more about these workshops at ZiplinetoSuccess.com.

Now it's time for you to prepare a Zipline Business & Marketing Strategy and Plan. You know what to do. Examine and evaluate your company and identify what needs to be developed, refined, or revised. Download and use the template from our website at ZiplinetoSuccess/Resources. Complete it, and start riding the zipline using successful fast-track marketing strategies and efforts that will accelerate your sales and profits.

Whether you implement your company's marketing strategies independently, partner with a colleague who will help keep you accountable, or work with a trained Zipline Coach, the Zipline Resource online materials, combined with this book, will give you the outlines, guidance, and tools you need to approach and implement your business marketing in a much smarter, more productive, and more cost-effective way. The next steps are entirely up to you.

If we can be of service to you in the future, please don't hesitate to contact us. I'd like to hear from you about a specific tool, strategy, tactic, or idea that you ziplined with and how it worked for your business. I love to celebrate success stories, and with your permission, will share it on our website and social media.

Remember: you can't ride the marketing *Zipline to Success* unless you take the necessary actions to create results. And once you do, it's going to be a great ride, filled with adventure, great views, and more ziplines to explore.

I know you can do it!

To your success!

Claudia Newcorn
Award-Winning Consultant ~ Author ~ Speaker ~ Coach
Acorn Enterprises / Zipline To Success
AcornMarketing.com / ZiplineToSuccess.com
Claudia@ZiplineToSuccess.com

 ## Part 7 – Zipline Highlights

✂ **Fill in the gaps.** Nobody is good at everything when it comes to running or managing a business. Admitting this is the hallmark of the smart business individual. Fill in the gaps through outsourcing, delegating, or hiring. After all, is it really sensible to be spending 60% of your time doing $10/ hour work?

✂ **Don't forget to look ahead.** Day-to-day business keeps owners and managers focused on the immediate issues. Schedule "coming up for air" as part of sound business practices so you can adjust company strategies and plans, and keep the zipline ride smooth and profitable.

✂ **Create your Zipline Plan for Success.** Download our free Zipline Plan for Success template from ZiplinetoSuccces.com/Resources and get your strategy and plan organized to accelerate sales and profits!

The 27 Zipline Essentials to Successful Marketing

 I know how busy you are. So to make it more convenient, here's a summary of all the Zipline Essentials outlined in this book. Call it a bit of value-added (and, having read this book, I know you know what I'm talking about!).

1. You must understand your customers' "reasons why to buy."

2. Change is permanent—so enjoy the ride.

3. Knowing your competitors can give you the competitive edge.

4. Always look at things from your customer's viewpoint.

5. Make buyers focus on your value, not just your price.

6. Marketing is *not* a synonym for advertising and promotion.

7. Clearly define how your product or service uniquely solves a customer's problem.

8. Advertising and promotion are only two of the ways to market to your customers.

9. Smart pricing is essential to delivering decent profits.

10. "Doing" marketing without a strategy or plan = poor results.

11. Be proactive, not reactive, when it comes to business growth.

12. Choosing the wrong pricing strategy can be a costly mistake.

13. Your wholesale pricing strategy is all about how much money the retailer or reseller is going to make.

14. Understand how your buyer speaks to write more effective marketing messages.

15. Customer surveys can be gold mines if done properly.

16. Your brand "look" and "message" should be consistent across all marketing materials.

17. Advertising and promotion can be big financial drains when done without purpose.

18. Don't buy any media without a plan in place.

19. Reach without Frequency = wasted $$ / Frequency without targeting = wasted $$.

20. Create added value from the buyer's perspective to motivate them to take action.

21. Avoid ready, fire, aim. Cost out a promotion *before* you do it.

22. Digital marketing must target where *your* buyers are.

23. Don't treat social media primarily as a sales platform.

24. Online reviews are critical influencers in how people shop.

25. Do not succumb to snarling in negative social currency situations.

26. Don't sacrifice sales on the altar of creativity.

27. You can't manage it if you can't measure it.

About the Author

Claudia Newcorn has over 30 years of successful corporate consulting, planning, and marketing experience with such large firms as Gillette, E&J Gallo, FoodSaver, and Delicato Family Vineyards. She developed her unique *Zipline to Success* system to help businesses identify opportunities, make critical marketing decisions, zip through roadblocks, and shift into high gear to achieve outstanding results and gain a competitive edge.

An award-winning consultant, author, speaker, and coach, Claudia has worked with hundreds of companies, from entrepreneurs and small to mid-sized firms to large organizations. President and founder of Acorn Enterprises, a respected business and marketing consulting firm in California, she was the recipient of the inaugural Small Business Administration (SBA)/University of California-Merced Small Business Development Center (SBDC) 2016 Center Impact Award for consulting excellence.

Claudia is a certified Ice House Entrepreneurship Program facilitator, taught marketing at St. Mary's College in California, and was the host of the Central Valley Business Workshop TV series. She earned her BA in English & Psychology from Wellesley College, and her MBA with a concentration in Marketing and International Business from Northeastern University.

I invite you to connect with me!

To take advantage of all the Zipline free resources, and learn about workshops, seminars, upcoming events, and more, join my email list and follow me on social media.

✎ Join my mailing list at Claudia@ZiplineToSuccess.com

f Facebook.com/AcornMarketing

in Linkedin.com Claudia Newcorn

Websites:

ZiplineToSuccess.com

AcornMarketing.com

Made in the USA
San Bernardino, CA
07 September 2017